I0901774

IMAGES
of America

FILIPINOS OF GREATER PHILADELPHIA

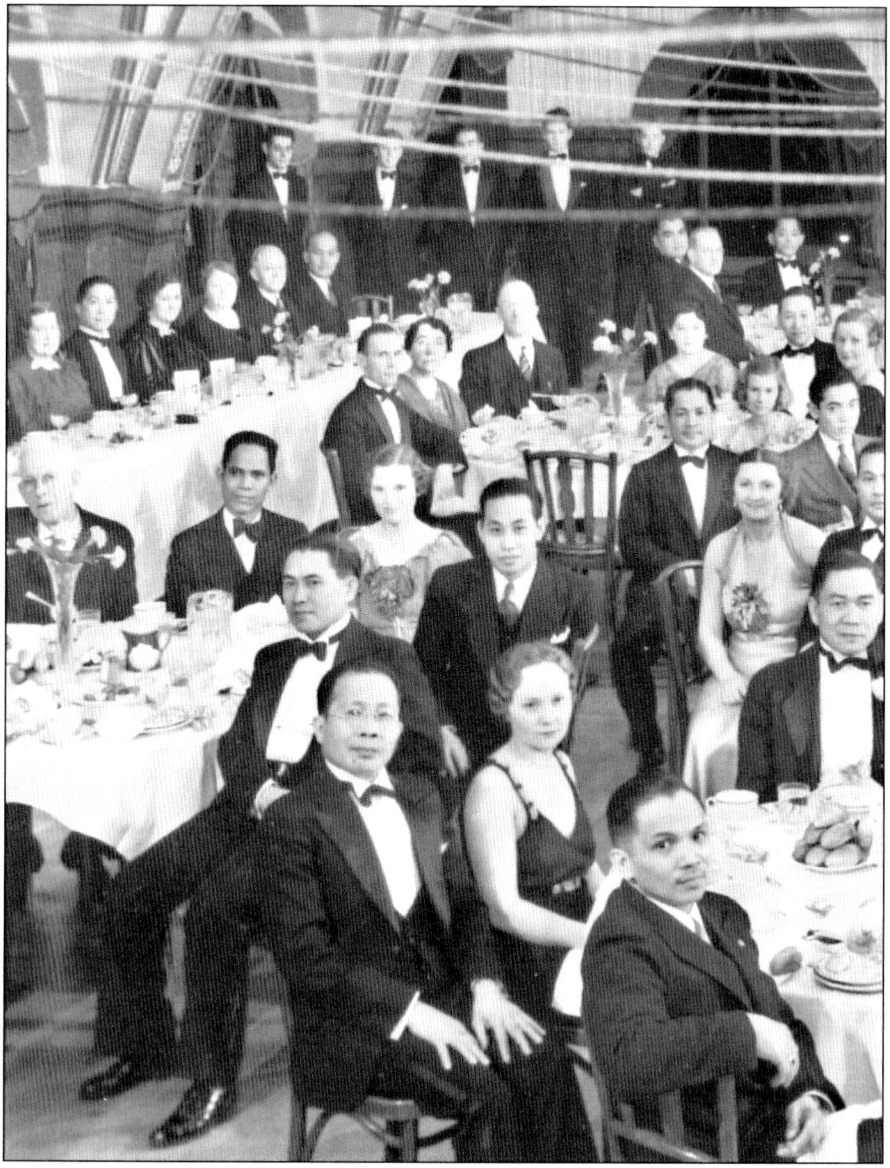

During the 1936 Rizal Ball at the Lorraine Hotel, Agripino M. Jaucian was seated at the presidential table (second from left in rear, wearing bowtie) across from Theodore Roosevelt Carino, who was still a teenager (right edge of photograph, in gray suit). Theodore shared stories about FAAPI with his daughter Dr. Patricia Carino Pasick shortly before his passing in January 2012, just a week prior to the completion of the manuscript for this book. (Courtesy of Patricia Carino Pasick.)

On the Cover: A group of Filipinos and their families invite readers to enjoy home cooking with touches of their homeland cuisine in 1934. Most Filipinos in Philadelphia developed harmonious marriages with Caucasian women despite the antimiscegenation laws in America. From left to right are (standing) Florence Carino (not shown), Laura Carbonel Laeno, and Catherine Academy; (sitting) Lucian Pineda (1st), Zacarias Gomez (2nd), Mabel Quinto (3rd), Terrance Quinto (5th), Jose Sallez (6th), Ella Santos Pineda (10th), and Petra Carino (12th). (Courtesy of Patricia Carino Pasick.)

IMAGES
of America

FILIPINOS OF GREATER PHILADELPHIA

Eliseo Art Arambulo Silva for the Filipino
American Association of Philadelphia, Inc.
Foreword by Victorina Alvarez Peralta
Message from Dr. Rommel L. Rivera

ARCADIA
PUBLISHING

ISBN 978-0-7385-9269-5

Published by Arcadia Publishing
Charleston, South Carolina

Printed in the United States of America

Library of Congress Control Number: 2012933017

For all general information, please contact Arcadia Publishing:
Telephone 843-853-2070
Fax 843-853-0044
E-mail sales@arcadiapublishing.com
For customer service and orders:
Toll-Free 1-888-313-2665

Visit us on the Internet at www.arcadiapublishing.com

Eliseo Art Silva dedicates this book to his parents, siblings, and their children; to the memory of Theodore Roosevelt Carino, the last of the pioneer Filipino Philadelphians; and to over a million martyrs of the 1898 War of Philippine Independence.

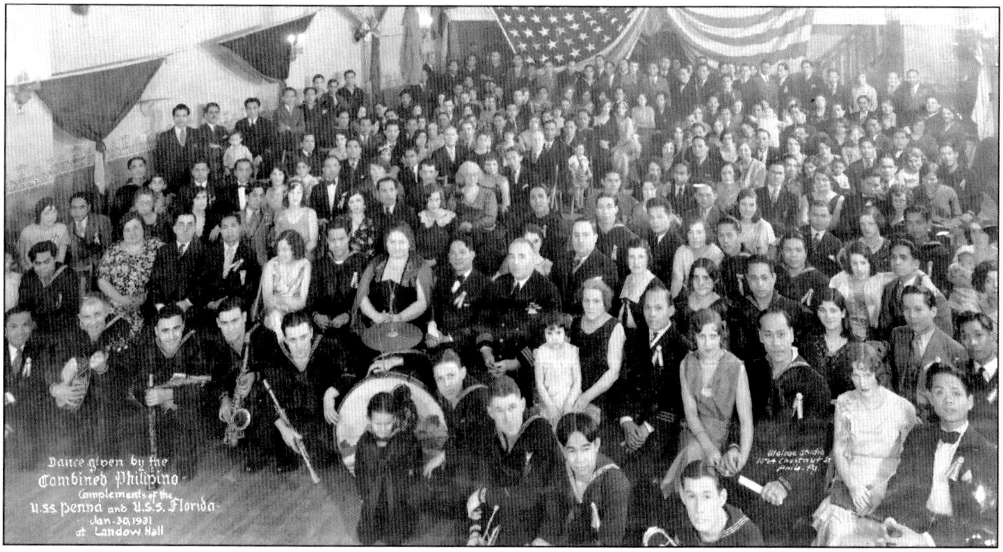

Pictured here is a dance party at Landow Hall in Philadelphia given by the combined "Philipino" crew of the USS *Florida* and USS *Pennsylvania.* The *Florida* was decommissioned at the Philadelphia Navy Yard in 1931, while the *Pennsylvania* saw action in one of the greatest naval battles in history, the Battle of Leyte Gulf in the Philippine Sea. This photograph shows some of the first American-born Filipino Philadelphians in the City of Brotherly Love. (Courtesy of Filipino American National Historical Society.)

Contents

Foreword

When I immigrated to Philadelphia in 1966, I found the Filipinos of Philadelphia a strong, close-knit community, thanks to the dedicated work of FAAPI, founded by Agripino Jaucian in 1912. This organization has kept alive the spirit of our rich and meaningful beliefs and traditions and has successfully highlighted our rightful identity as Filipinos.

I arrived as a 44-year-old widow with a 20-year-old son, who obtained a full scholarship to Temple University, resulting in a master's in speech therapy. The Philadelphian Filipinos welcomed us and made us feel at home. Quakers employed me as the program director of their Philadelphia Center for Older People. The respect and appreciation I received were a most pleasant experience. They regarded me as "a hardworking, knowledgeable, honest person with great dignity!"

At that time, Filipinos who lived in Philadelphia were mostly there under the Exchange Visitor's Program, as nurses, doctors, and medical technicians who worked in the hospitals, contributing to the improvement of health care services. There were no jobless or homeless Filipinos. Pete Supelana, owner of a printing press and bulk mailing company, readily gave Filipinos jobs. Likewise, Danny Peralta, owner of a Filipino grocery and gift shop in Philadelphia's Chinatown, gave jobs to whoever needed one. Maria Velez-Umali opened her spacious home, located in University City, to boarders at a price they could afford, and so did Prexy Oxinio in North Philadelphia.

During the 1960s, through the US Department of Housing and Urban Development, Filipinos were able to buy homes on North Marshall Street, which had seven blocks populated by Filipinos, with a down payment of $50 and a monthly mortgage of $40. Their monthly socials and festivities promoted friendly and positive relationships within their community.

Elias Dungca organized the first Filipino Knights of Columbus San Rafael Council; this was done so that Filipino Americans could participate in key parts of the 1975 Eucharistic Congress in Philadelphia. More importantly, the discriminatory "doctor's examination" that was administered to foreign medical graduates was dispelled through the assertive advocacy of Filipino doctors based in the Greater Philadelphia region.

This important book written by Eliseo Art Silva is a highly commendable and meaningful undertaking. I extend my sincere congratulations and heartfelt thanks for a job well done. It is a great pleasure to be a part of it!

—Victorina Alvarez Peralta
Philadelphia, Pennsylvania

President's Message

Like many, I am an immigrant from the Philippines. Like many, my story is laden with hardships, sacrifices, opportunities, joys, and successes. Like many who came here as professionals, I traveled for many years to establish myself again. My journey took me across the United States, from California where I landed with my wife, Aida, to Oregon where my children were born, to Florida, and, eventually, to the Keystone State, Pennsylvania. I earned the opportunity to train at the following prestigious medical centers in the country: the University of Miami-Jackson Memorial Hospital, Temple University Hospital, and the Hospital of the University of Pennsylvania. I found work and a home for my family and saved my earnings to give my children the best opportunities to succeed. My hard work and struggles paid off as I was finally living the American dream, like many before me did.

After settling into my profession as a psychiatrist and getting more control of my week's schedule, I began meeting with some of my *kababayans*, or fellow countrymen. If truth be told, my success as a physician made me a leader in local Filipino civic organizations. I was thrust into what would be a second job. These leadership roles, however, gave me opportunities to give back, to empower, and to enrich my communities here and back in the Philippines. I served as a two-term president of the area's umbrella organization, the Filipino Executive Council of Greater Philadelphia. My work ethic and leadership appealed to the elders of the community. I enjoyed the extra work so much that I accepted to lead the Filipino American Association of Philadelphia, Inc. (FAAPI). I realized that "if I do this, I am taking over almost 100 years worth of an organization." It was definitely a daunting task, being asked to follow such a long succession of leaders, but I was up for it. It was my destiny to lead the oldest ongoing Filipino American association in the United States and to be its president at its centennial celebration.

Part of being the president of an organization almost 100 years old is awareness that you have almost 100 years of history you are responsible for. I am currently in possession of the original charter signed by our founder, Agripino Jaucian. I have photographs of Filipinos long since passed. I have seen records that prove that some of my fellow Filipino friends have roots going back decades. Each and every item has a story to tell, just like the story I have to tell about myself and my family. On the following pages of *Filipinos of Greater Philadelphia*, you will get a glimpse of more than 100 years of history. Each photograph holds in it a story, just a piece of the big picture that is the history of Filipino Americans in the Delaware Valley. The book tells the story of my people. We are like any immigrant of America. We are also in many ways a unique breed of people. We are hard working and resilient. We are fun loving and God fearing. We respect our parents and elders. We value life and education. I congratulate Eliseo Art Silva for his tenacity and resolve in compiling an organized tablet of the history and culture of Filipinos in Greater Philadelphia. Thank you for empowering us all.

Mabuhay tayong lahat! (Long live to all!)
—Rommel L. Rivera, MD, President
Filipino American Association of Philadelphia, Inc.

Filipino-American Association of Philadelphia, Inc.
100 Years of Filipinos in Philadelphia
1912–2012

ACKNOWLEDGMENTS

I am honored to have the support of countless organizations and individuals in sharing their photographs and the stories that accompany them. First and foremost, thanks go to the following officers and members of the Filipino American Association of Philadelphia, Inc. (FAAPI): Purita Acosta, Auring Dungca, Maria E. Dungca-Agkoz, Mary Faustino, Virginia Luz, Dr. Rommel Rivera, Raymond Soriano, and Stephen Spadaro. Secondly to the Filipino American National Historical Society (FANHS): Fred and Dorothy Cordova, Timoteo Cordova, Eloisa Borah, Nestor Palugod Enriquez, Emily Lawsin, and Mel Orpilla. Special thanks to: Noel Abejo, Imelda Alpas, Roslyn Arayata, Charisse Baldoria, Raymundo Benitez, Arnaldo Dumindin, Restituto EstacioJose de los Santos Galura, Abraham Ignacio, Jonny Itliong, Emma de Jesus, Minette Manalo, Dr. Lita Mangubat, Sister Loretto Mapa, R.A., Humberto Mendez, M.S.W., L.C.S.W., Ambeth Ocampo, Patricia Carino Pasick, Vicky Peralta, Darlene Ragucci, Philip Reyes, Greg Santillan, Dr. April Talangbayan, Rose Tibayan, Dnvzs Zjzllg, and Emilio Aguinaldo Museum.

Also, thanks go to the following people for their assistance in acquiring images: Ernesto Arcilla, Joan May Cordova, Elizabeth Clemens (Walter P. Reuther Library), Aurora Deshauteurs (Free Library of Philadelphia), Nestor Enriquez, Mary Faustino, Vic Fernandez (Seaman's Church Institute), Gilbert de Jesus (Filipinas Heritage Library, Ayala Foundation, Philippines), Megan Good (Independence Seaport Museum), Linda Gross (Hagley Museum and Library), Cora & Victoria Lopez (Courtesy of Lopez of Balayan, Batangas Foundation / the Lopez family history Facebook page), Lourdes Marzan, Mary Mecartney (United Farm Workers of America), Nancy Miller (University of Pennsylvania Archives), Anne Mosher (Temple University Urban Archives), Darlene Ragucci, Lee Samuels (Top Rank Boxing), Linda Nietes, Edward de los Santos (pinoykollektor.blogspot.com), Rob Sieczkiewicz (Drexel University Archives), Skip Voluntad, Norma Yabut, and Shawn Weldon (Philadelphia Archdiocesan Historical Research Center). University of Pennsylvania Filipino students source: *1908 Scope*, pp. 76, 102, University of Pennsylvania Medical School Yearbook, Philadelphia.

My heartfelt appreciation to Van and Ven Kalugdan, Rick and Norma Yabut, and Auring Dungca for their selfless support, as well as Carolina Goodman and Virginia Luz for reviewing the manuscript.

I am thankful for *Tita* Virgie Luz for her research and advocacy and to *Mammy* Vicky Peralta for writing the foreword, as well as to Dr. Raymond Soriano for his expertise with local history. In addition, this book also led us to the wonderful great grandchildren of Agripino Jaucian, who shared loving memories of their great grandparents.

I am thankful for Dr. Patricia Pasick's photographs, which altogether comprise a highlight of the collection. She also gifted us with restored photographs capturing Rizal banquets, which were heirlooms passed on from her father, Theodore Roosevelt Carino, to whom this book is dedicated.

Introduction

Memory is the most important ingredient in nation-building.

—F. Sionil Jose

The most effective way to destroy people is to deny and obliterate their own understanding of their history.

—George Orwell, 1984

This book documents the perspective of Filipinos on the east coast of the United States. Presenting history is very much like artwork resulting from a figure drawing class, where the same subject, viewed by various artists, yields multiple perspectives.

Being an artist and muralist, I understand that the art of sequential narrative is as powerful a tool for enhancing and empowering the social dynamic of communities as it was with ancient cave art. I intend to reconstruct the panoptic gaze of historians from the one who defines to the one who is being defined and to lift footnotes into the foreground. I have included historical photographs from the Philippines to provide context and a sense of the bigger picture. These photographs have an important connection to Philadelphia and also help to answer the question, what is Filipino?

As a weaver of history and heritage, I reconcile my lineage with the history of painting. It has always been my passion to integrate the Filipino perspective into mainstream discourse and mental maps. This book actually had its start in 2002, when I was contracted to paint the first of 35 murals in the City of Murals and neighboring cities. It was then that I discovered the dynamic Filipino community of Greater Philadelphia and its *bayanihan* spirit (neighborly cooperation).

The earliest recorded Filipinos in Philadelphia were volunteers in the Civil War who served as sailors on the USS *Conemaugh* and the USS *Little Ada*, which functioned as the Union's West Gulf blockade. In 1765, writing to the king of Spain, explorer Francisco Leandro de Viana described Filipino sailors in glowing terms: "There is not an 'indio' in those islands, who has not a remarkable inclination for the sea, nor is there at present in all the world a people more agile in maneuvers on shipboard or who learn so quickly nautical terms and whatever a good mariner ought to know."

The first Filipino to serve in the US Navy was Augustin Feliciano, a fact documented in the first monthly Filipino American publication, *The Filipino*, published by US government–sponsored Filipino students known as *pensionados*, and edited by Philadelphia's own Olivia Salamanca. The March 1906 article "The Largest Colony of Filipinos in America" describes receiving a subscription from a Filipino living in New Orleans: "The Filipino whom we addressed was Mr. Eulogio Yatar, and he sent us some most astonishing news; in fact, we feel almost as the ethnologist does who discovers a new race of people, for we find that there is a colony of 2,000 Filipinos in that Queen City in the South. This community has been established for about a hundred years, the first one who landed there being a native of Bicol by the name of Augustin Feliciano, who later served in the American navy in the war of 1812."

Theodore Roosevelt established his reputation in 1882 when he published *The Naval War of 1812*, which today remains the standard for the study of war. This conflict, matching the young nation against the powerful British Royal Navy, was a daunting victory in naval history. According to historian Nestor Palugod Enriquez, founding president of the Filipino American National Historical Society (FANHS) New Jersey, Roosevelt was the architect of US imperialism and may have been thinking of naval strategies and US naval power early on. It was assistant secretary of the navy Theodore Roosevelt who mobilized the USS *Olympia* to head toward Manila Bay in the Philippines without approval from Pres. William McKinley. The *Olympia* was commanded by Adm. George Dewey, previously a junior officer in the Union blockade of New Orleans during the Civil War. Dewey employed a successful naval blockade at the Battle of Manila Bay, which resulted in the sinking of the antiquated Spanish armada, aiding Filipino soldiers to liberate their country from 333 years of Spanish rule.

After the defeat of Spain, the United States had initially promised to be a protector of the Philippines, Asia's first constitutional republic. However, Filipinos soon found themselves in a much larger military conflict with a new imperial overlord, the United States of America. The Philippine-American War, or the War of Philippine Independence, ushered in the first phase of Asian nationalism vs. US imperialism. This war resulted in the largest number of US military defections and inspired the earliest anti-war mass demonstrations in the United States. The Anti-Imperialist League, led by prominent Americans such as Andrew Carnegie and Samuel Clemens (Mark Twain), opposed the war. The Anti-Imperialist League had two prominent Filipino spokespersons—siblings Sixto and Clemencia Lopez. According to the *Springfield Republican*, Sixto Lopez was given a grand reception in Philadelphia on December 22, 1900. He delivered a landmark speech on March 12, 1901, entitled "A Filipino's Plea for Liberty." Sixto was hailed as the Simon Bolivar of the Philippines. His sister, Clemencia, became the first Filipino to have an audience with a US president, Theodore Roosevelt, in order to make the case for US recognition of Philippine independence.

It is an interesting coincidence that two Filipino sailors from the same part of the Philippines, a century apart, would impact both Filipino American and US history. Augustin Feliciano came from Bicol, Philippines, as did Agripino Mallado "Pinoy" Jaucian, who settled in Philadelphia a hundred years later. Jaucian organized the oldest Filipino American organization in continuous existence: the Filipino American Association of Philadelphia, Inc. (FAAPI). Jaucian was one of the first Filipinos to join the US Navy in the Philippines, in 1907. He is the first on record to use the term *Pinoy*, a derivative of his nickname and an informal demonym referring to the Filipino people. A magician, boxer, linguist, and musician, he was known as the "Old Maestro" and also conducted the local FAAPI orchestra. Pinoy Jaucian dedicated his life to helping those in need, both in Philadelphia and in the Philippines. A library and a major street are named after him in his hometown in the Philippines.

During the 1930s, a significant number of the 25,000 Filipinos who enlisted in the US Navy and Merchant Marines were assigned to Philadelphia's shipyards. Several Filipino barbershops and restaurants were established in Philadelphia's Chinatown. After World War II, the US Census listed 1,000 Filipinos living in Metro Philadelphia; that number continued to increase after the 1946 Philippine independence when Filipinos were granted US citizenship. After World War II, thousands of Navy and Coast Guard recruits from the Philippines arrived to work as mess attendants or cooks, filling the jobs vacated by African Americans as a result of executive order No. 9981 signed by President Truman on July 26, 1948, which ended racial segregation in the armed forces and provided equal opportunities to all military personnel. An agreement made in 1952 allowed Filipino citizens to stay in the United States and work as long as they were in the service.

According to Ray Burdeos, author of the memoir *Flips in Philadelphia in the Fifties*, the weekend population of Filipinos in Philadelphia could swell to twice the number of the local population, especially when the Navy shipyard was still in operation. Oftentimes, Filipino sailors from the US Naval Academy in Annapolis, Norfolk Naval Station, and New London's submarine base and Coast Guard Academy would drive to Philadelphia to meet women during their "liberty" breaks. Philadelphia had a reputation among Filipinos for having single women who did not discriminate against "Flips" (a racial slur directed to Filipinos in America). The ratio of Filipino males to Filipino women was 30 to 1, hence the high number of interracial marriages in Philadelphia. The children of these mixed marriages were called *mestizos*. Among the famous mestizas and mestizos are Philadelphia Eagles quarterback Roman Gabriel, whose mother was Irish, and Philadelphia's very own Barbara Magallanes, principal dancer in Dick Clark's *American Bandstand*, whose mother was Scottish/Welsh.

I hope that the reader will come away with a better understanding of what it was like to be a Filipino of Greater Philadelphia. More importantly, the reader will hopefully begin to ask the question, what is American? Philadelphia is the perfect place to refresh our understanding of the ideas that created and anchored the United States as a political concept, ideas forever enshrined in the Declaration of Independence. In the same manner, the ideas that anchored the Philippines as a political concept and birthed Asia's first modern nation are enshrined in Jose Rizal's novels *Noli Me Tangere* and *El Filibusterismo*.

There are no tyrants where there are no slaves.

—Jose Rizal, *El Filibusterismo*

One

Filipino Philadelphia in the Land of Liberty

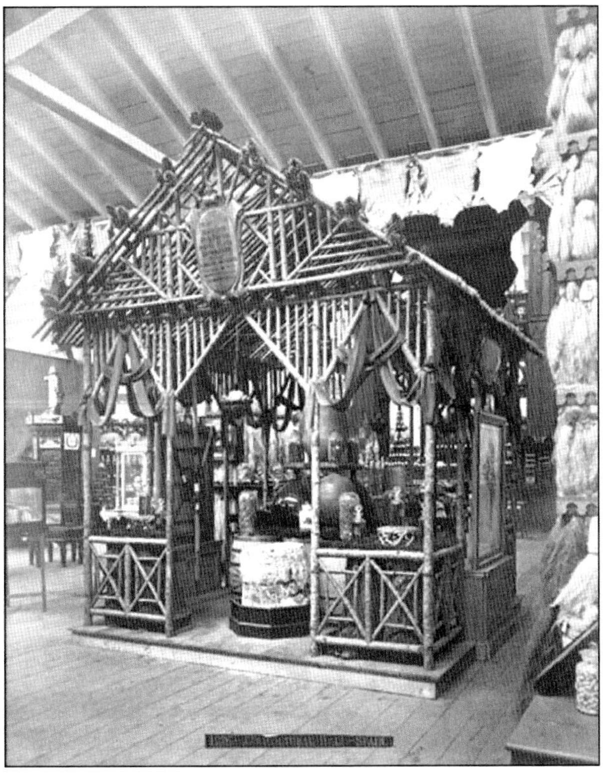

At the 1876 Philadelphia Exposition, the Philippine Exhibit of the Spanish Pavillion featured an archetype of a traditional Philippine hut known as a *bahay kubo*. Graciano Lopez Jaena was the first Filipino to document 19th century Filipino Philadelphians. In the February 25, 1889, issue of *La Solidaridad*, Jaena wrote, "In a town near Barcelona live quite a number of Filipino sailors. I also know that in almost all the ports of England, France, and America, particularly in New York and Philadelphia, there are many Filipino sailors." (Courtesy of the Free Library of Philadelphia.)

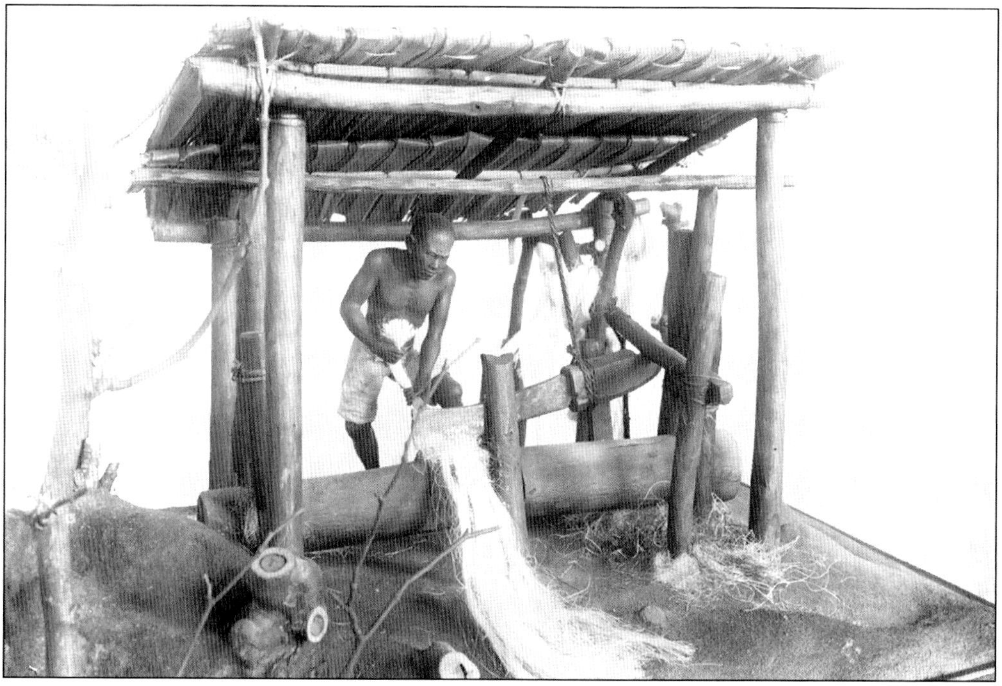

Here is an exhibit of a laborer heckling hemp at the Philadelphia Commercial Museum. Manila hemp was used to create Manila paper and folders, patented in 1843 by John Mark and Lyman Hollingsworth, who had come to Milton, Massachusetts, from Delaware. They discovered that they could utilize hemp from Manila rope cut from old sails. This rope proved to be of exceptional strength and was brought by Filipino sailors settling on the east coast in the 1700s. (Courtesy of Independence Seaport Museum.)

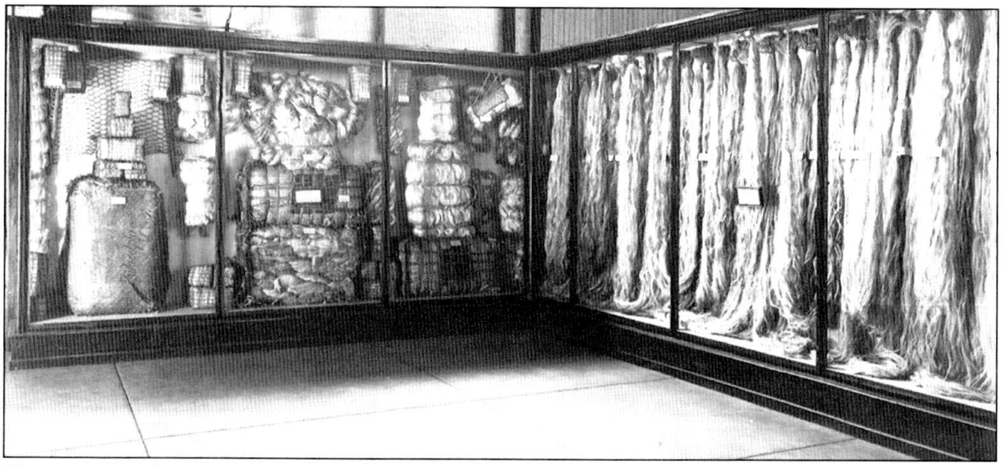

Shown around 1910 is a Manila hemp exhibit at the Commercial Museum featuring various products sourced from Manila hemp. According to Carlos Quirino, Filipinos found their way to the eastern seaboard of the United States via clippers that visited the ports of Manila during the late 1700s. Three Philadelphians, Andrew Bellino, Joseph Bernardo, and John Henry, in the 1864 roster of Civil War volunteers, were from Manila. Joseph Bernardo worked on the USS *Conemaugh*, a side-wheel steamer with a crew of 125 that was assigned as a gunboat in the Union blockade during the Civil War. (Courtesy of Nestor Palugod Enriquez.)

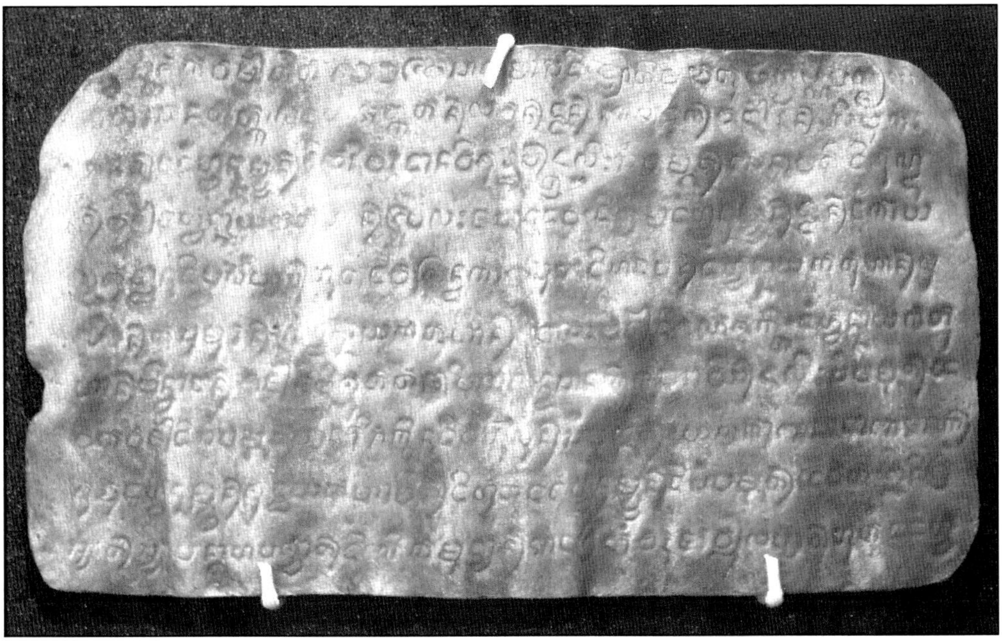

The Laguna Copperplate, dated to Monday, April 21, 900 A.D., is the earliest historical document of the Philippines. This national treasure confirms the existence of the Indianized Kingdoms of the Philippines and a vibrant and dynamic culture that connected the archipelago with the rest of Southeast Asia. This predates the colonization of the Philippines by the Spanish Empire in 1571 by 600 years. (Courtesy of Roslyn Arayata.)

Known as a *piloncito*, this conical gold nugget was the currency used by early Filipinos. Inscribed on the base of each piece is the syllable *Ma*, which refers to *Ma-yi*, the Chinese name for the Philippines. In 1225, Zhao Rugua said: "Ma-yi is north of Borneo, natives live in large villages where metal images are scattered about. When trading ships enter the harbor, they stop in front of the official plaza, where merchants present white umbrellas as gifts to the local officials." (Courtesy of Edward de los Santos.)

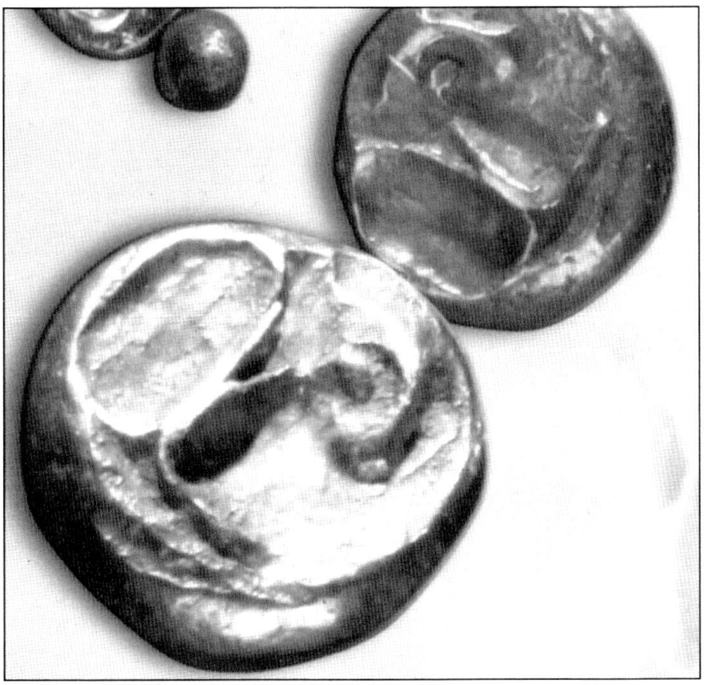

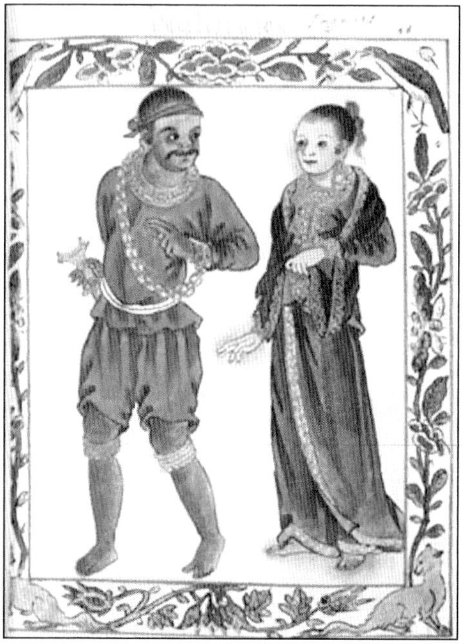

The illuminated *Boxer Codex*, a c. 1595 manuscript, contained illustrations of Filipinos at the time of contact with Spain. At least 15 illustrations depict Filipinos; this image presents a Tagalog couple. The man and woman pictured were a part of the native royalty known as *Maharlika*. In 1902, Clemencia Lopez said, "In almost all relations of life, our women are regarded as equals. Prior to the Spanish occupation, the people were already civilized, and this respect for and equality of women existed." (Courtesy of Lily Library.)

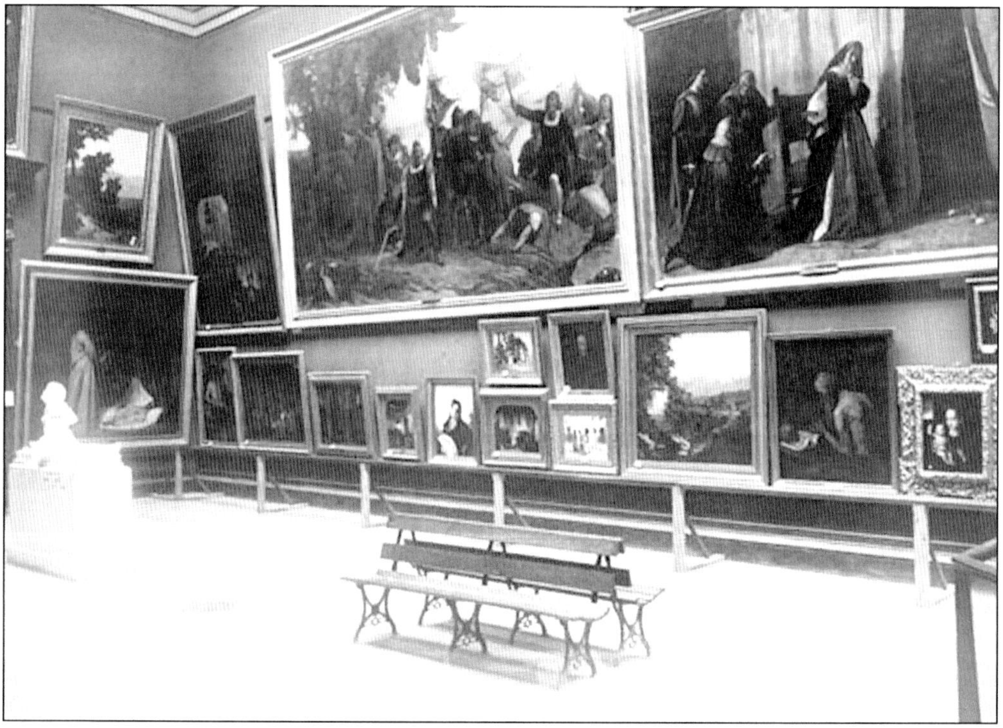

Here are paintings from Spain inside Memorial Hall. The 1876 Exposition was the country's first major exposition, drawing nine million visitors. An entry by the Filipino artist Simon D. Flores, *Orquesta en un Pueblo de la Provincia de Pampanga*, won the silver medal, which made Flores the first Filipino to win international acclaim. As documented in *Lista Preparatoria del Catalogo de los Expositores de Espana, 1876*, under *Islas Filipinas*, the whereabouts of Flores's entry are unknown. (Courtesy of Free Library of Philadelphia.)

Here is a self-portrait of Simon De la Rosa Flores (October 28, 1839, to March 12, 1902). Simon Flores was among the first students and one of the most outstanding graduates of the Academia de Dibujo y Pintura, the first art school in the Philippines, founded by Damian Domingo in 1821. In this school, there was no racial discrimination. Flores set up his own studio after four years of studies and, later, was commissioned to paint several church murals in Pampanga. (Courtesy of Filipinas Heritage Library, Ayala Foundation, Philippines.)

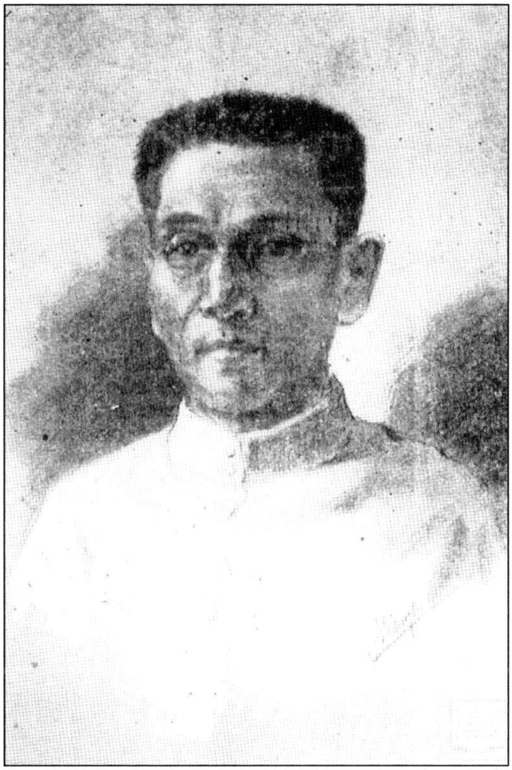

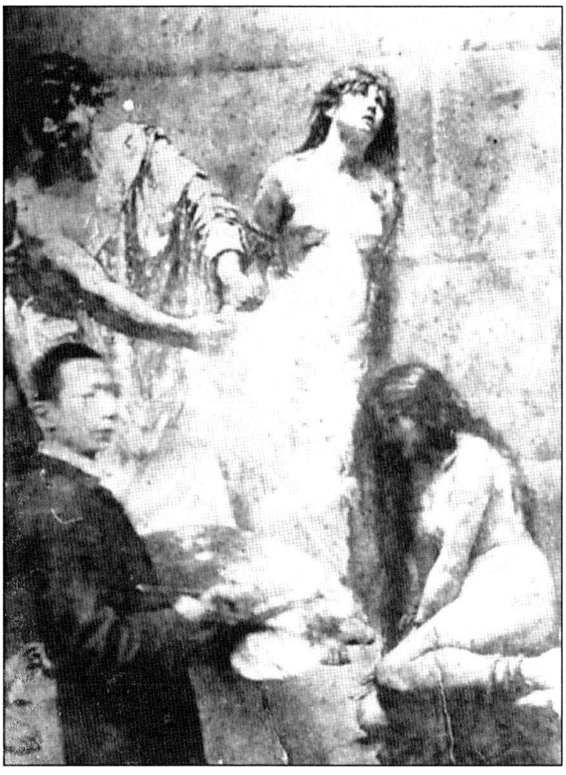

Felix Resurreccion Hidalgo's painting, *Las Virgenes Cristianas Expuestas al Populacho* (The Christian Virgins Exposed to the Populace), was awarded a silver medal at the 1884 Exposición General de Bellas Artes in Madrid. It showed a group of boorish looking males mocking semi-naked female Christians, one of whom is seated in the foreground, with her head bowed in misery. In the same exposition, Juan Luna's *Spoliarium* was awarded a gold medal. (Courtesy of Ambeth Ocampo.)

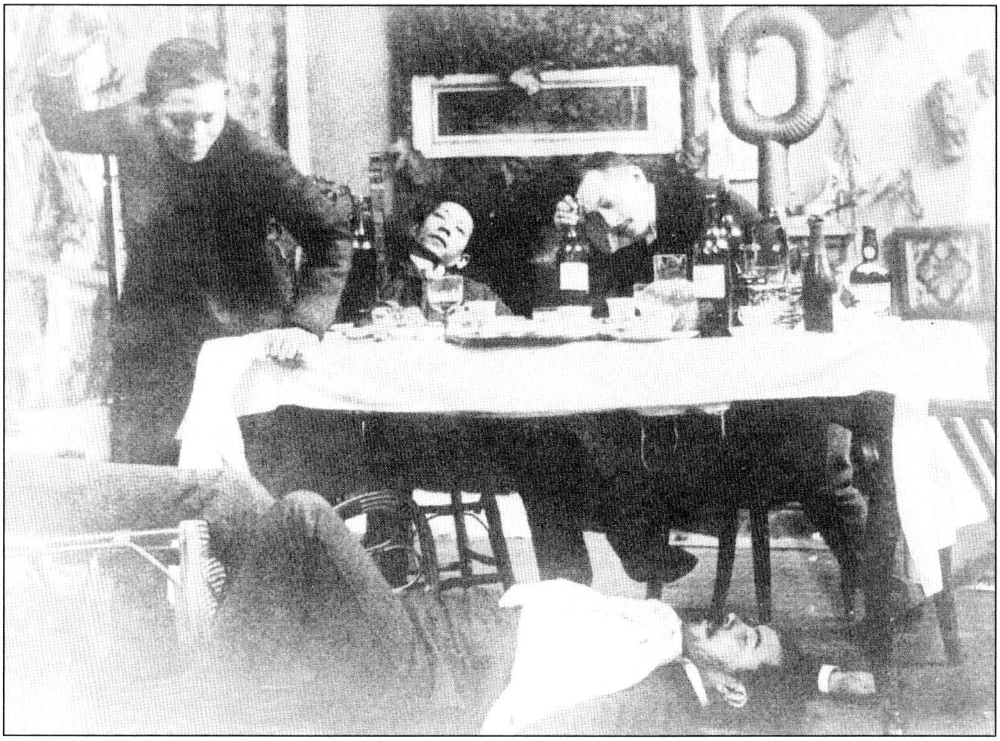

Around 1887 in Madrid, Jose Rizal (standing at left), with Felix Hidalgo (center) and Pardo de Tavera (sitting) and Juan Luna (laying on the floor), are enjoying camaraderie and fellowship. Luna's and Hidalgo's achievements in the world of art laid the cultural foundation for the Philippine Revolution, prompting 22-year-old Rizal to write the *Noli Me Tangere*. At the 1884 toasting speech Rizal delivered in honor of Luna and Hidalgo's dual triumph, he proclaimed: "The eastern chrysalis from the orient is emerging from its cocoon." (Courtesy of Ambeth Ocampo.)

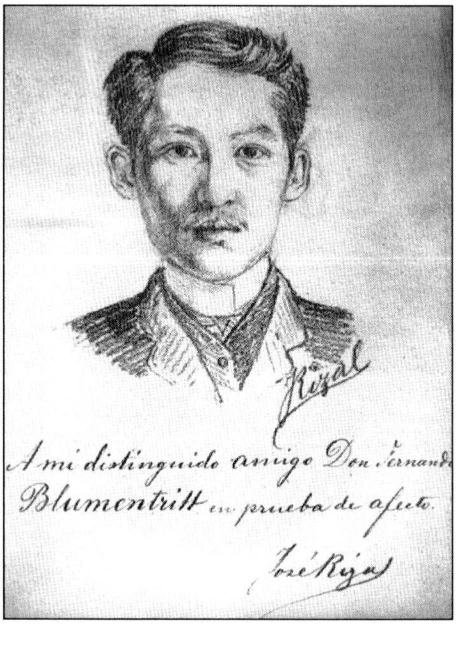

After Rizal completed *Noli Me Tangere*, he drew his self-portrait using a mirror and gave it to Ferdinand Blumentritt, of the Czech Republic, who became his best friend. A true Renaissance man, Rizal was a polymath and was fluent in 22 languages. In 1891, Rizal organized La Liga Filipina, which eventually became an organization that launched the 1896 revolution. Gandhi read *Noli Me Tangere* and *El Filibusterismo* and acknowledged Rizal as a forerunner. Gandhi manifested the following Rizalian ideas as gleaned from *El Filibusterismo*: "There can be no tyrants were there are no slaves." The great Spanish philosopher Miguel de Unamuno called Rizal "The Tagalog Christ." (Courtesy of Ambeth Ocampo.)

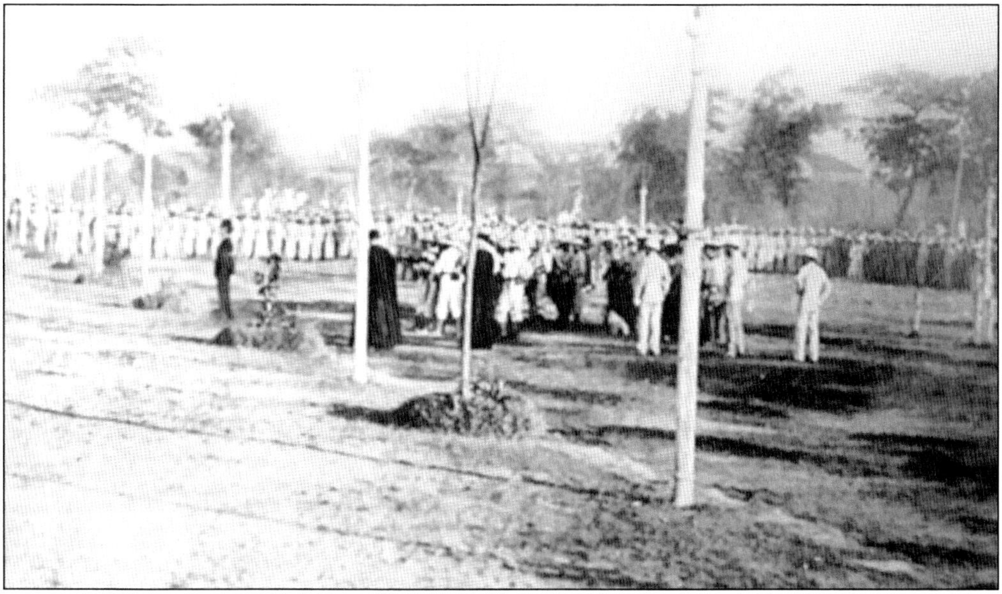

This photograph capturing the execution of Jose Rizal was discovered in 1897 in a flea market in Pennsylvania. It was taken seconds before Rizal was shot. Tradition dictated that traitors be shot in the back; Rizal requested that his head be spared, enabling him to turn around once shot and face the firing squad. After the order to fire was given, Rizal exclaimed, "Consummatum est!" (It is finished), which were also the last words of Jesus Christ. Rizal fell to the ground with his head facing the sunrise. (Courtesy of Arnaldo Dumindin.)

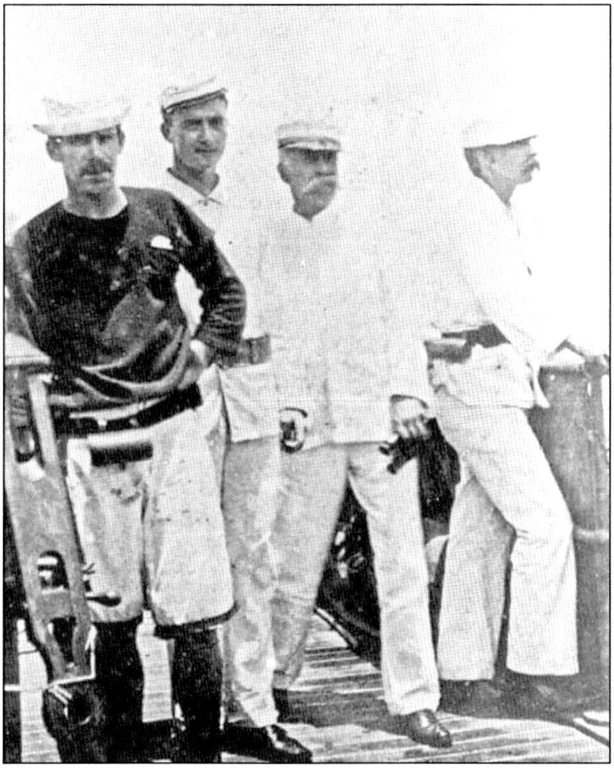

On May 1, 1898, Adm. George Dewey (center) won a naval victory in Manila Bay, sinking the Spanish armada. In the meantime, Filipino soldiers of independence welcomed the American victory, hoping that the land of Lincoln would be the protector of a new nation emerging in a world still hostile to non-white governments. The resulting war between Asian nationalism and American imperialism triggered the earliest antiwar demonstrations in the United States as well as the largest defection of American soldiers. (Courtesy of Arnaldo Dumindin.)

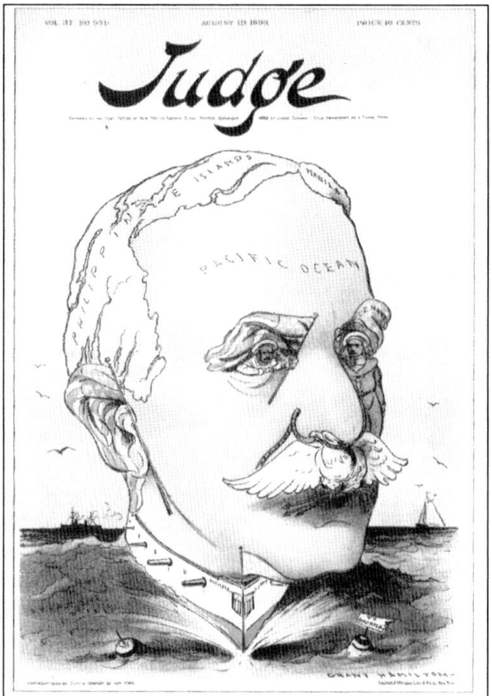

"THE CHIEF FEATURES OF ADMIRAL DEWEY."
Judge, Judge Company,
New York, August 19, 1899 [artist: Grant Hamilton]

Admiral Dewey's victory in the Battle of Manila Bay captured the imagination of the American people. On August 4, 1898, the mayor of Minneapolis offered $10 to anyone who named his or her daughter "Manila Philapina" in honor of the American victory in the Battle of Manila Bay. In addition, Walt Disney named one of Donald Duck's nephews "Dewey" after the Admiral, the latest American hero. (Courtesy of Edward de los Santos)

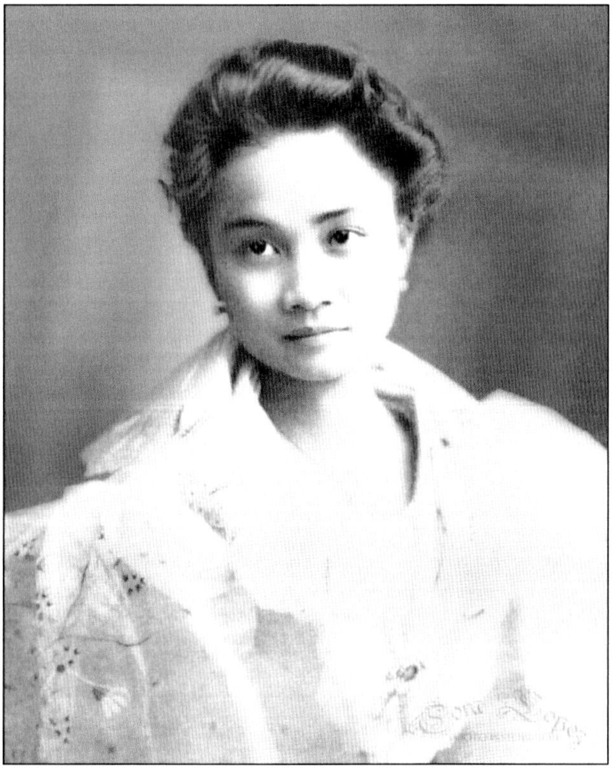

The "Mother of History," Clemencia Lopez figured prominently in the movement of dissent in the United States when she testified before a US Senate hearing and was granted an audience in the White House by Pres. Theodore Roosevelt to plead for US recognition of Philippine independence. In 1902, she said: "You ought to understand that we are only contending for the liberty of our country, just as you once fought for the same liberty for yours." (Courtesy of Lopez of Balayan, Batangas Foundation / the Lopez family history Facebook page.)

The declaration of independence, signed by 98 Filipinos on June 12, 1898, was proclaimed at 4:15 in the afternoon outside the window of Gen. Emilio Aguinaldo's home in Kawit, Cavite. Just as the United States of America was the first to declare its independence in the West, the Philippines was the first in the East. The iconic symbols of the Philippines that birthed the Filipino nation as a political concept were created on this day. (Courtesy of Arnaldo Dumindin.)

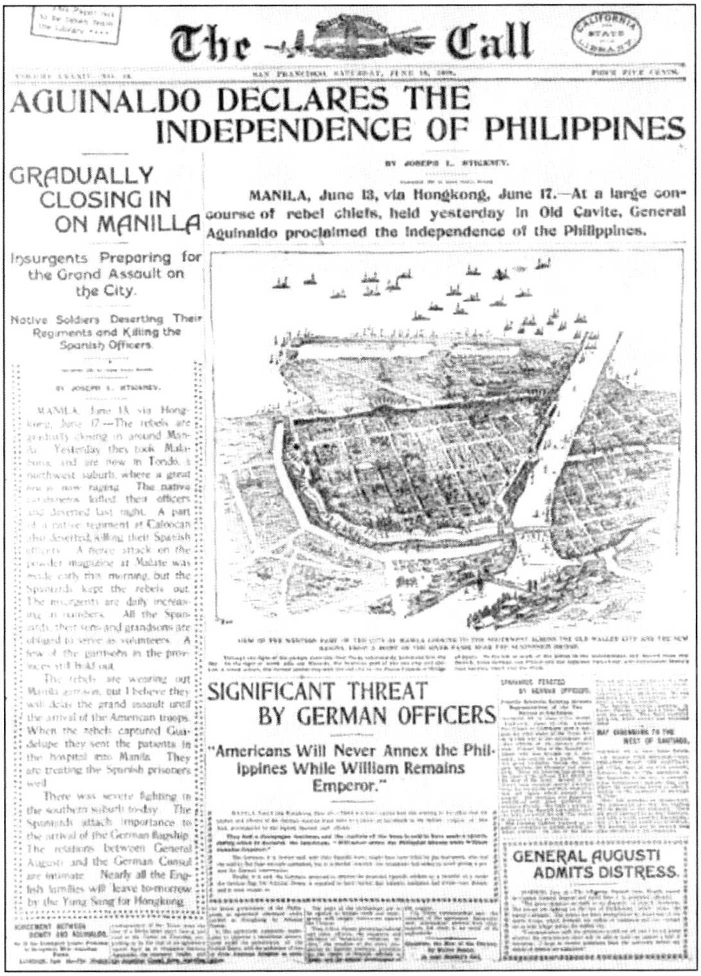

The Call

AGUINALDO DECLARES THE INDEPENDENCE OF PHILIPPINES

BY JOSEPH L. STICKNEY.

MANILA, June 13, via Hongkong, June 17.—At a large concourse of rebel chiefs, held yesterday in Old Cavite, General Aguinaldo proclaimed the independence of the Philippines.

GRADUALLY CLOSING IN ON MANILLA

Insurgents Preparing for the Grand Assault on the City.

Native Soldiers Deserting Their Regiments and Killing the Spanish Officers.

BY JOSEPH L. STICKNEY.

MANILA, June 13, via Hongkong, June 17.—The rebels are gradually closing in around Manila. Yesterday they took Malabon, and are now in Tondo, a northwest suburb, where a great fire is now raging. The native [illegible] killed their officers and deserted last night. A part of a native regiment at Caloocan also deserted, killing their Spanish officers. A fierce attack on the powder magazine at Malate was made early this morning, but the Spaniards kept the rebels out. The insurgents are daily increasing in numbers. All the Spaniards, their sons and grandsons are obliged to serve as volunteers. A few of the garrisons in the provinces still hold out.

The rebels are wearing out Manila garrison, but I believe they will delay the grand assault until the arrival of the American troops. When the rebels captured Guadelupe they sent the patients in the hospital into Manila. They are treating the Spanish prisoners well.

There was severe fighting in the southern suburb to-day. The Spaniards attach importance to the arrival of the German flagship. The relations between General Augusti and the German Consul are intimate. Nearly all the English families will leave to-morrow by the Yung Sang for Hongkong.

SIGNIFICANT THREAT BY GERMAN OFFICERS

"Americans Will Never Annex the Philippines While William Remains Emperor."

GENERAL AUGUSTI ADMITS DISTRESS.

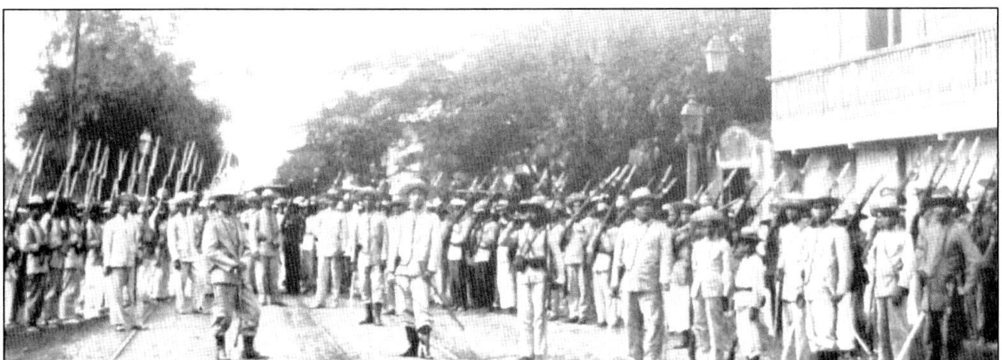

Filipino soldiers of independence await their commander-in-chief, Gen. Emilio Aguinaldo, in Malolos, Bulacan. Aguinaldo's army consisted of barefoot farmers and fishermen, including children. On the right, in the dark uniforms, is the army's elite force, known as the Tiradores de La Muerte (Sharpshooters of Death), credited with America's highest-ranking casualty, Gen. Henry Lawton, and defeat at the Battle of San Mateo on December 19, 1899. (Courtesy of Arnaldo Dumindin.)

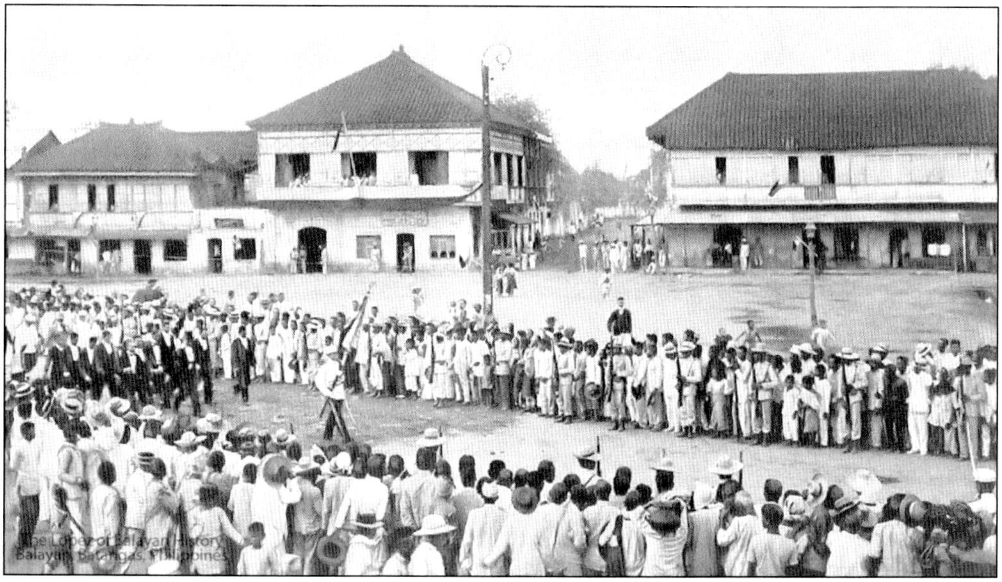

Emilio Aguinaldo, the committee of congress, and his cabinet led a parade through the town plaza of Malolos, Bulacan, the country's new capital. On this day, January 21, 1899, Emilio Aguinaldo was sworn in as president, and Asia's first republican constitutional democracy was born. By 1900, the Philippines were second to Japan in economic prosperity, gaining for the United States nearly unlimited resources as well as a market for US products in Asia. (Courtesy of the Lopez family history Facebook page.)

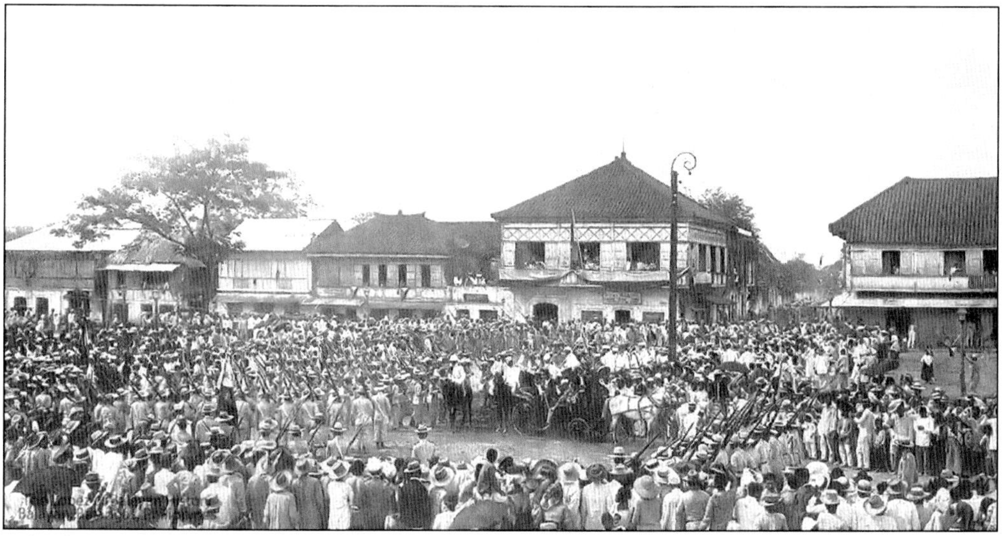

After being sworn in as president and publicly reading the constitution, Aguinaldo presented a parade of troops, celebrating the proclamation of the Republic of the Philippines. Despite the odds, 50 delegates ratified the Constitution of the Philippines, which granted basic civil rights and the separation of church and state and called for the creation of an assembly of representatives that would act as the legislature. Upon the inauguration of the republic, Aguinaldo granted executive clemency to all Spanish civilians being held prisoner. (Courtesy of the Lopez family history Facebook page.)

The June 12 declaration of independence was signed by 98 Filipinos representing the entire archipelago of 7,100 islands claimed by Spain, except for parts of Mindanao and the Cordillera region. This document was ratified by the Philippine Congress convened in Malolos, Bulacan, on September 29, 1898, after which the Philippine constitution was drafted and ratified on November 29, 1898, and promulgated by Aguinaldo on January 22, 1899. Congress declared war against the United States on June 12, 1899. (Courtesy of Ambeth Ocampo.)

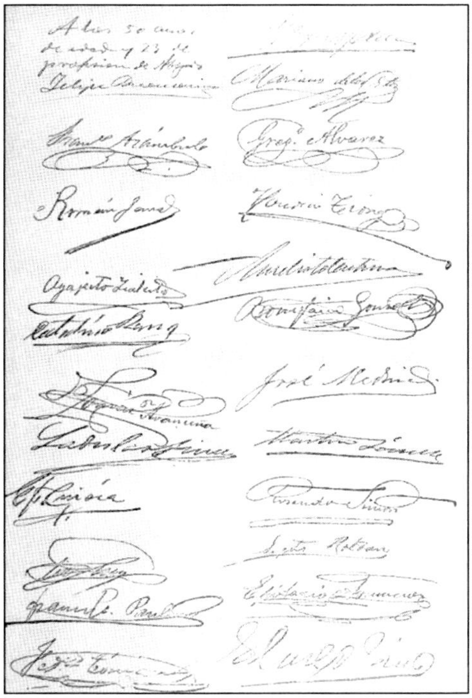

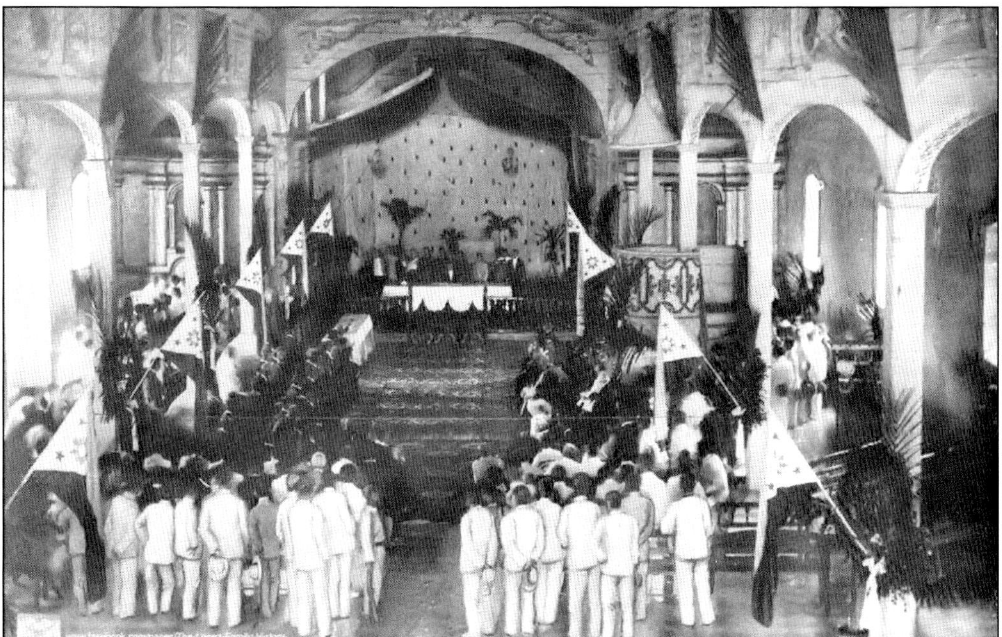

The inauguration of the Philippine Republic was highlighted with the swearing in of 29-year-old Gen. Emilio Aguinaldo as the country's first and youngest president. Delegates to the Assembly of Representatives, representing nine million Filipinos, approved the constitution. It guaranteed separation of church and state with basic human rights for its citizens. Congress passed a law allowing the Philippines to borrow 20 million pesos from banks and the establishment of the Universidad Literatura De Filipinas. (Courtesy of the Lopez family history Facebook page.)

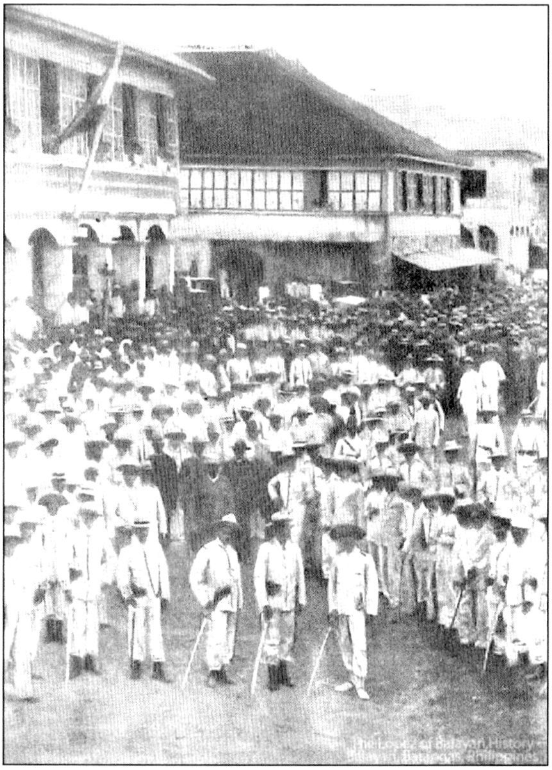

Here is Aguinaldo's army in Iloilo, Philippines. Prior to becoming the next imperial overlord of the Philippines in 1899, the United States actually supported the independence of the Philippines, and on June 16, 1898, in a nationwide press release, Oscar Williams, American consul in Manila, applauded Aguinaldo: "[He] has organized a government . . . and from that day to this he has been uninterruptedly successful in the field and dignified and just, as the head of his government." (Courtesy of the Lopez family history Facebook page.)

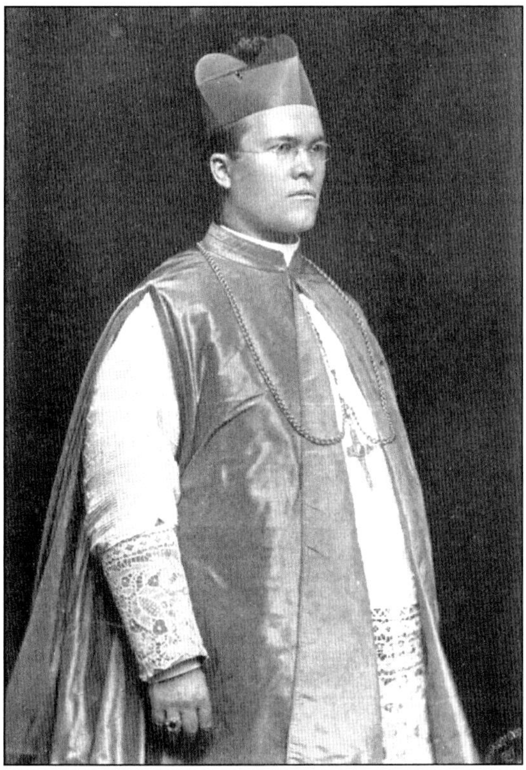

After serving as a priest in Philadelphia, Cardinal Denis Dougherty was appointed bishop of Nueva Segovia, Philippines. He took back the Catholic population from Gregorio Aglipay. Aglipay founded the Philippine Independent Church, setting out to change all baptized Spanish names and convert them to Filipino. Traveling through jungles, Dougherty visited leper colonies and brought Aglipay's revolution to a halt. He then became bishop of Jaro, Philippines, on April 19, 1908. (Courtesy of Philadelphia Archdiocesan Historical Center.)

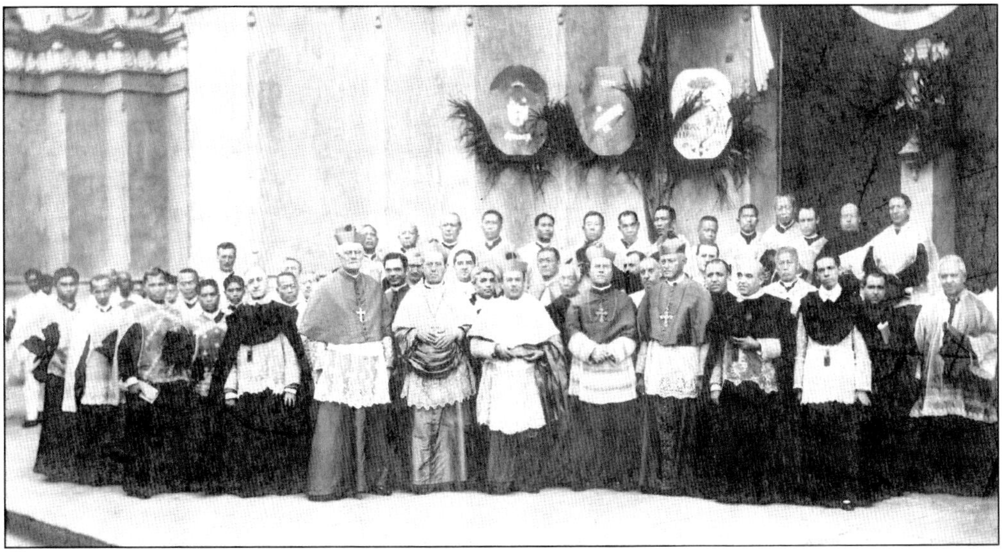

Here is a provincial council of Manila in 1907. Whenever Dougherty drove past the Navy yard, he would point to Dewey's flagship and say, "There's the reason I became a bishop." He confirmed over 70,000 in his first years in the Philippines. He reopened a girls' academy, renamed it Sisters of the Assumption, and built another one in Tuguegarao. This religious order of women was to become the first women's community to enter Philadelphia. (Courtesy of Philadelphia Archdiocesan Historical Center.)

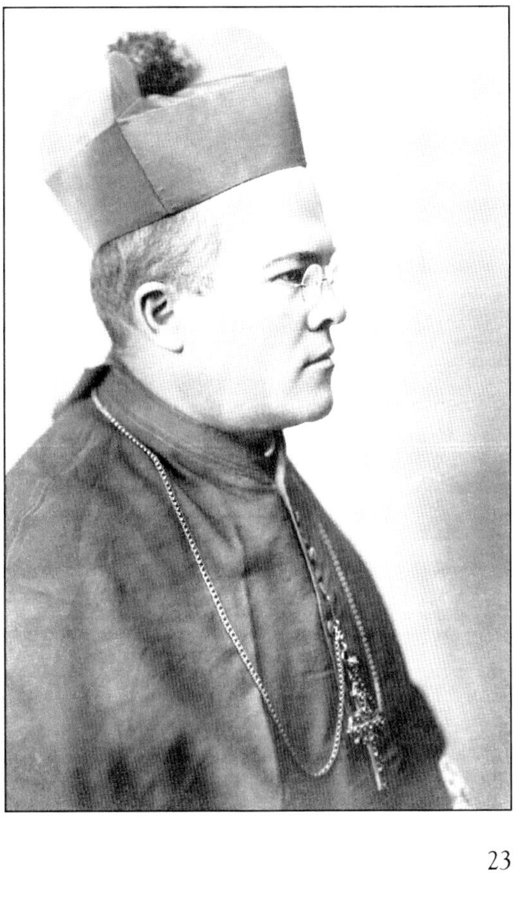

In 1915, Cardinal Dougherty returned as bishop of Buffalo, New York, and in Philadelphia as archbishop. In 1937, Pope Pius XI sent Dougherty to the Eucharistic Congress in Manila, the first time an American presided over a church meeting as representative of the Pope. In Philadelphia, he called himself "God's Bricklayer," establishing numerous parishes, parochial schools, Catholic high schools, four Catholic colleges, hospitals, and homes for the elderly, and ordained over 2,000 priests. (Courtesy of Philadelphia Archdiocesan Historical Center.)

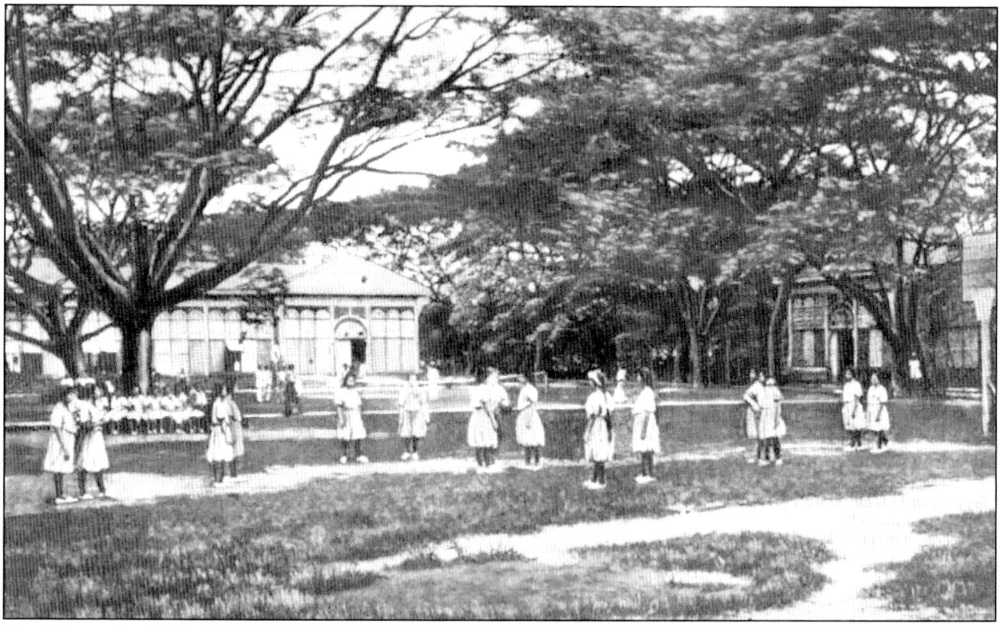

On November 3, 1903, the first 100 *pensionados* (students) arrived in the United States. Not long after, a dozen attended the best universities in Philadelphia. This photograph shows the front side of a postcard, written by Genoveva Llamas and sent to her teacher. Dated 1913, it accompanied a jar of mango preserves. Other Drexel students include Carlos Barretto (Manila), Olivia Salamanca (Cavite), and Luisa Sison (Pangasinan), all graduates of 1908. By 1912, a total of 209 Filipinos under the program cost the United States $479,940. (Courtesy of Drexel Institute Archives.)

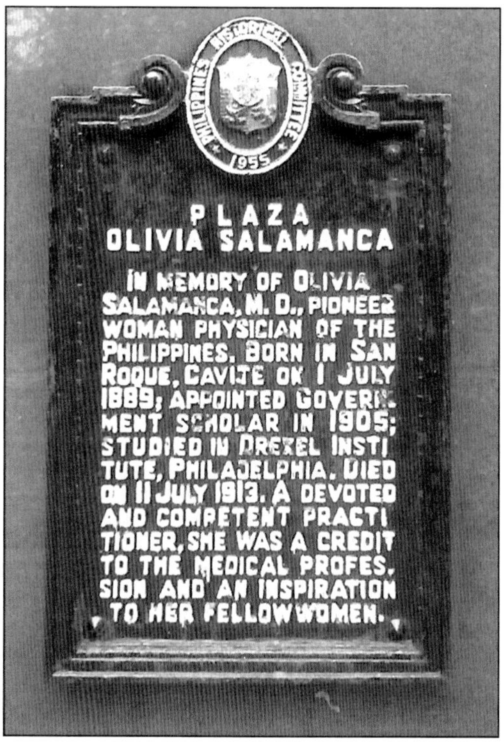

Pictured here is a plaque located in Olivia Salamanca Plaza at the corner of Taft and Gen. Luna Streets in Ermita, Manila, in honor of a pioneer Filipina doctor who studied at Drexel Institute. Dr. Olivia Salamanca, from Cavite, Philippines, went to Drexel for her secondary course and graduated with a medical degree from the Women's Medical College in Philadelphia in 1910, the second Filipina to earn a medical degree in the United States.

In April 1900, a student-run theater group of the University of Pennsylvania, called the Mask and Wig Club, produced a theatrical satire on Gen. Emilio Aguinaldo, entitled "Mr. Aguinaldo of Manila." In its July 6, 1931, issue, *Time* magazine stated that "Emilio Aguinaldo was a bloody name with which to frighten US children after dark." (Courtesy of University of Pennsylvania Archives.)

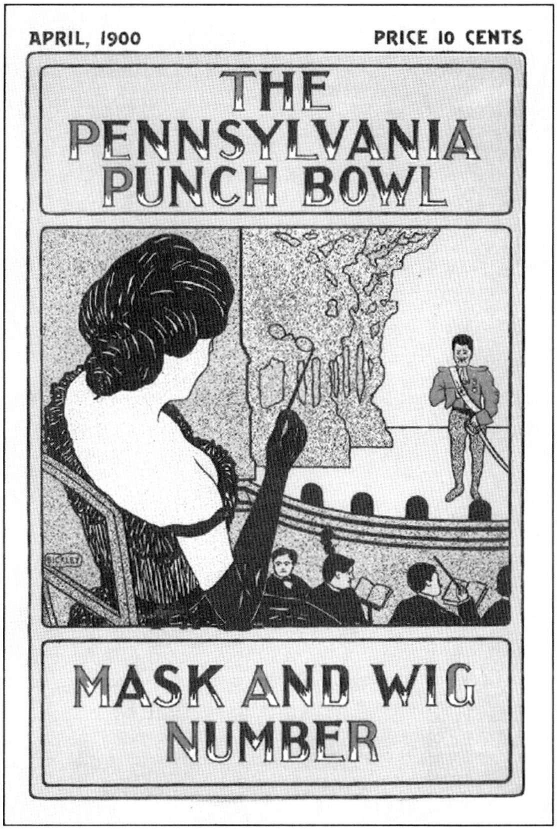

Pacifico Laygo was a student from Batangas who, according to the text accompanying this photograph, endured discrimination during his time in America. Most of the students hosted by families in Philadelphia came from aristocratic Filipino families. In 1906, *pensionados* published *Filipino* magazine, the first Filipino publication in the United States. Philadelphia's own Olivia Salamanca was the editor for women. Published in Washington, D.C., each edition was 20¢ or $1 for a one-year subscription. (Courtesy of University of Pennsylvania Archives.)

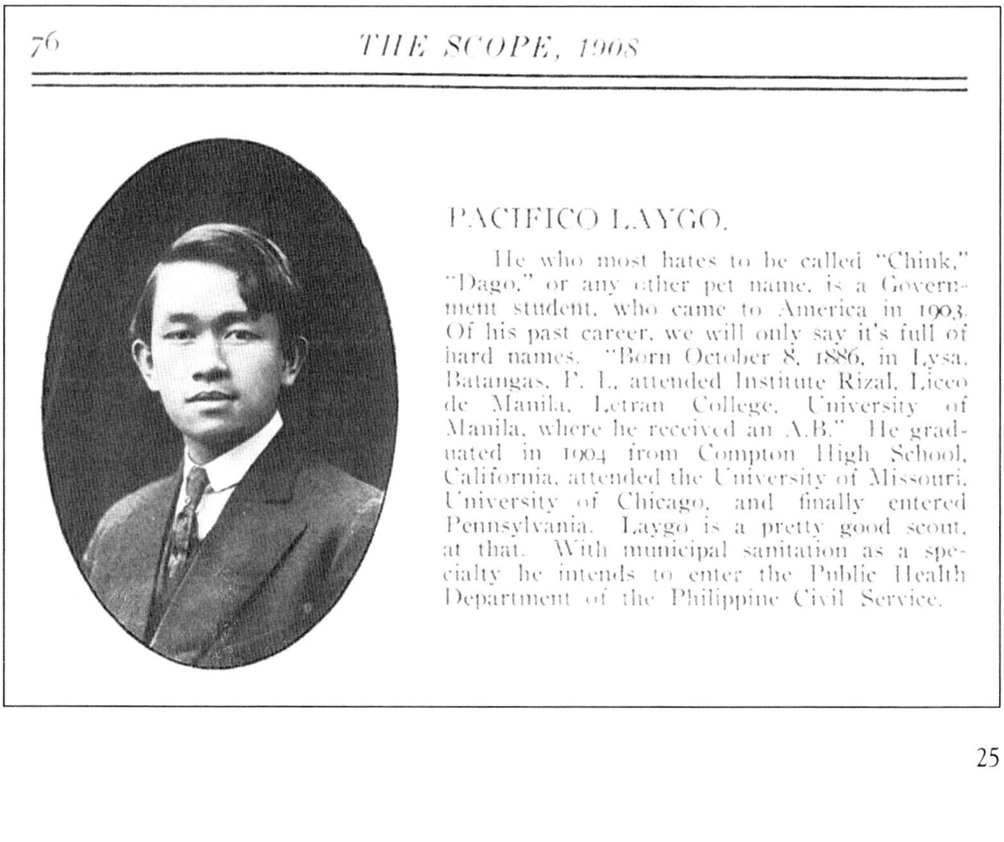

76 *THE SCOPE, 1908*

PACIFICO LAYGO.

He who most hates to be called "Chink," "Dago," or any other pet name, is a Government student, who came to America in 1903. Of his past career, we will only say it's full of hard names. "Born October 8, 1886, in Lysa, Batangas, P. I., attended Institute Rizal, Liceo de Manila, Letran College, University of Manila, where he received an A.B." He graduated in 1904 from Compton High School, California, attended the University of Missouri, University of Chicago, and finally entered Pennsylvania. Laygo is a pretty good scout, at that. With municipal sanitation as a specialty he intends to enter the Public Health Department of the Philippine Civil Service.

102 *THE SCOPE, 1908*

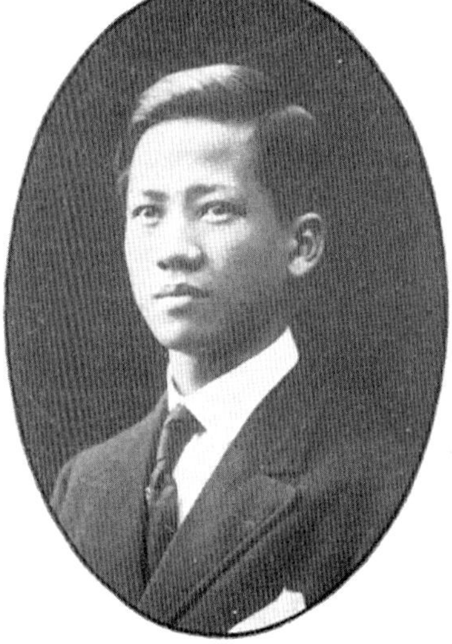

ANTONIO G. SISON.

Sison hails from the Philippines, where he was born February 11, 1883. He prepared at a private school and later entered the "Liceo de Manila," and still later Letran College of Manila, where he snatched an A.B. in 1903. Just as he was taking up his first year in the medical department of the University of Manila, the Philippine government appointed him to one of the government scholarships, and sent him to the United States to pursue medicine. He took his freshman year at the University of Missouri, but hearing of the fame of Pennsylvania, came East and joined us in our second year. Sison is a diligent and a conscientious student and fully deserves the scholarship that he holds from the Government. He expects to enter the Philippine Civil Service on his return home.

A 1908 graduate of the University of Pennsylvania, Antonio Sison became the chief of the medical staff of the Philippine General Hospital. During the great influenza epidemic in 1918, Dr. Sison returned to Philadelphia to volunteer at the university's hospital since help was sorely needed. The Filipino Association of Philadelphia, led by Agripino Jaucian and his wife, Florence Marvel Jaucian, a registered nurse, voluntarily rendered services to Filipinos and other residents of Philadelphia during the great influenza epidemic as well. (Courtesy of University of Pennsylvania Archives.)

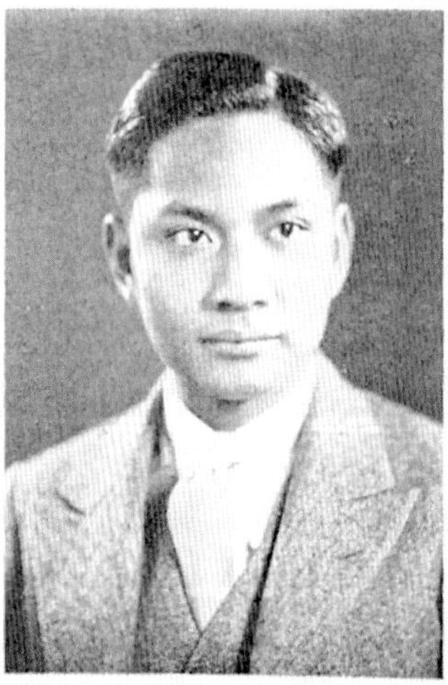

CASIMIRO MARCOS VALDEZ
"Miro"
Batac Ilocos Norte, Philippine Islands
WHARTON

Ilocos Norte High School; Vice-President Filipino Students Club; Treasurer, International Students' Council; L'Academie Cosmopolite.

JOSEPH VOCATURO
Nutley, N. J.
COLLEGE

Casimiro Valdez Marcos was born in the same province (Batac, Ilocos Norte) as Mariano Marcos, the father of future president Ferdinand E. Marcos. In another photograph taken outside the provost's house, Casimiro is pictured with other University of Pennsylvania foreign students from India, New Zealand, Bulgaria, and British West Indies in attendance at the Provost Penniman's 1936 annual Christmas dinner. Some Filipino students never returned to their mother country, becoming pioneers of Filipino communities in America. (Courtesy of University of Pennsylvania Archives.)

Two

Manifest Destiny and Dissenting Filipinos

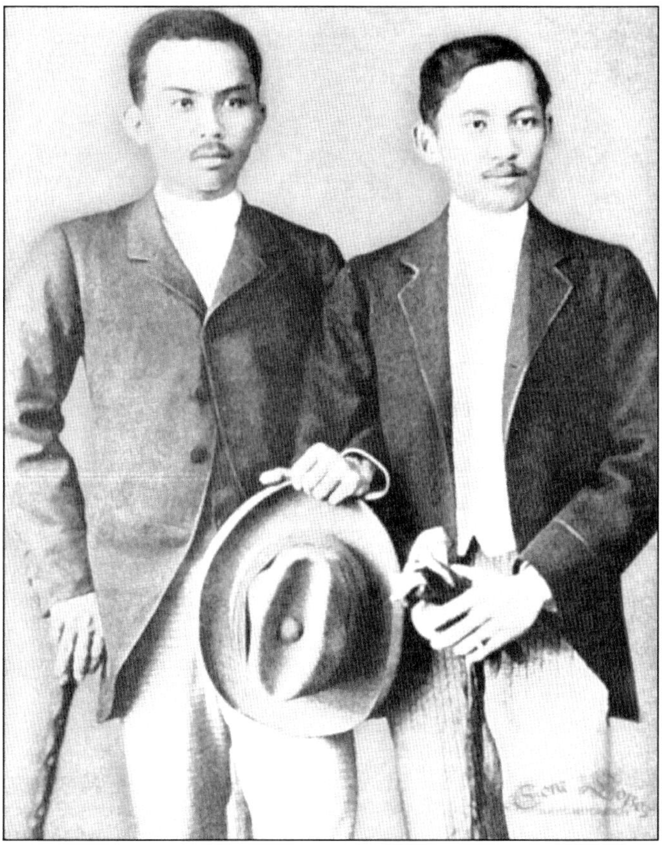

Sixto Lopez (left) and Jose Rizal (right) were the most effective voices in the movement of dissent against the US imperial war on the Philippines. Though martyred in 1896, Rizal's writings were the foremost arguments used to dispel hostility toward non-white governments. Sixto was secretary to the diplomatic commission, created the same day Aguinaldo proclaimed Philippine independence in 1898. After hostilities broke out, Sixto wrote in numerous publications and delivered public speeches throughout the east coast, including Philadelphia. (Courtesy of Lopez of Balayan, Batangas Foundation / the Lopez family history Facebook page.)

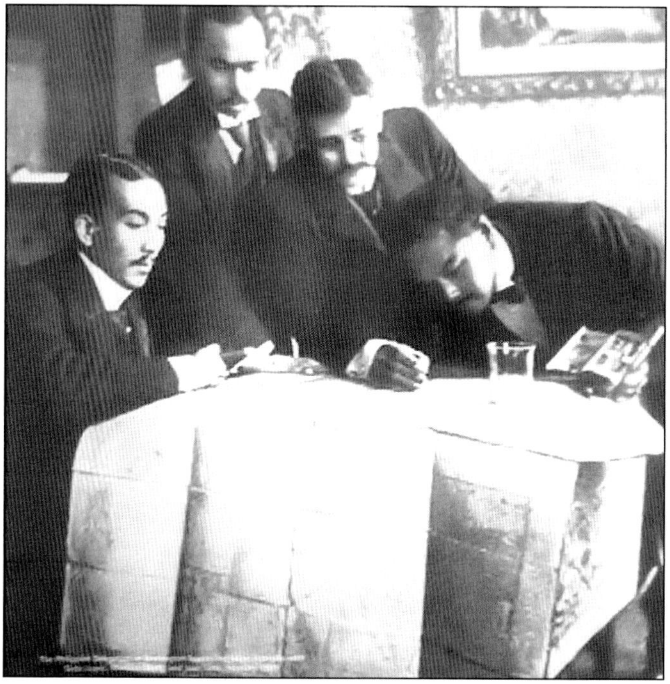

From left to right, Felipe Agoncillo, Sixto Lopez, and two unidentified Filipinos prepare their arguments blocking the passage of the Treaty of Paris and encouraging the global recognition of the new Philippine Republic. Felipe Agoncillo headed this diplomatic commission, with Sixto as his secretary. Agoncillo, the first Filipino diplomat, took the bar exam in Manila in 1905 and attained a perfect score of 100 percent, an achievement that has remained unmatched to the present day. (Courtesy of Lopez of Balayan, Batangas Foundation / the Lopez family history Facebook page.)

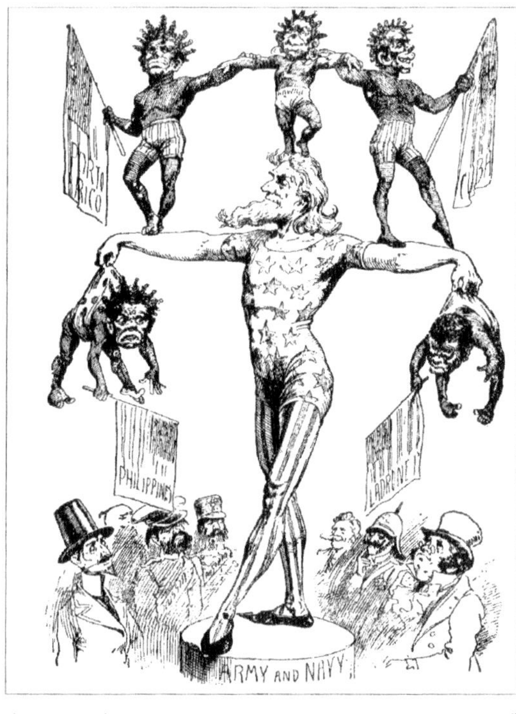

"UNCLE SAM'S NEW CAUGHT ANTHROPOIDS, HOLDING HIS END UP."
"JOHN BULL—'It's really most extraordinary what training will do. Why, only the other day I thought that man unable to support himself.'"[3]

Philadelphia Inquirer, also published in *The Literary Digest*, Vol. XVII, No. 8, August 20, 1898, p. 215 [artist: unknown]

This editorial cartoon, published by the *Philadelphia Inquirer*, portrays non-white governments as African natives regardless of what continent the nation is from. Racist depictions of Filipinos and Aguinaldo dominated US media at a time before televised news. Manifest Destiny was a widely held belief that the United States was destined to expand westward across the North American continent, from the eastern seaboard to the Pacific Ocean. This is a belief in an American mission to promote and defend democracy throughout the world. (Courtesy of Abraham Ignacio.)

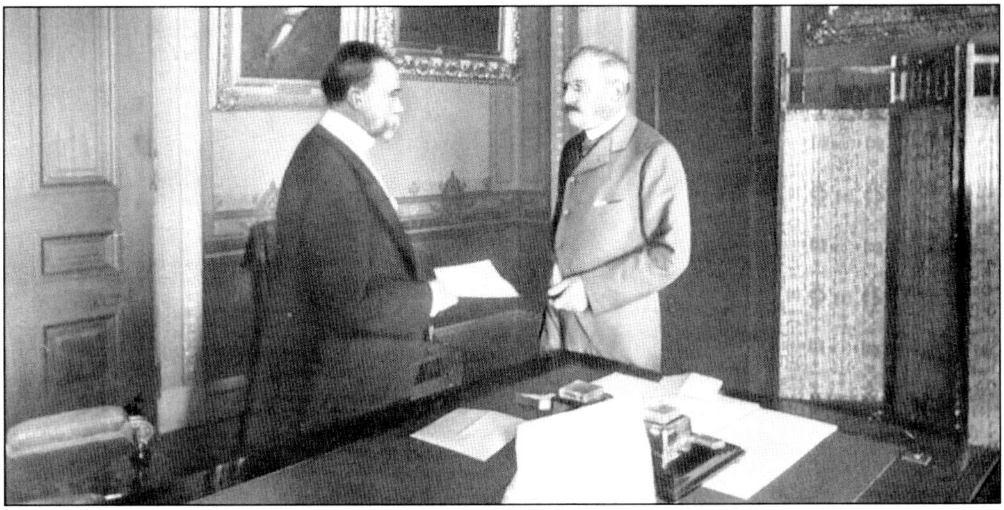

On May 1, 1899, a total of $20 million was handed over by US secretary of state John Hay to French ambassador Jules Cambon, under the terms of the Treaty of Paris, which ended the Spanish-American War. The more costly war with Asian nationalists that followed was erased as a footnote. There has yet to be a national memorial honoring the 10,000 Americans wounded and almost 5,000 who died in the US military campaign from 1898 to 1913. (Courtesy of Arnaldo Dumindin.)

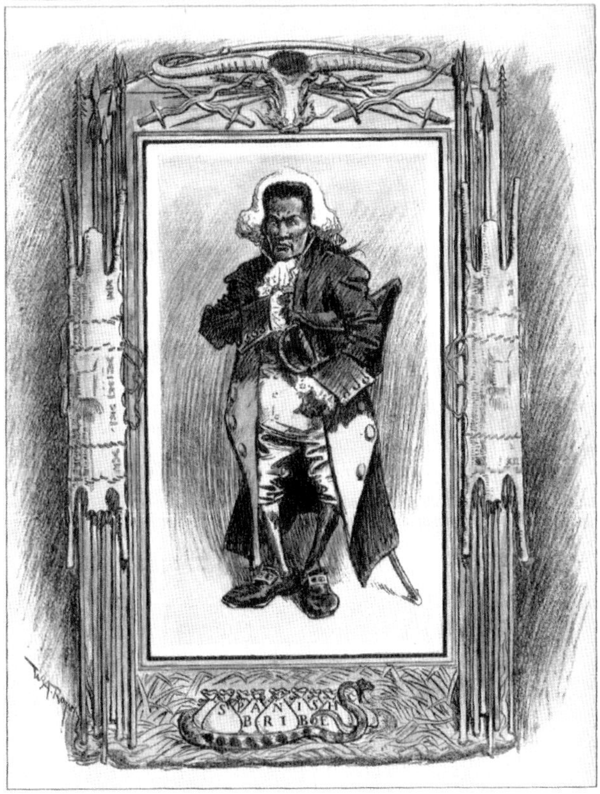

"A PORTRAIT OF GEORGE WASHINGTON DISCOVERED NEAR FANEUIL HALL. (ATTRIBUTED TO THE ATKINSON SCHOOL OF WORD-PAINTERS.)"[7]
Harper's Weekly, Harper & Brothers, New York, February 24, 1900 [artist: William A. Rogers]

Inflicting the severest blow against American imperialism, Aguinaldo is depicted here in the least flattering manner. Unfortunately, Filipinos today perceive Aguinaldo in similar fashion, resulting in a damaged culture that weakens solidarity behind the Philippines. Mark Twain compared Aguinaldo with Joan of Arc and said, "The people worshipped him, covering his path with flowers, the children dropped on their knees at his approach and the natives doffed their hats in reverence." (Courtesy of Abraham Ignacio.)

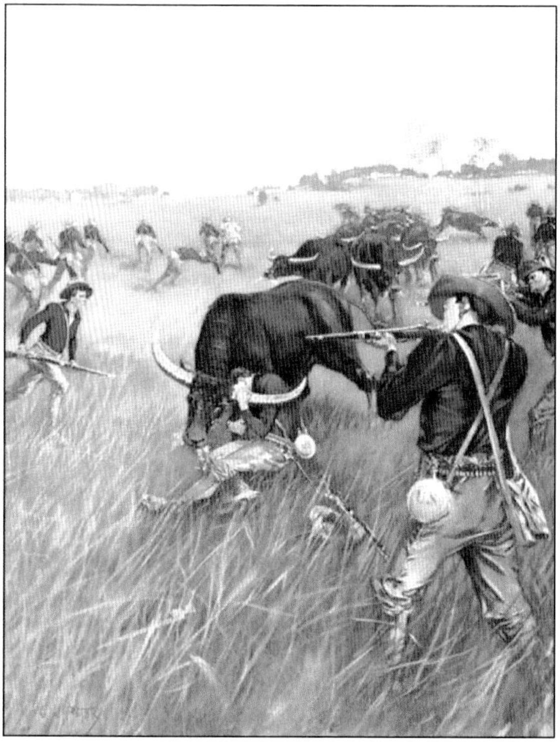

The 1900 Carabao Charge happened in Santa Cruz, Laguna, during the Philippine-American War when a herd of water buffaloes, or *carabao*, was caught in the volley of fire between Filipino and American lines. These farm animals started a stampede that inflicted massive casualties on the US side. Interestingly, a similar incident occurred in 1899 in the same province with the same outcome. In 1900, the Military Order of the Carabao was established in the United States. (Courtesy of Ambeth Ocampo.)

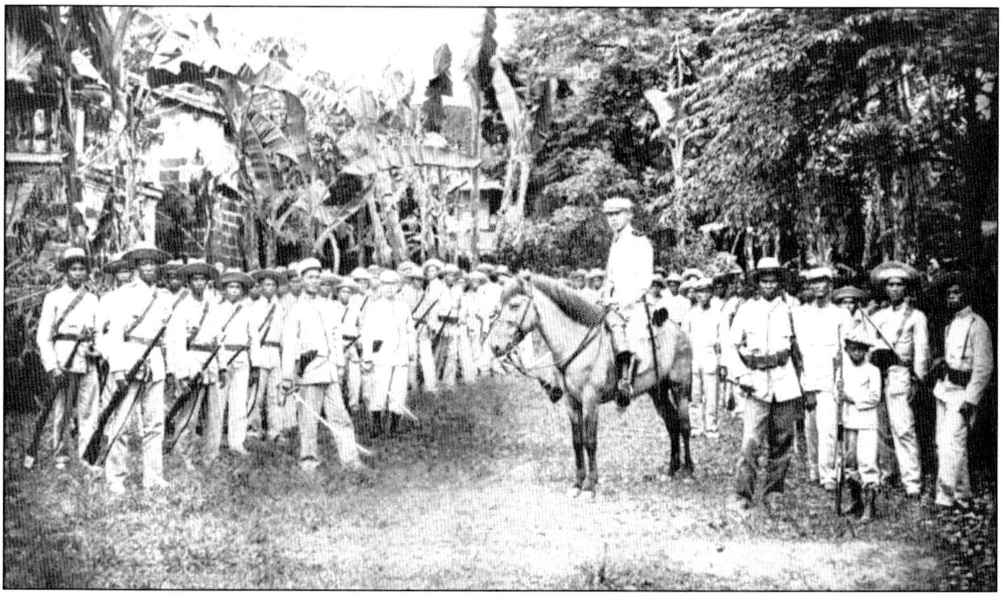

The Battle of Tirad Pass, led by 24-year-old Gen. Gregorio del Pilar, is the Filipino equivalent of the Battle of Thermopayle. In an epic battle above the clouds, Pilar succeeded in blocking the advance of 500 Texas Rangers for five hours with only 60 soldiers under his command, securing safe passage for Aguinaldo's army into the Cordillera mountains and launching the guerilla war. Similar victories against the United States were achieved by Filipinos in Quingua (Plaridel), Bulacan; Mabitac, Laguna; Makahumbus Hill, Cagayan de Oro; Pulang Lupa, Marinduque; and San Mateo, Rizal. (Courtesy of Arnaldo Dumindin.)

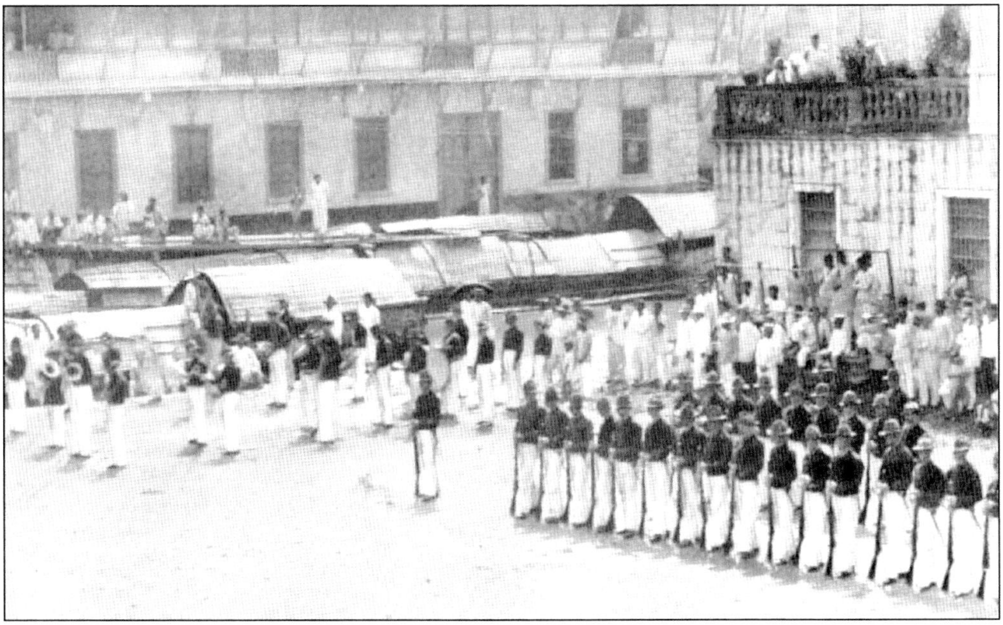

India's Gandhi and Jawarhal Nehru, along with China's Sun Yat Sen, were stunned at the developments of the US war in the Philippines and inspired the Asian independence movement. With no foreign alliance necessary for a prolonged war, shiploads of soldiers were consistently sent to defeat Aguinaldo. By March 1902, the US military campaign cost $400 million, with about 10,000 wounded and 5,000 dead. There has yet to be a memorial for the 126,000 US veterans of this forgotten war. (Courtesy of Arnaldo Dumindin.)

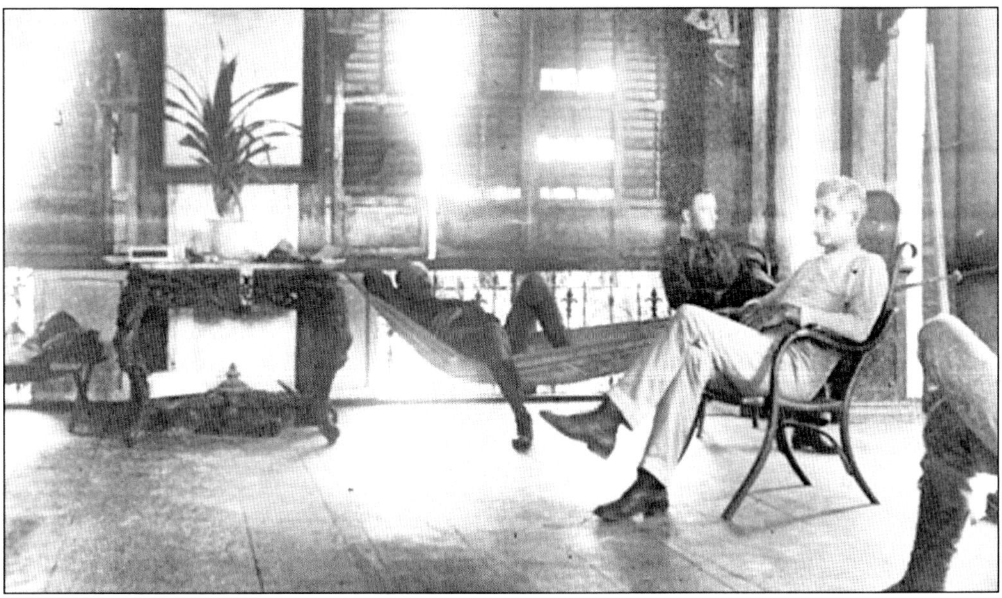

Gen. Henry Lawton was the highest-ranking American casualty of the war. Having claimed fame in 1886 as the captor of Apache chief Geronimo, Lawton lost his life to forces led by Filipino Gen. Licerio Geronimo in 1899. In a correspondence prior to his defeat, Lawton praised the Filipinos: "Taking into account the disadvantages they have to fight against in terms of arms, they are the bravest men I have ever seen." (Courtesy of Arnaldo Dumindin.)

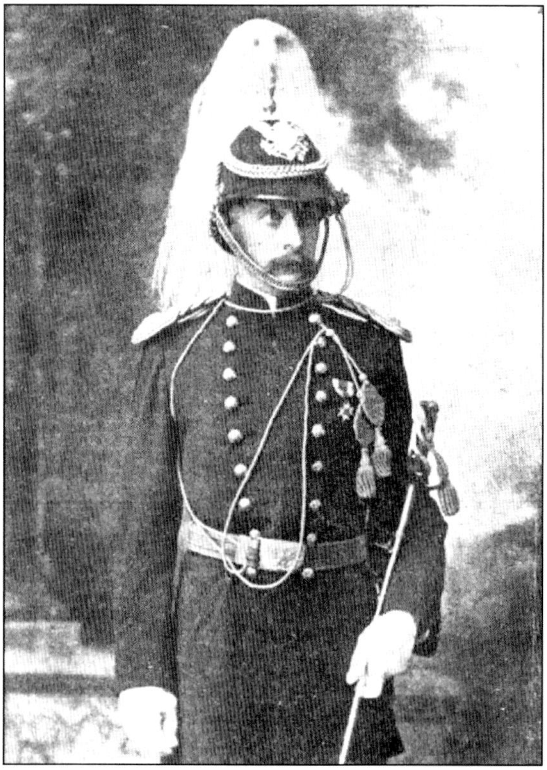

Gen. Jacob Smith was court martialed for ordering his men to "Kill everyone over 10!" in retaliation for the US defeat in the Battle of Balangiga led by Filipino general Vicente Lukban. Smith became known as the "Butcher of Samar," turning the province into a "howling wilderness." Similar to the Seige of Catubig in Samar a year earlier, where about 20 to 30 US soldiers were killed, Balangiga cost the United States 31 lives. (Courtesy of Dnvzs Zjzllg.)

Here is an editorial cartoon appearing in the *Philadelphia Inquirer* after the capture of Aguinaldo in March 1902. Prominent Americans, including Andrew Carnegie and Mark Twain, founded the Anti-Imperialist League in Boston. They organized the earliest antiwar demonstrations in the United States. This war also inspired the defection of 20 American soldiers, the largest in US history. Five of them were Buffalo Soldiers, including Pvt. David Fagen, who was promoted to general by Aguinaldo. (Courtesy of Abraham Ignacio.)

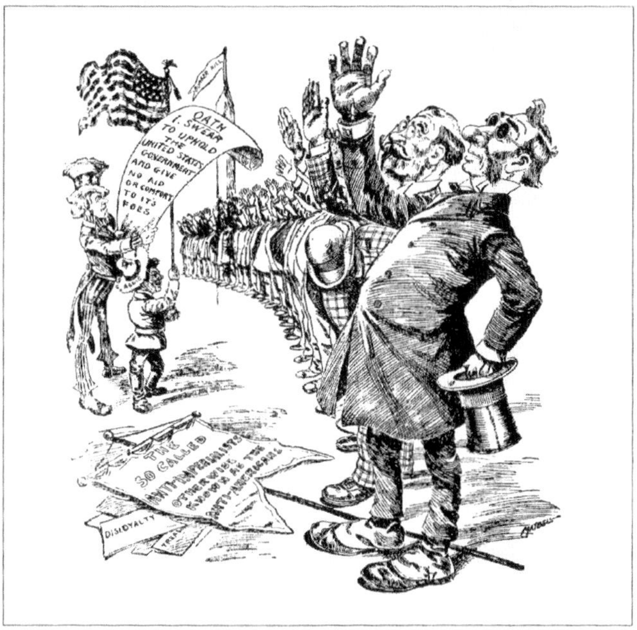

"NOW LET THE BOSTON INSURGENTS FOLLOW AGGIE'S EXAMPLE AND TAKE THE OATH OF ALLEGIANCE."

Philadelphia Inquirer, also published in *The American Monthly Review of Reviews*, Vol. XXIII, No. 5, May 1901, p. 547 [artist: Claudius Maybell]

Sixto Lopez (left) is pictured with Fiske Warren. Warren invited Lopez, Aguinaldo's member of the diplomatic commission created to secure American recognition of Philippine independence, to the United States. During the guerilla war, US casualties escalated. Arthur MacArthur said, "I have been reluctantly compelled to believe that the Filipino masses are loyal to Aguinaldo and the government which he heads. This unique system of warfare employed by the Filipino Army depended upon almost complete unity of action of the entire native population." (Courtesy of Lopez of Balayan, Batangas Foundation / the Lopez family history Facebook page.)

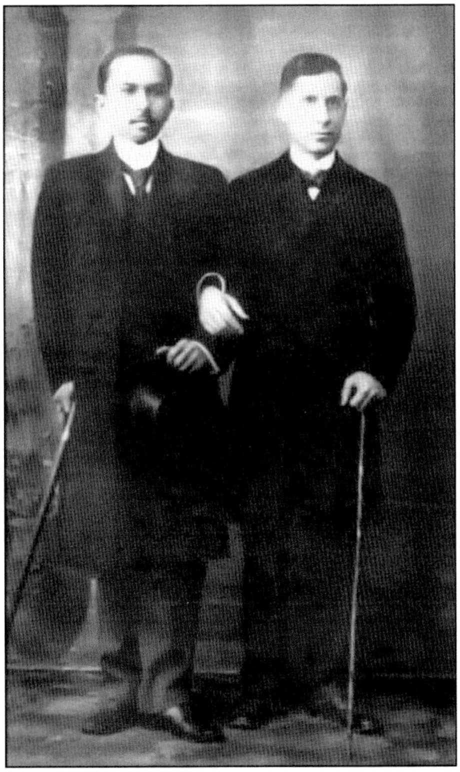

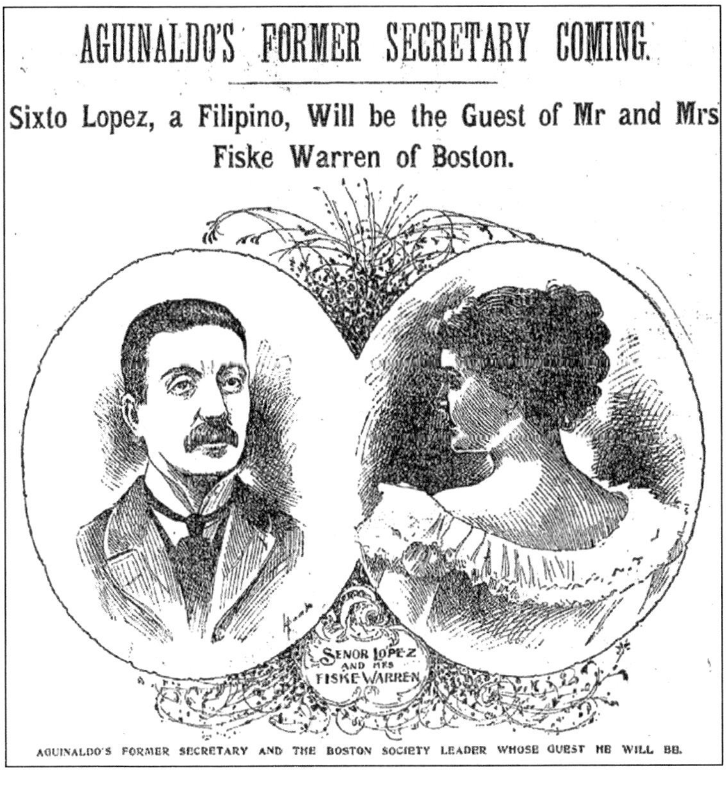

AGUINALDO'S FORMER SECRETARY COMING.

Sixto Lopez, a Filipino, Will be the Guest of Mr and Mrs Fiske Warren of Boston.

SENOR LOPEZ AND MRS FISKE WARREN

AGUINALDO'S FORMER SECRETARY AND THE BOSTON SOCIETY LEADER WHOSE GUEST HE WILL BE.

Sixto Lopez wrote numerous essays and delivered countless speeches throughout the east coast, including Philadelphia, where he stayed for an extended period as a guest of the American League of Philadelphia. "Had the Filipinos been white and fought as bravely as they have, the war would have ended and her independence granted long ago," stated Bishop A. Wuthers in a speech to the National African American Congress on September 2, 1899. (Courtesy of the Lopez family history Facebook page.)

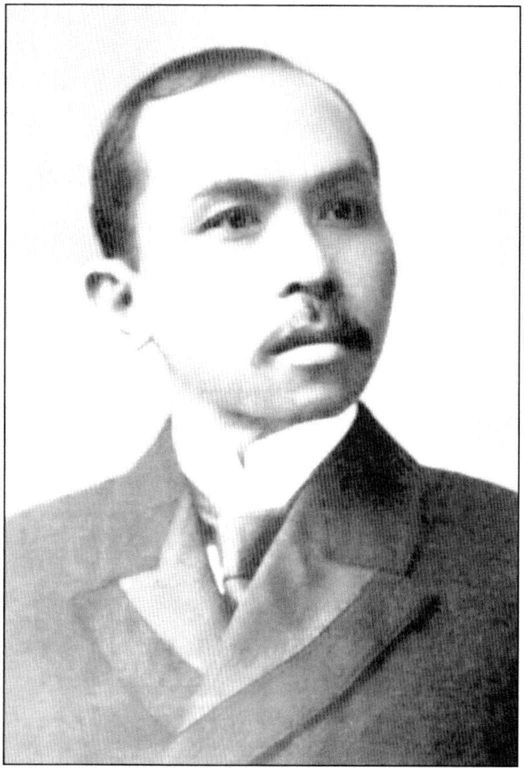

Sixto Lopez from Balayan, Batangas, became known in US media as the "Filipino Agitator" or the "Simón Bolívar of the Philippines," depending on the perspective of the source. These nicknames reflect how deeply divided the Americans were on their first colonial adventure overseas. On General Aguinaldo's capture and swearing of US allegiance, Sixto Lopez said, "It all depends under what circumstances . . . if he took it believing it would be the quickest way of obtaining independence, then he would be personally justified." (Courtesy of the Lopez family history Facebook page.)

AN APPEAL FOR JUSTICE

SIXTO LOPEZ, AT PHILADELPHIA, "EXPLAINS THE DESIRES OF HIS COUNTRYMEN"

SAYS THE WAR IS NEEDLESS

Draws a Parallel With the Days of George III. of England and the War for American Independence.

PHILADELPHIA. Senor Sixto Lopez, a native Filipino, addressed a mass meeting of citizens of Philadelphia at the New Century hall this evening, he having accepted an invitation to "Explain the desires of his countrymen." He said, in part:

"My mission in this country is not only to tell the ruth about the Philippines, but to obtain peace. The way out of the present difficulty may be summed up in one phrase:

" 'Do unto others as you desired George III. should do unto you. Be great enough to determine to do right, no matter what may be thought or said by other nations, who are too busy doing wrong to ever regard it as dignified to do right.'

"Admit that the Filipinos have the same rights which you yourselves enjoy. Admit that there have been mutual misunderstandings. If wrong has been done, admit that also, and rectify it. It is nobler to admit a wrong than to persist in it. Had congress declared its intentions towards the Philippines, conformable with Philippine independence, the clash of arms would have been heard no more and strife would have ceased between two peoples who ought never to have been other than friends. Let the Filipinos re-establish the government which they have instituted with the consent of the governed; take whatever means are necessary to protect your interests and to discharge your international obligations. You will then be surprised, though perhaps it will not be a surprise to some, to find that all your fears about anarchy and disunity and failure will have proved to be groundless. Another example will have been given to kings, showing that the people may be trusted to govern themselves, and we shall be able to look up at 'Old Glory' knowing that it is the symbol of liberty—liberty, not only to this people, but to all mankind."

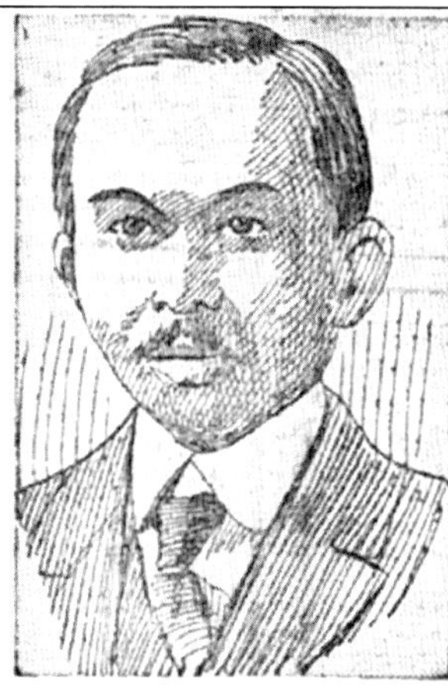

SIXTO LOPEZ.

"Had Congress declared its intentions toward the Philippines, conformable with Philippine Independence, the clash of arms would have been heard no more . . . you will then be surprised, to find that all your fears about anarchy, will have proved to be groundless," said Sixto Lopez in Philadelphia on March 12, 1901. At another mass rally in 1901, Sixto declared, "As long as they retain their self-respect they will never submit to a master, however benevolently inclined they may be." (Courtesy of the Lopez family history Facebook page.)

Clemencia Lopez captured the United States with her natural beauty and charmed Americans with her wit and character. In a farewell banquet before Clemencia's return to Batangas, Wellesley professor Katareine Coman highlighted her influence: "Wellesley College has had abundant opportunity to prove the civilization of the Filipinos . . . we have found Senorita Lopez a most delightful, courteous, charming and responsive student. We are indebted to Miss Lopez for the demonstration she has given for the possibilities of that people." (Courtesy of the Lopez family history Facebook page.)

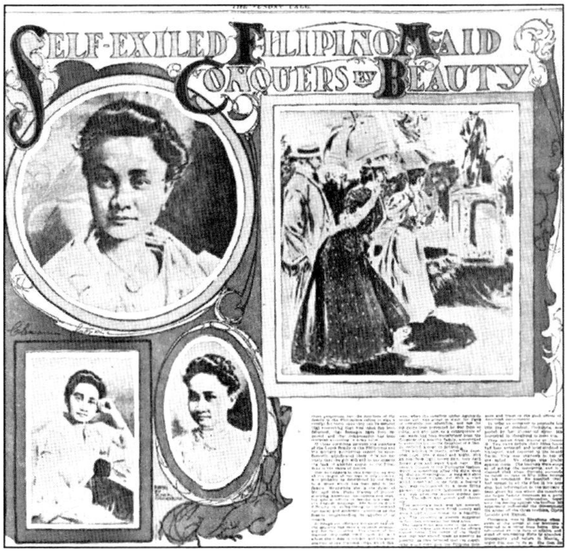

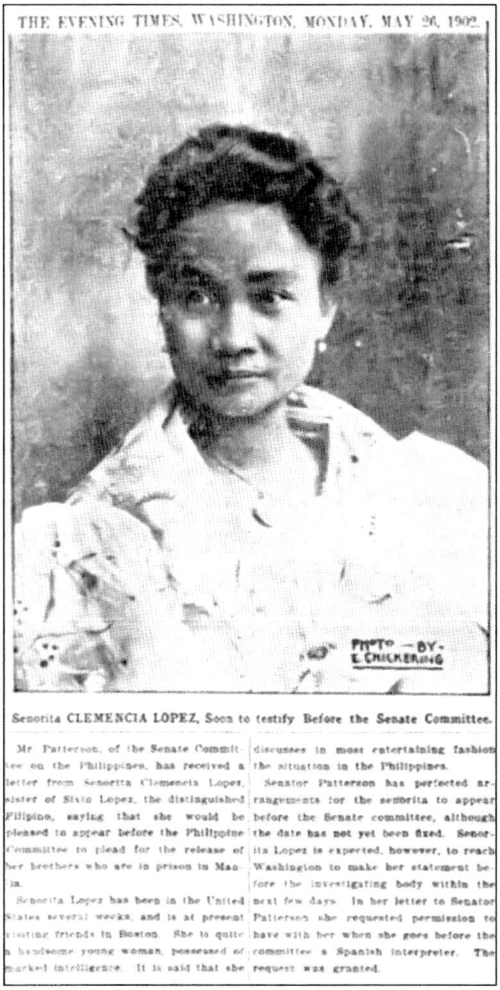

THE EVENING TIMES, WASHINGTON, MONDAY, MAY 26, 1902.

Senorita CLEMENCIA LOPEZ, Soon to testify Before the Senate Committee.

Mr. Patterson, of the Senate Committee on the Philippines, has received a letter from Senorita Clemencia Lopez, sister of Sixto Lopez, the distinguished Filipino, saying that she would be pleased to appear before the Philippine Committee to plead for the release of her brothers who are in prison in Manila.

Senorita Lopez has been in the United States several weeks, and is at present visiting friends in Boston. She is quite a handsome young woman, possessed of marked intelligence. It is said that she discusses in most entertaining fashion the situation in the Philippines.

Senator Patterson has perfected arrangements for the senorita to appear before the Senate committee, although the date has not yet been fixed. Senorita Lopez is expected, however, to reach Washington to make her statement before the investigating body within the next few days. In her letter to Senator Patterson she requested permission to have with her when she goes before the committee a Spanish interpreter. The request was granted.

Clemencia was granted an audience with Pres. Theodore Roosevelt in March 1902 to plead for US recognition of Philippine independence and an end to the unjust deportation and imprisonment of her brothers who refused to pledge allegiance to the United States. She became the first Filipino to enter the White House and the first to testify before a US Senate hearing as a representative of her subjugated people. (Courtesy of the Lopez family history Facebook page.)

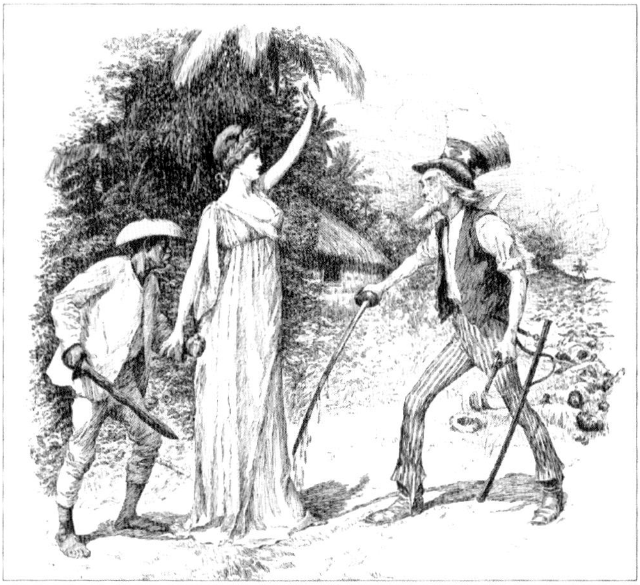

"LIBERTY: STOP THIS BLOODY WORK, SAM! HE IS THE ONE WHO IS FIGHTING FOR *ME*."

Life, Life Publishing Company, New York, June 8, 1899
[artist: William H. Walker]

On June 19, 1902, Congressman Cooper of Wisconsin recited the Charles Derbyshire translation of Jose Rizal's *Mi Ultimo Adios* inside the halls of US Congress in its entirety, enabling the passage of the Philippine Organic Act, granting civil rights to Filipinos and creating Asia's first elected legislature at a time when non-white American citizens had yet to be granted their own civil rights. This poem was recited by Filipino—and much later, Indonesian—soldiers of independence before going into battle, fulfilling Rizal's larger vision of an Asian Renaissance, embodied in his 1889 *Redemption of the Malay Race*. (Courtesy of Abraham Ignacio.)

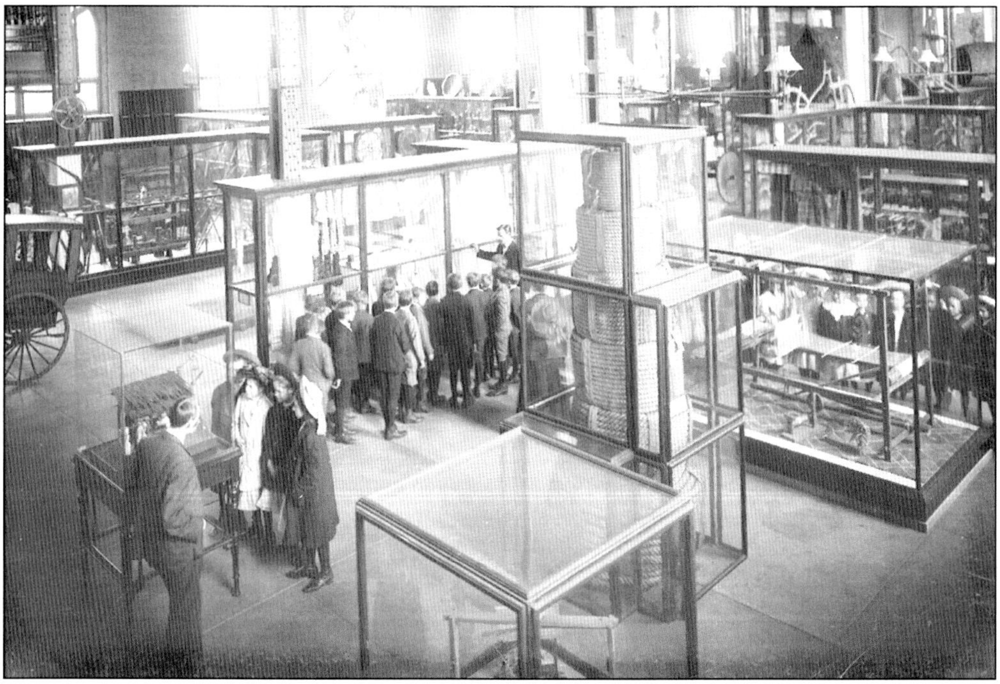

Here, a public school class views the Philippine Collection at the Philadelphia Commercial Museum in 1910. Dr. William Wilson, founder of the Commercial Museum, was tasked to put together a Philippine Exhibit for the 1909 World's Exposition in Nancy, France; it featured 1,200 live dioramas of native Filipinos. The inanimate portions of the attraction were displayed permanently in Philadelphia. Just like the 1904 St. Louis World's Fair, the Philippine Exhibit proved to be the largest attraction of the fair. (Courtesy of Independence Seaport Museum.)

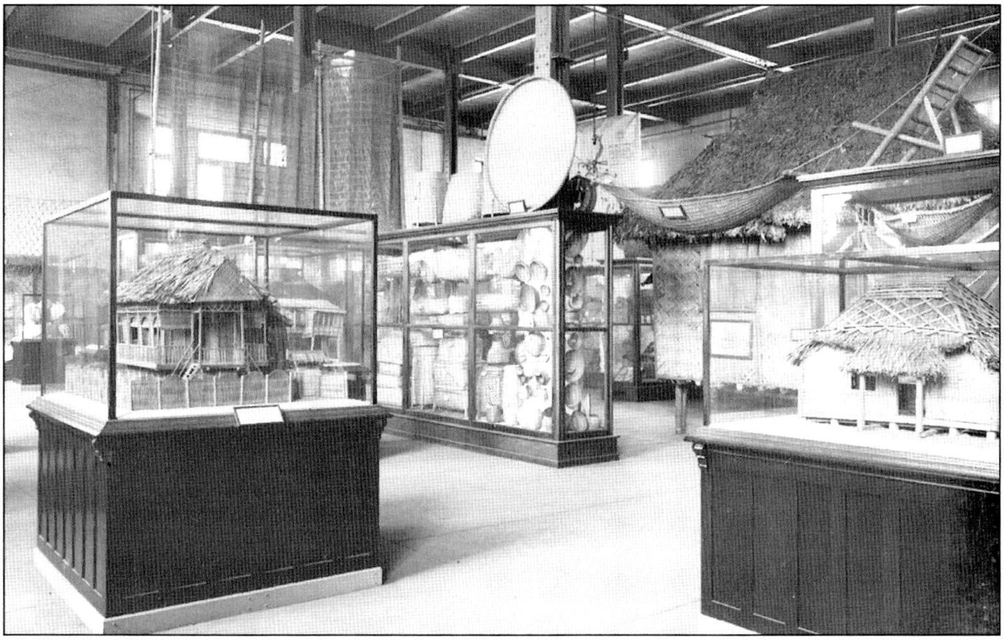

Here is a panoramic shot of the Philippine Collection at the Philadelphia Commercial Museum. The whereabouts of images of the living Filipinos used for the American-sponsored Philippine Exhibit in France are unknown. The closest one can get to imagining the Philippine Exhibit in France is by viewing photographs of the 42-acre Philippine Exhibit at the 1904 St. Louis World's Fair, featuring 1,100 live Filipino displays that were designed to reinforce racial stereotypes. (Courtesy of Independence Seaport Museum.)

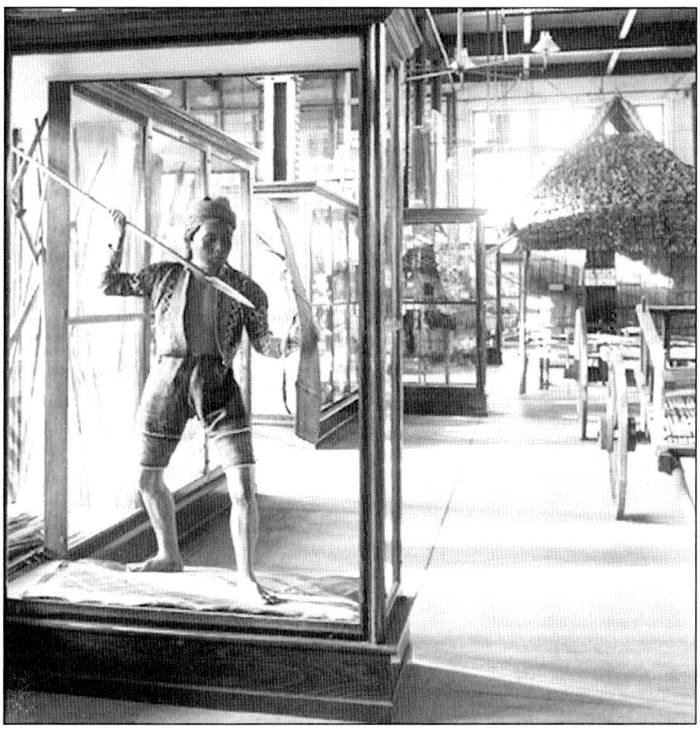

This view of the Philippine Collection at the Philadelphia Commercial Museum shows a life-size model of a Bagobo warrior. These so-called anthropological exhibits were arranged to emphasize the superiority of Caucasian accomplishments as a civilizing force and the Filipinos as savages in need of the civilizing presence of the white man. In this case, the force resided in the American government, which had taken over Asia's first constitutional democratic republic. (Courtesy of Independence Seaport Museum.)

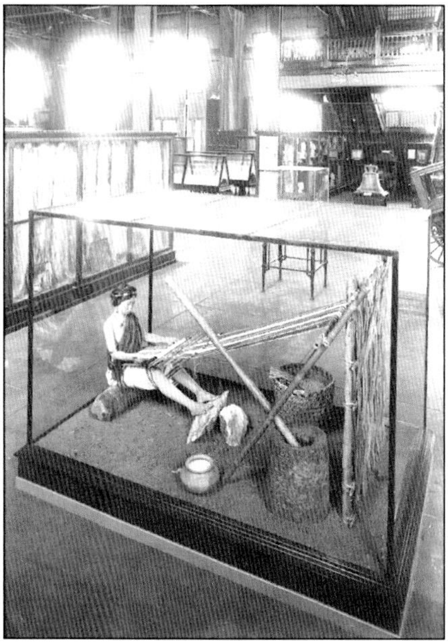

Found in the Philippine Collection at the Commercial Museum is a life-size model of an Igorot woman weaving. The 1904 St. Louis World's Fair exhibit's main draw was the live consumption of dogs within the Igorot Village. Total admission returns for the Igorot Village alone were $200,387.18. An estimated 600 dogs were choreographed to be consumed on a daily basis at the live display, even though their culture only performs these acts in an entirely different context. (Courtesy of Independence Seaport Museum.)

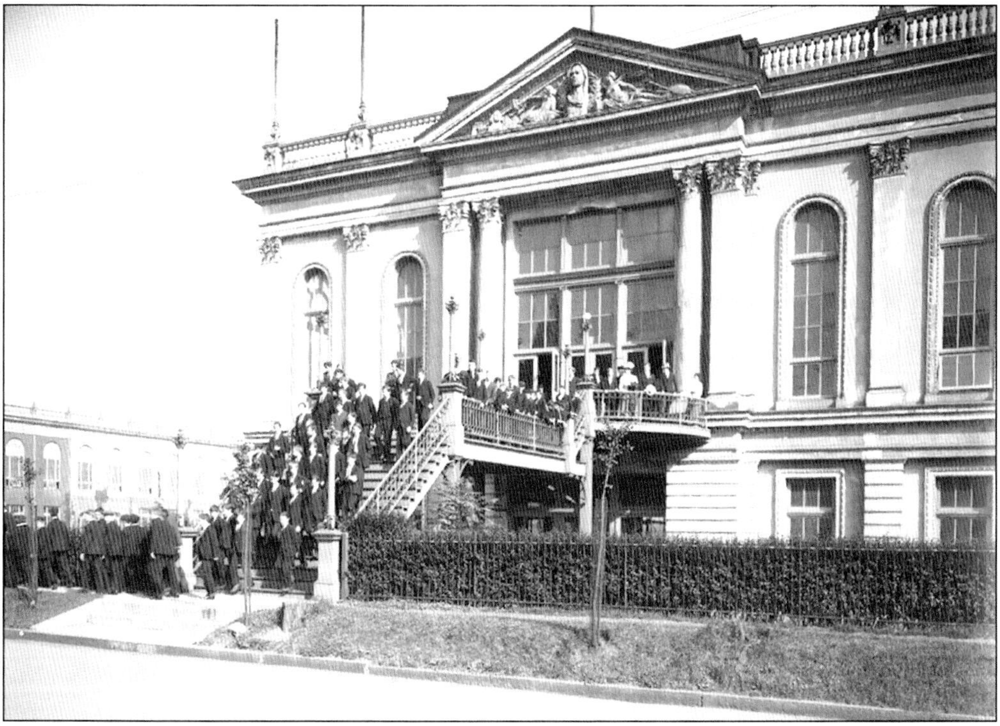

Here, a public school class is leaving the Commercial Museum. The USS *Olympia*'s return not only brought back memories of a war that Americans chose to forget but also introduced cultural connections that forever bind the two nations together. For example, the following represent a small portion of what is shared between the cultures: the word boondocks (from the Tagalog word *bundok*), the yo-yo (introduced by Pedro Flores), Manila folders (from Filipino sailors), and even the term "hot dog," which got its name only after the so-called "Bow-Wow Feast" at the 1904 World's Fair. (Courtesy of Independence Seaport Museum.)

Three

CREATING COMMUNITY IN THE CITY OF BROTHERLY LOVE

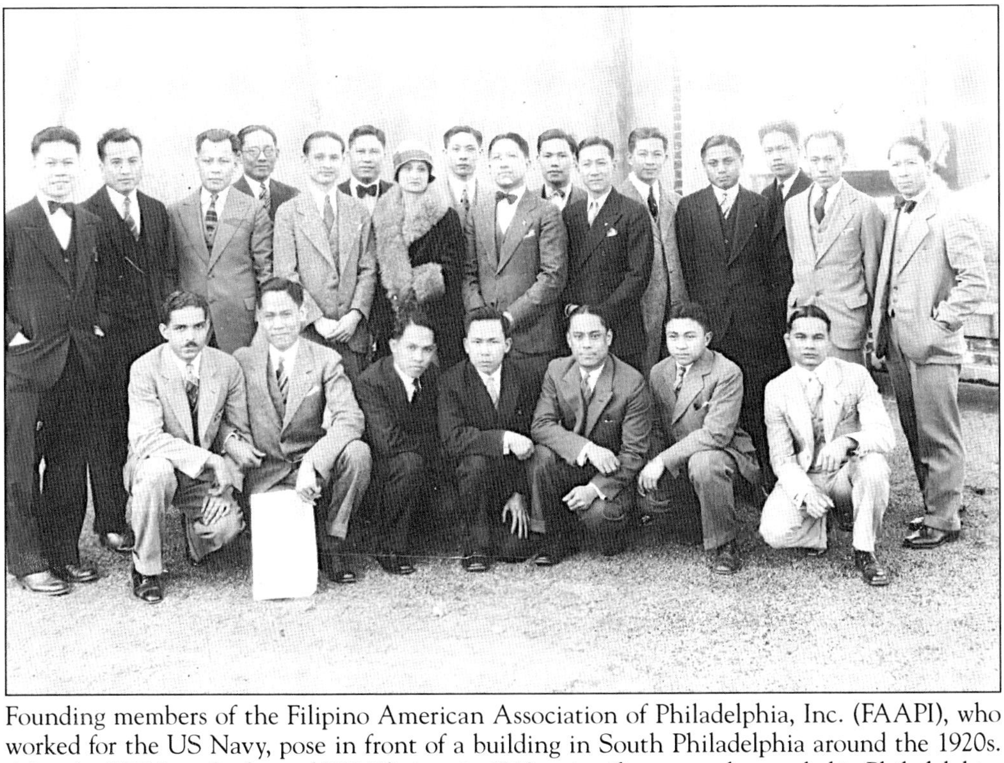

Founding members of the Filipino American Association of Philadelphia, Inc. (FAAPI), who worked for the US Navy, pose in front of a building in South Philadelphia around the 1920s. After the US Navy discharged 200 Filipinos in 1912, a significant number settled in Philadelphia. There was an imbalance of one Filipina woman for every 30 Filipino men, and the organization's founder, 23-year-old Agripino Jaucian, stands right next to the only female member, highlighting her importance to the organization. (Courtesy of FAAPI.)

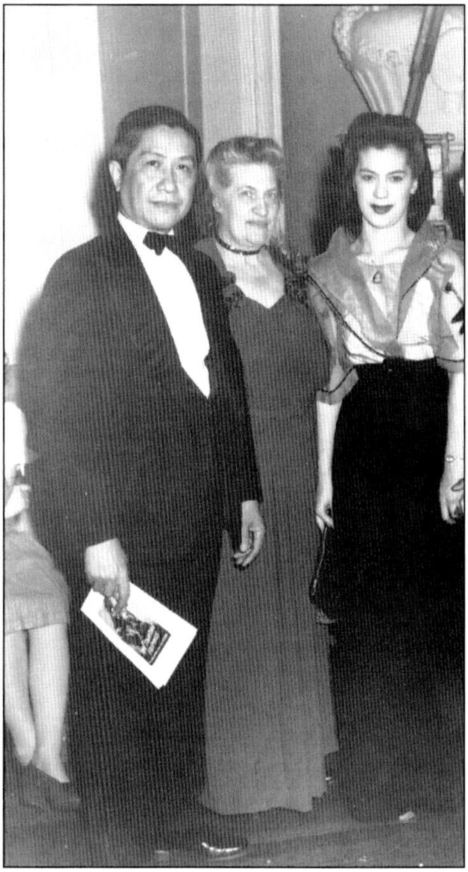

From left to right are Agripino "Pinoy" Mallado Jaucian, his wife Florence Marvel Jaucian, and their second youngest daughter, Fe Jaucian, attending FAAPI's 10th anniversary celebration of the Philippine Commonwealth on November 17, 1945, at the North Garden Ballroom of the Bellevue-Stratford Hotel in Philadelphia. Jaucian was born November 9, 1889, in Daraga, Albay, and joined the US Navy in October 1908. Among the crew in Roosevelt's "Great White Fleet" traveling the globe to demonstrate US naval power, he started at the bottom and was promoted to midshipman. (Courtesy of FAAPI.)

This photograph is of Asia's oldest secondary institution, the Colegio de San Juan de Letran, established in 1620 in Intramuros, Manila, where Jaucian earned his degree. His father was *alkalde*, mayor of Albay, and fifth born of nine children. His nickname was "Pinoy," and he would have been an educator or a boxer had he not joined the US Navy. Employed by the US Postal Service, he was not only known as "Old Maestro," director of orchestras, but was also a linguist fluent in Spanish, Mandarin Chinese, English, Tagalog, and several Filipino dialects. A gifted magician as well, he was a pioneer member of the Society of American Magicians founded in 1917. (Courtesy of Arnaldo Dumindin.)

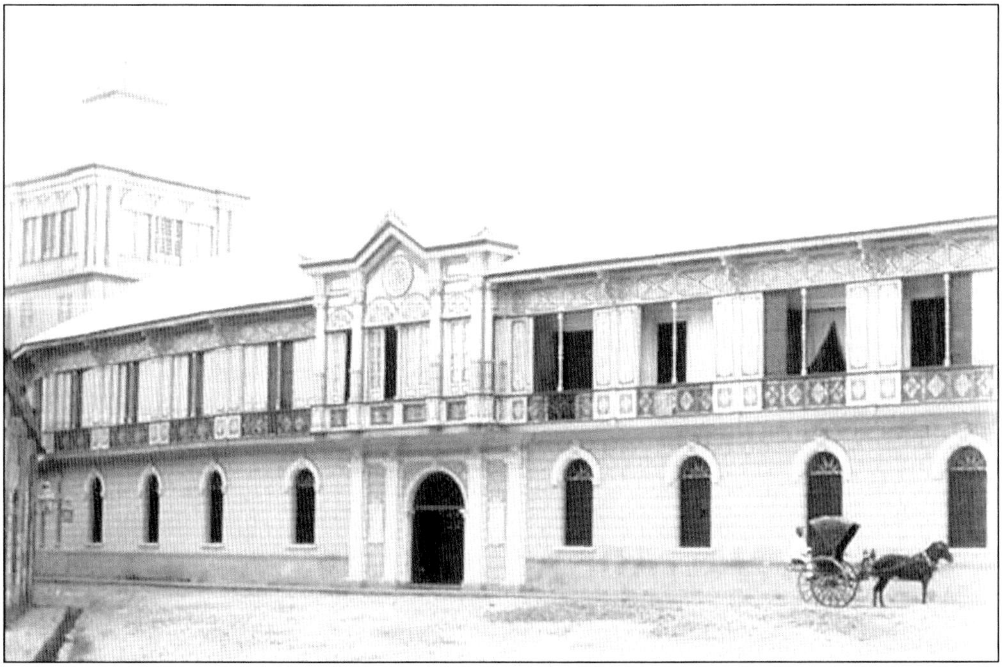

Here is a wedding picture of Mariano and Laura Nagele Carbonel. Jaucian's wife was a charming niece of the governor of the state of Delaware and worked as a registered nurse at Wilkes-Barre General Hospital. They were married on August 15, 1916, at the circuit court of Cecil County, Maryland, before settling in Philadelphia. During the influenza pandemic of 1918, Florence and Agripino Jaucian voluntarily rendered medical services to the Filipino community. (Courtesy of Patricia Carino Pasick.)

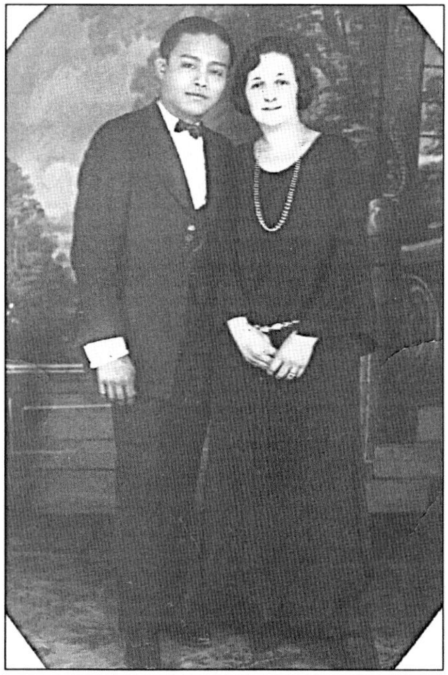

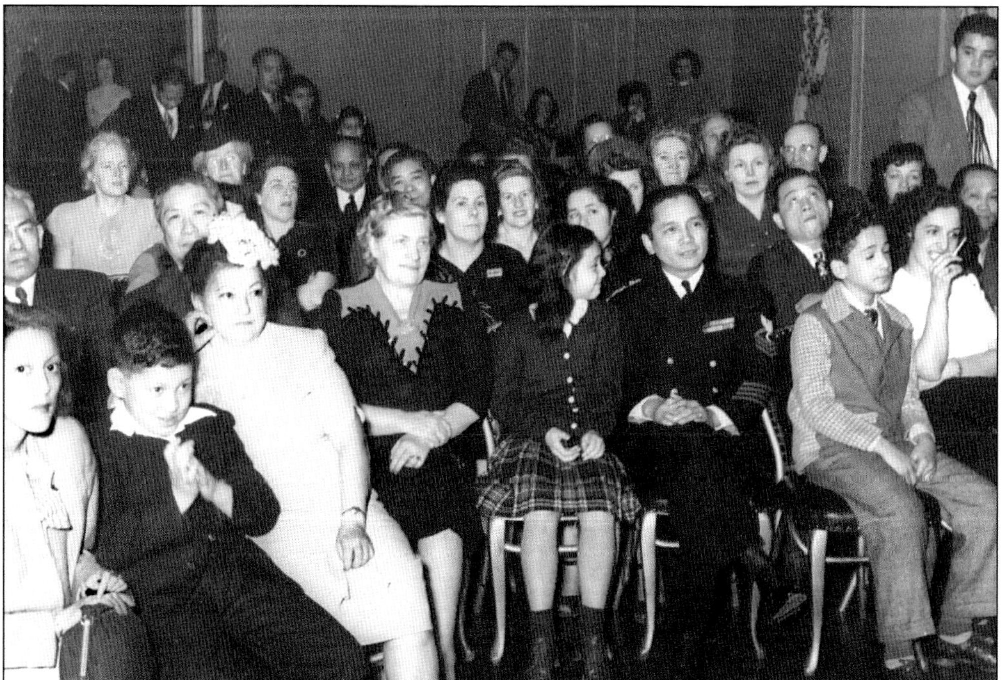

FAAPI members are seen at a social event. Sometime between 1912 and 1916, Jaucian (second row, second from left) was offering his seat to an elderly lady on an elevator when she responded, "Thank you, Chink." That event compelled him to organize a group to address such attitudes. They met at his home at 2026 North Carlisle Street, forming the Filipino Association of Philadelphia. It was incorporated in 1917, and chartered in the Commonwealth of Pennsylvania on September 17, 1925. (Courtesy of FAAPI.)

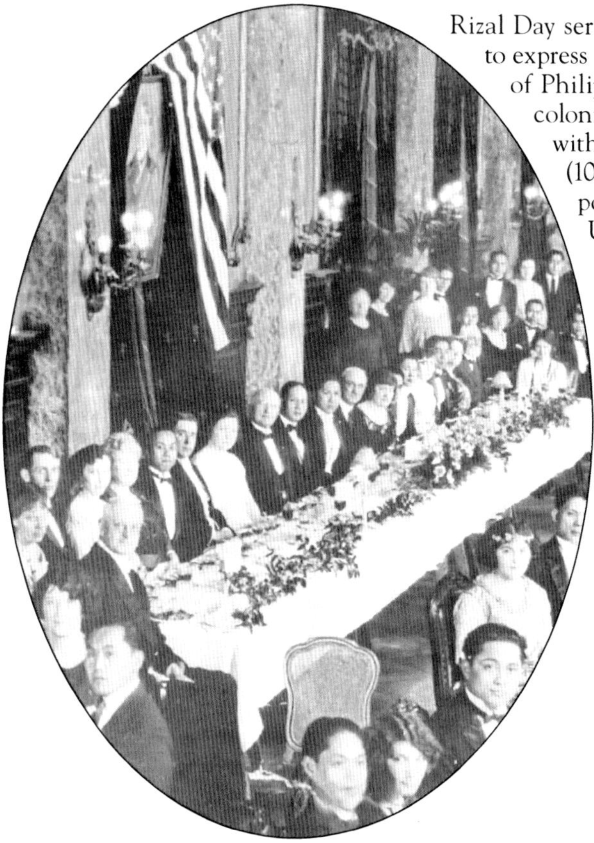

Rizal Day served as a stage for Filipino Americans to express their sentiments about US recognition of Philippine independence from American colonial rule. Behind the presidential table, with Agripino Jaucian seated at the center (10th from the left), is a large oil-on-canvas portrait of Dr. Jose Rizal, draped with the US and Philippine flags. When Pres. Howard Taft visited Philadelphia around 1914, he personally congratulated Agripino Jaucian for his civic activities. (Courtesy of Patricia Carino Pasick.)

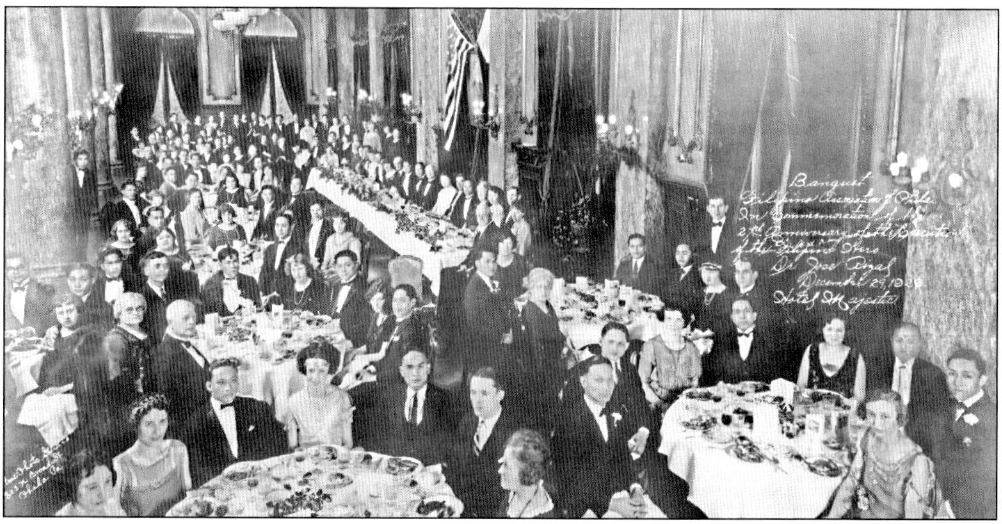

People are all dressed up to honor Dr. Jose Rizal during a formal FAAPI dinner at the Hotel Majestic on December 29, 1923. Many of these Filipinos were US Navy personnel and Merchant Marine seamen married to Americans. Others worked for the US Postal Service. These dinner-dances usually started at 7:00 p.m. and lasted until 2:00 a.m. Socials are usually held at the Penn Square Club, while formal events, such as elections and meetings, are held at the International Institute. (Courtesy of Patricia Carino Pasick.)

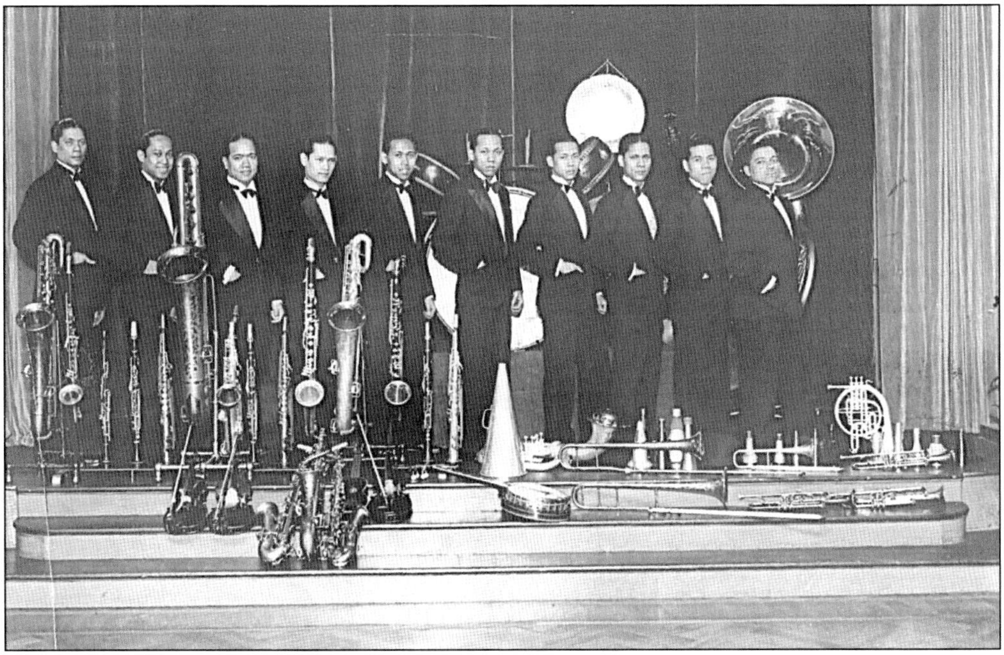

The Manila Serenaders pose at a FAAPI event around 1925. Filipinos satisfied American demand for exotic music from distant islands during the Roaring Twenties. One program touted "Enchanting melodies of native music," while another said: "there is a melodious cadence and sweetness of tone in the native Filipino music . . . it is truly music borne of the soul even more distinctive and even more beautiful than the alluring Hawaiian melodies so popular in America." (Courtesy of FAAPI.)

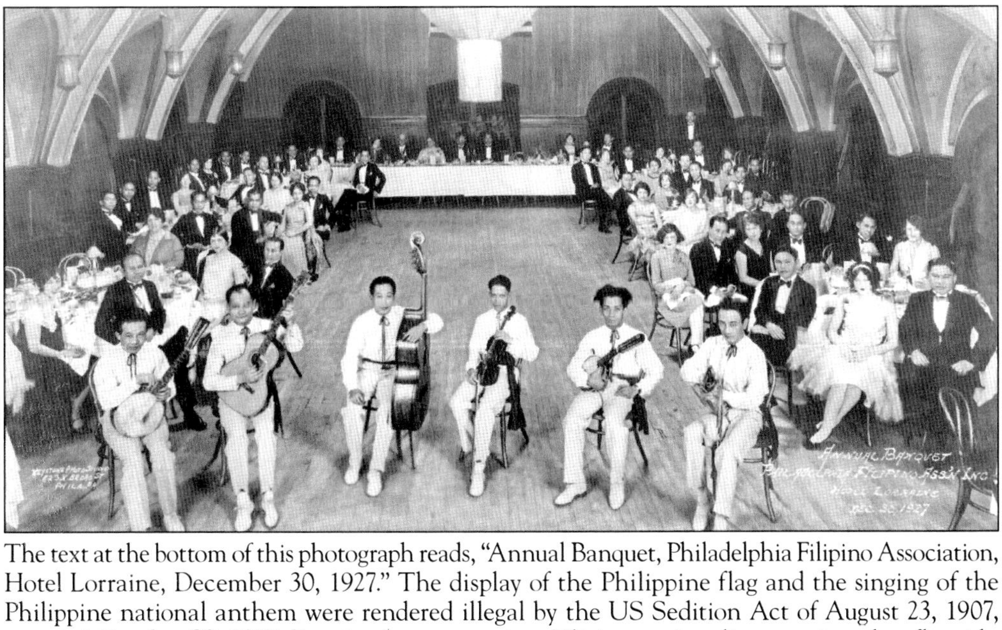

The text at the bottom of this photograph reads, "Annual Banquet, Philadelphia Filipino Association, Hotel Lorraine, December 30, 1927." The display of the Philippine flag and the singing of the Philippine national anthem were rendered illegal by the US Sedition Act of August 23, 1907, repealed October 30, 1919. Despite the suppression, Filipino nationalism continued to flourish. Rizal Day was the annual event when Filipino Americans expressed their love for their motherland and their desire to finally set it free. (Courtesy of Patricia Carino Pasick.)

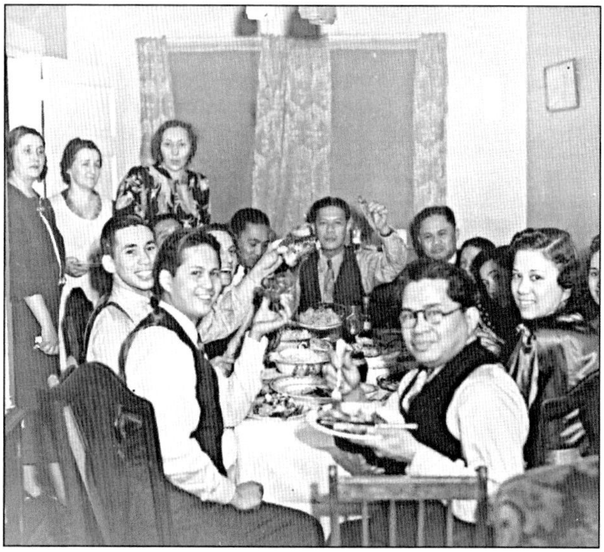

Among their must-haves is *tuyo*, a traditional Filipino dried, smoked fish served with vinegar. This photograph was taken by Pete Academy at 804 Johnson Street, Philadelphia. Enjoying a sumptuous meal are, from left to right, (standing) Florence Carino, Laura Carbonel Laeno, and Catherine Academy; (sitting) Lucian Pineda (1st), Zacarias Gomez (2nd), Mabel Quinto (3rd), Terrance Quinto (5th), Jose Sallez (6th), Ella Santos Pineda (10th), and Petra Carino (12th). (Courtesy of Patricia Carino Pasick.)

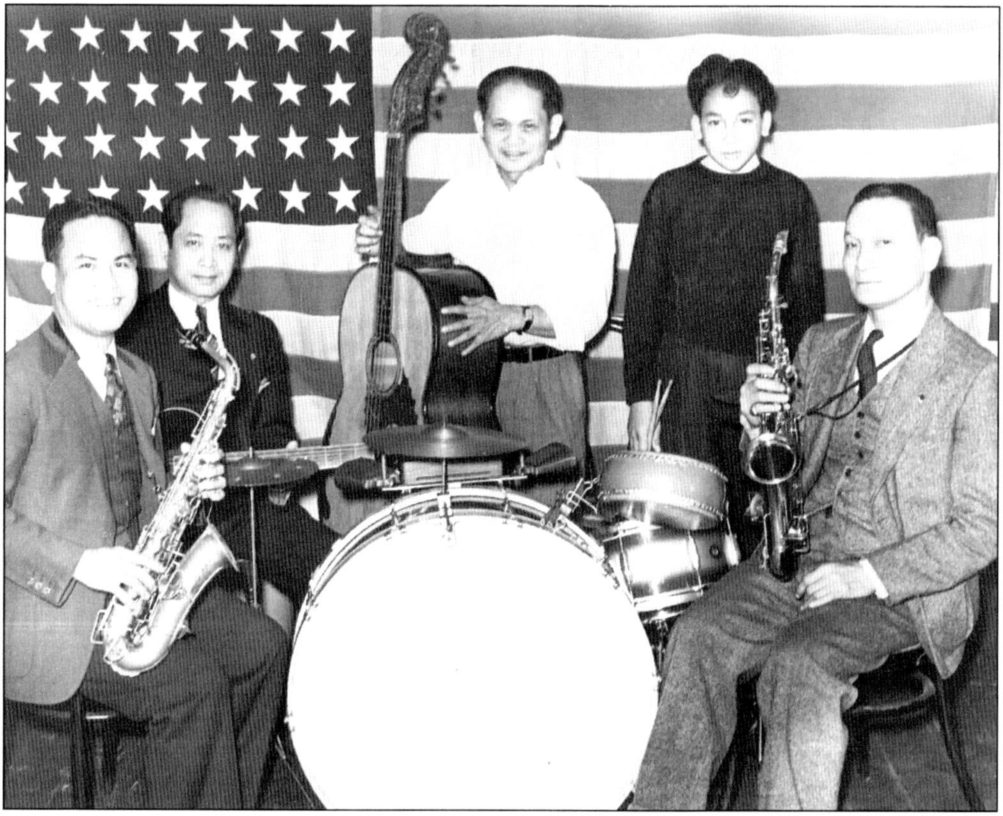

Here is Pete Academy (far right) with a band in the 1930s. FAAPI's main annual event is the Rizal Banquet, but there are many others, such as picnics, relief work, fundraisers, scholarships awarded to deserving students, and welcome and farewell dinners for important guests. Held on May 31, 1947, one particular dinner and dance honored three departing Filipina students and exemplified FAAPI's commitment to uphold the dignity of the Filipina, as embodied in the current FAAPI traditions of Mother of the Year and Miss Maria Clara. (Courtesy of Patricia Carino Pasick.)

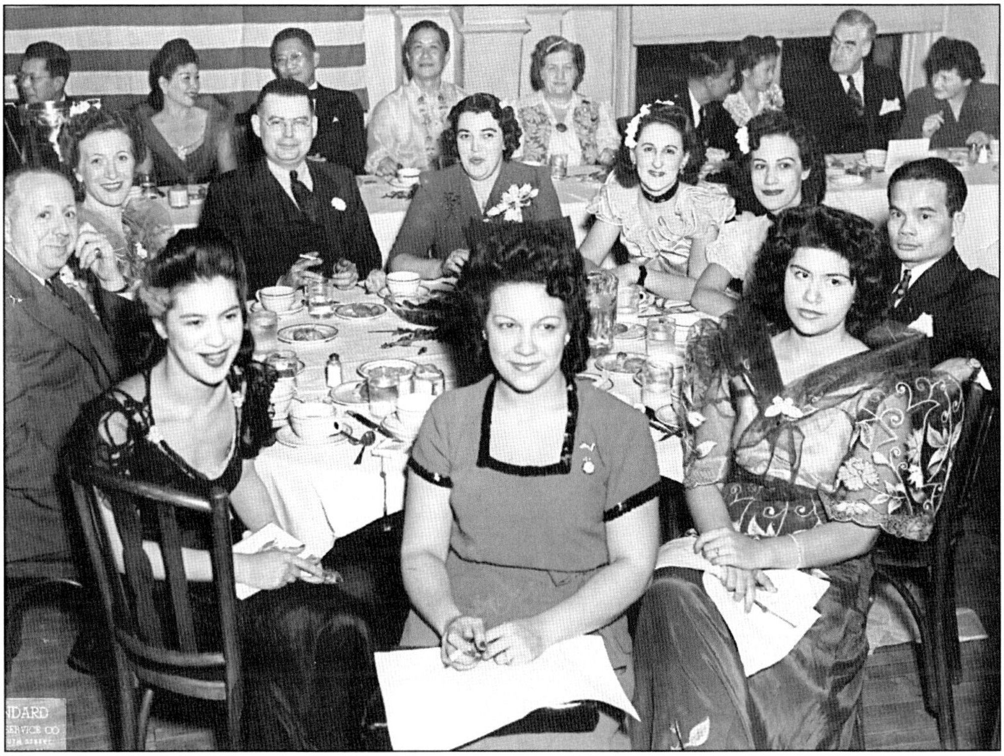

To host events, FAAPI shares the International Institute, located at 645 North Fifteenth Street. According to the FAAPI newsletter, the "Old Maestro" Jaucian directed an orchestra during these socials, where "Johnny Academia sang a romantic ballad accompanied on his guitar. The ladies tingled with delight listening to his mellow, tuneful voice. The orchestra was superb for it could not be any better when the Old Maestro is directing it." Pictured are the Juacians with their daughters Florence, Joan, Doris, and Fe, along with adopted son Jimmy. (Courtesy of FAAPI.)

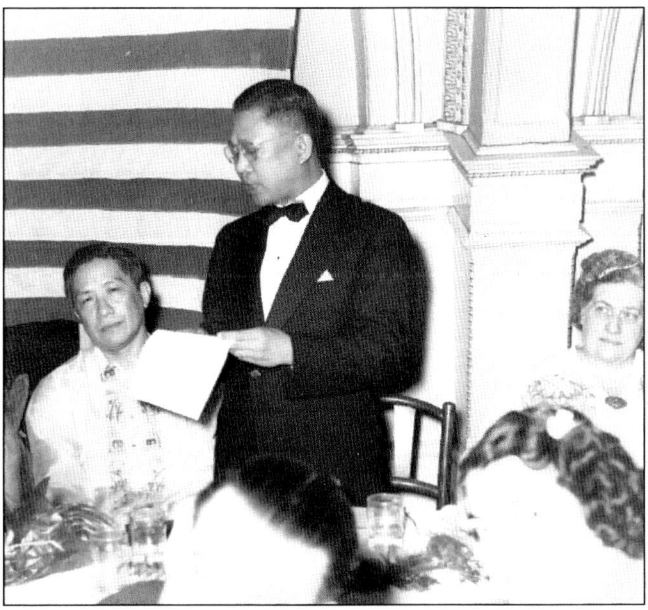

A distinguished diplomat from the Philippines addresses the Filipino community of Philadelphia, with FAAPI president A.M. Jaucian looking on in the 1920s. The founder of the Filipino American Association of Philadelphia, Inc., Agripino Jaucian proudly wears a *barong tagalog*, the national attire of the Philippines. The Filipinas in the event wear the traditional attire called *Maria Clara*, named after a fictional character in one of Rizal's novels. (Courtesy of FAAPI.)

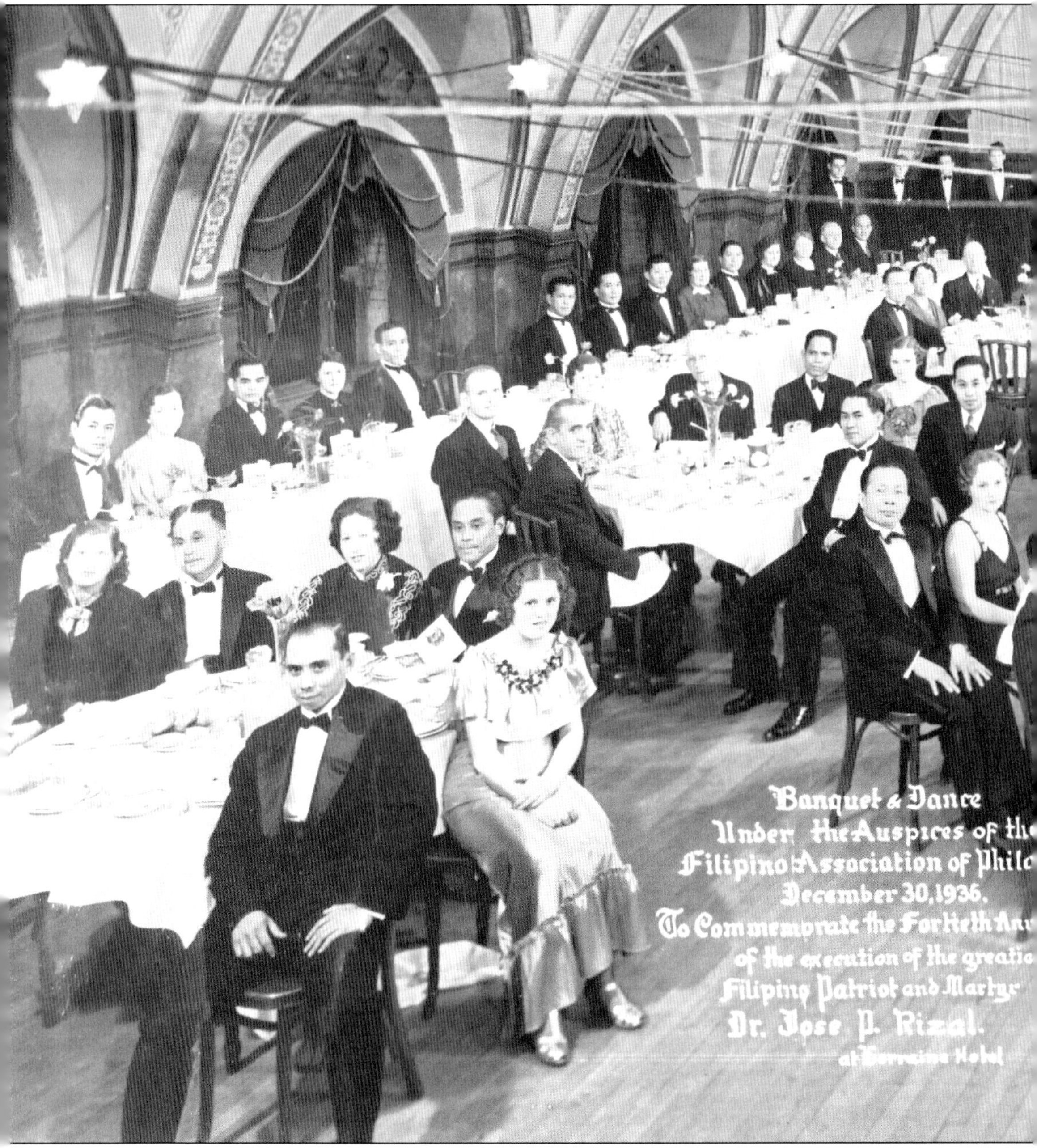

Before 1946, Rizal Day was the Filipino community's national day and was usually a day of unforgettable events and celebrations. Seen at the back of room is a bust of Rizal, along with the US and Philippine flags. This event combined socials, musical numbers, the placement of a wreath on Rizal's bust, the reading of the *Ultimo Adios* and an account of Rizal's life, and speeches espousing United States recognition of Philippine independence, plus the New Year's Eve celebration. From

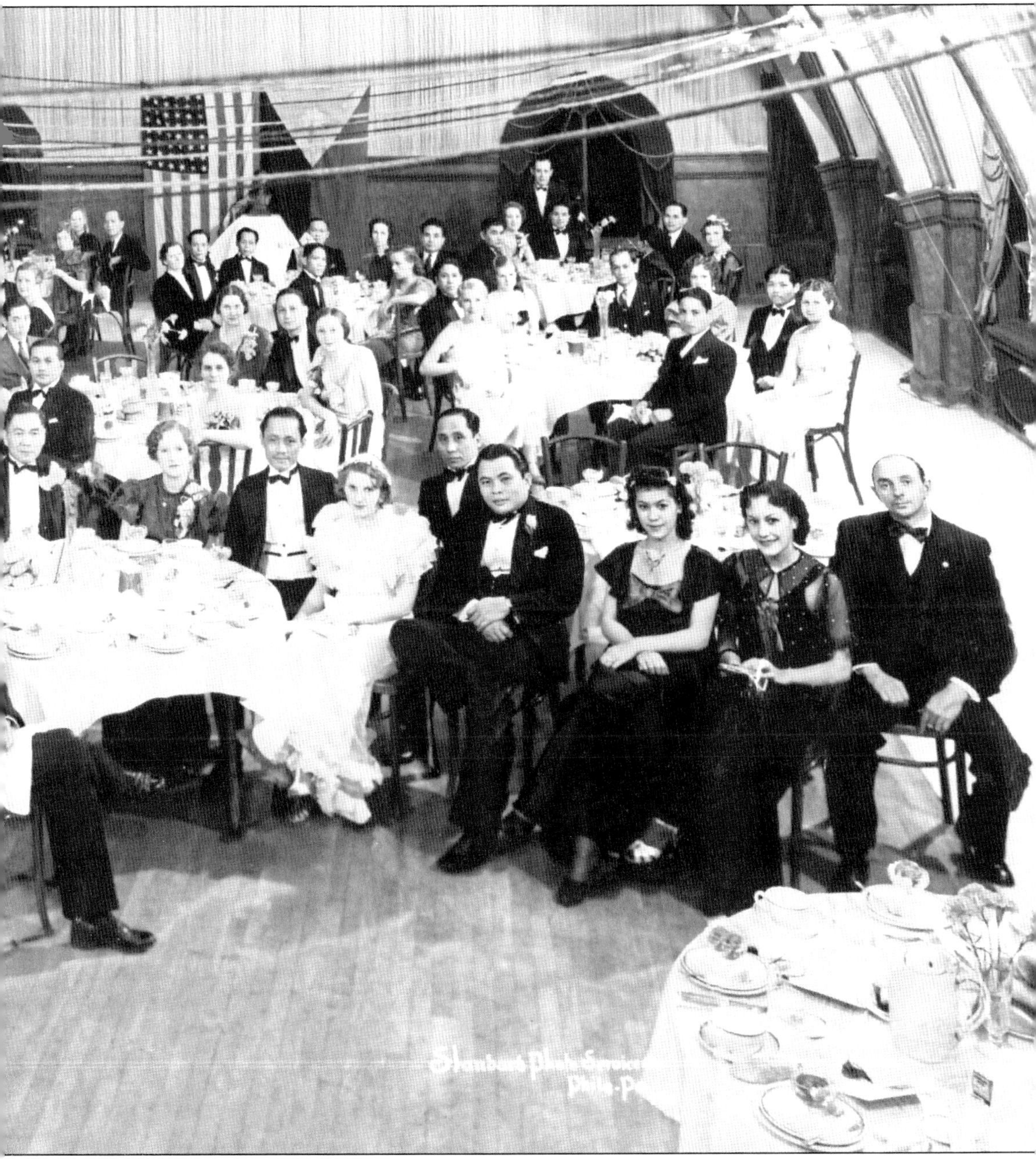

1923 to 1927, Clyde Tavenner published a monthly magazine in Washington, D.C., called the *Philippine Republic*, in which Jose Rizal was touted as the "Greatest Filipino" icon in support of full Philippine independence. Rizal was the magazine's most effective argument against the prevailing cultural and racial biases in opposing the independence movement, which also benefited Filipino Americans' goal of attaining full citizenship. (Courtesy of Patricia Carino Pasick.)

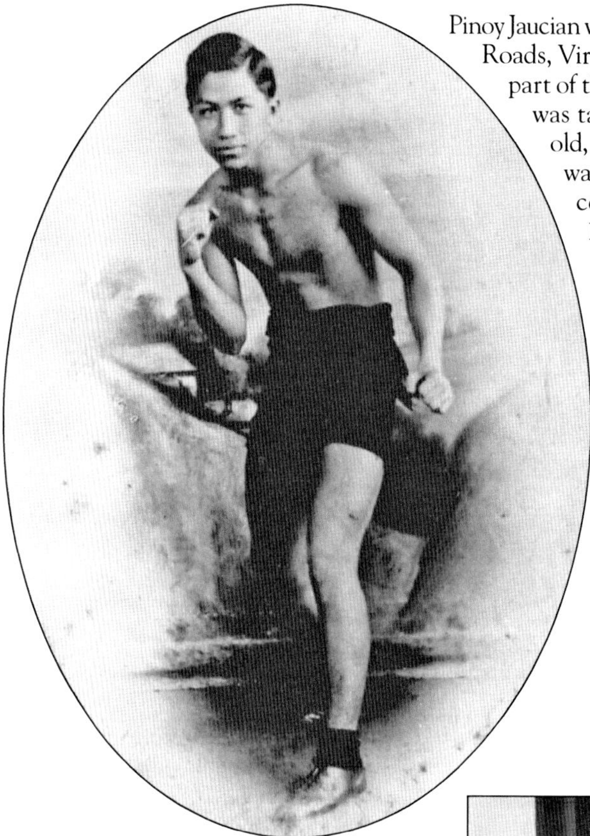

Pinoy Jaucian was discharged in March 1909 in Hampton Roads, Virginia, having served the USS *Kansas* as part of the Great White Fleet. This photograph was taken in 1918, when Pinoy was 29 years old, and reveals his real passion: boxing. He was a practicing boxer in the Philippines, continuing in Philly from 1909 to the 1920s. His generation produced hundreds of Filipino boxing stars from the 1920s to the 1940s, including hall of famer Francisco "Pancho Villa" Guilledo and middleweight champion Ceferino "Bolo Punch" Garcia. This era became known as The Great Pinoy Boxing Era. (Courtesy of Darlene Ragucci.)

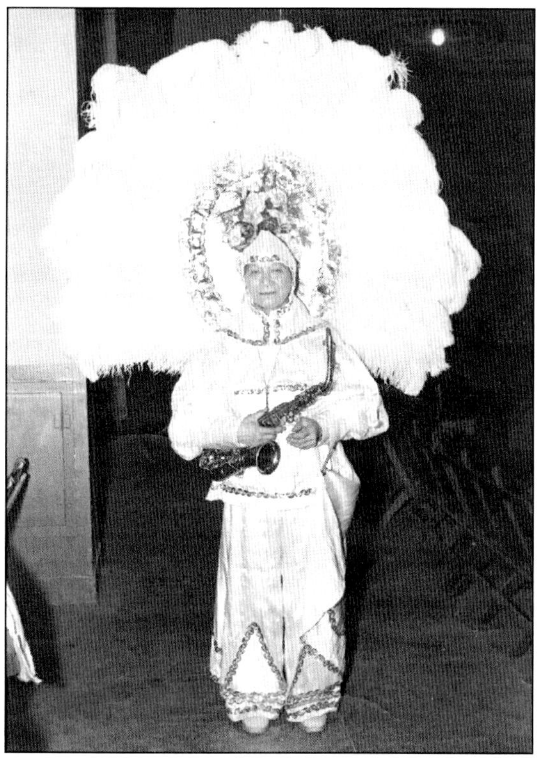

Pedro Academia, who later changed his name to Pete Academy, is seen dressed for the Mummer's Parade in Philadelphia. Being classified as a US national made Filipinos yearn for the day that they would truly belong and be counted as citizens. Traveling abroad prior to May 1, 1934, Filipinos' passports were stamped "American Citizen" at foreign ports of call. (Courtesy of Patricia Carino Pasick.)

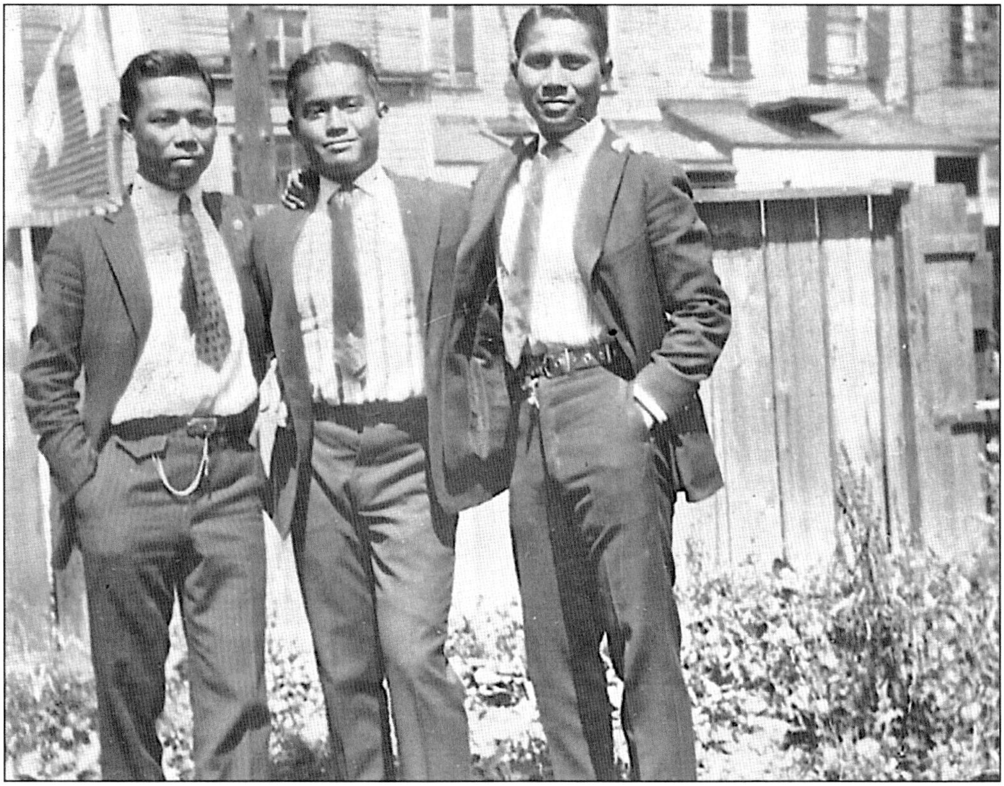

Mariano Carbonel (middle) is seen with his friends in South Philly. In 1934, the US Congress passed the Tydings-McDuffie Act, which reclassified Filipinos as aliens and severely restricted immigration to 50 annually. Prior to that, Filipinos had a unique status as nationals and were free to enter the United States without any restrictions. One of the difficulties that Filipinos experienced from the 1920s to the 1950s was finding housing. Most housing had a "Filipinos not wanted" policy, but FAAPI helped a lot of the new arrivals to overcome this hurdle. (Courtesy of Patricia Carino Pasick.)

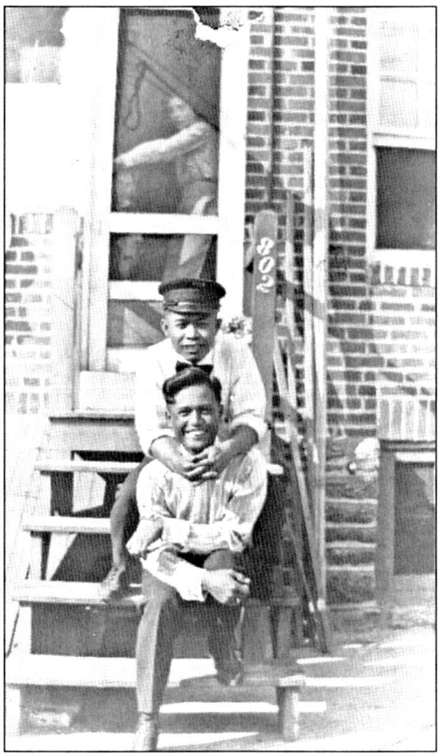

Filipino Americans were unique among Asian communities in the United States because they were not immigrants but nationals, meaning they were essentially colonial subjects of America. As such, they could not own property and did not have the right to vote. Pio Dimayuga Carino (wearing hat) hangs out with a friend after a day's work. Pio was a Navy steward who served in the Nicaragua War and World Wars I and II. After he retired, he worked as a chef in hotels. (Courtesy of Patricia Carino Pasick.)

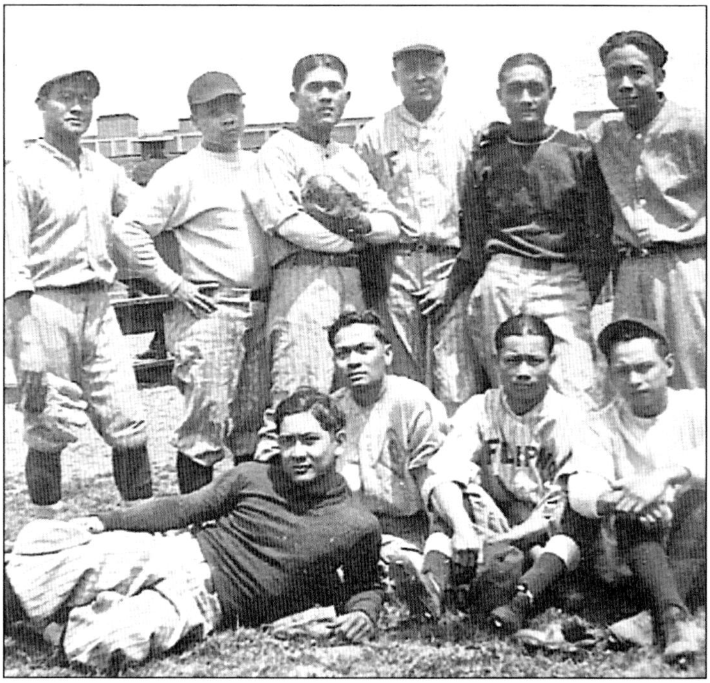

Standing on the far left of this US Navy Filipino baseball team picture is Mariano Carbonel. Although many Filipinos worked in the Navy yard, a significant number were employed by the post office. In the main post office alone, there were 23 Filipino employees in 1945. Being dependents of US Navy personnel, most Filipinos clustered around South Philadelphia due to its close proximity to the US Navy Shipyard (the first in the United States). (Courtesy of Patricia Carino Pasick.)

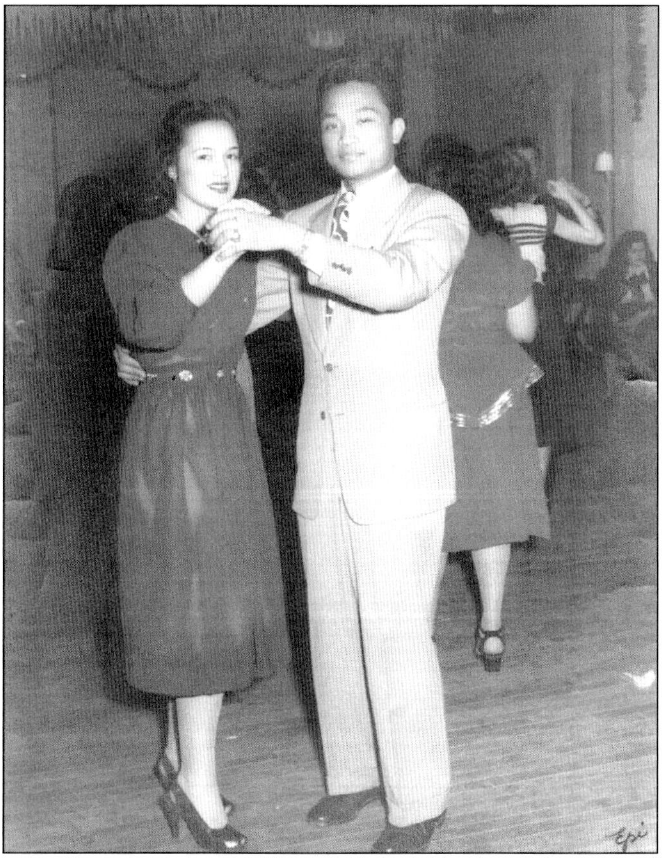

Audrey Carbonel dances in her first social event with Nick Aquino. The event was sponsored by the United Sons of the Philippines Club on January 30, 1948, at the International Institute on Fifteenth Street. Other Filipino groups in Philadelphia during the 1940s were the Filipino Athletic Club, Pvt. Tomas Claudio Post, Dr. Jose Rizal Beneficial Association, and the Philadelphia Bataan Post. (Courtesy of Patricia Carino Pasick.)

In 1925, Theodore Roosevelt Carino is shown with his bike on Johnson Street in South Philadelphia. Ted was born in 1920 in Brooklyn, New York, and spent his early and middle childhood in South Philadelphia. His love of music began when he saw his Uncle Pedro Academia, who settled in Philadelphia, play the saxophone in a local band. (Courtesy of Patricia Carino Pasick.)

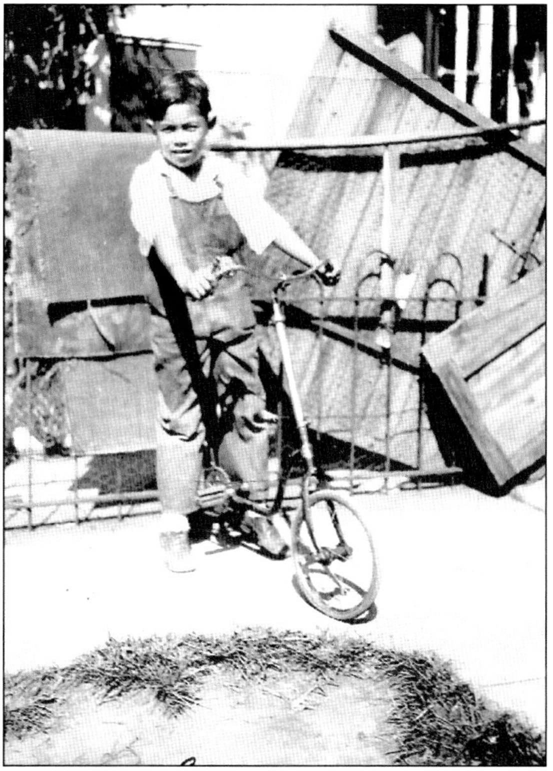

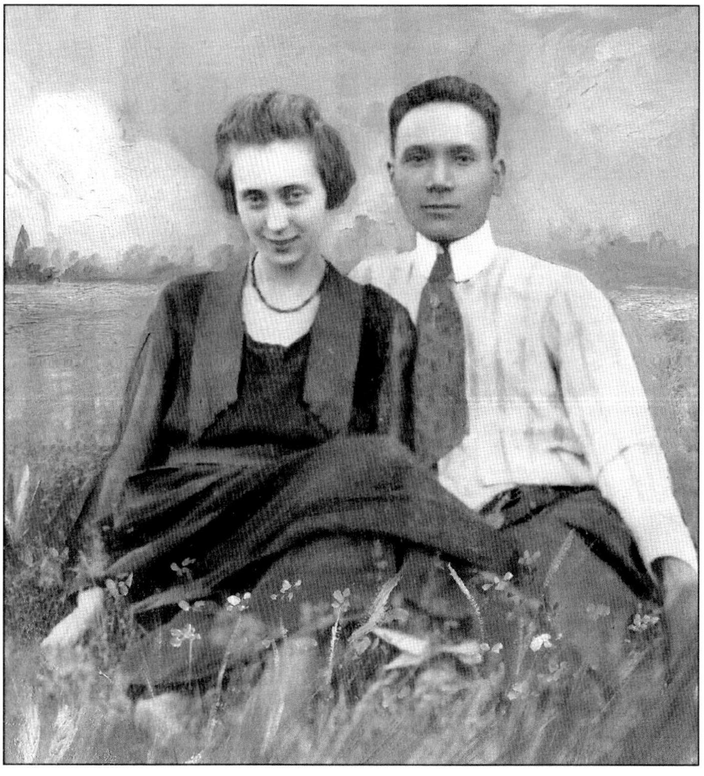

Catherine Atlakson and Pedro Academia posed for this engagement picture with the Philadelphia skyline in the background in 1918. One social event popular with FAAPI members is the Fourth of July Association Picnic, usually held in Rancocas Heights, New Jersey. A non-Filipino host, Herman Lieber, offers his estate to the FAAPI members. Another popular destination for FAAPI picnics is Burholme Park in the Fox Chase section of Philadelphia. (Courtesy of Patricia Carino Pasick.)

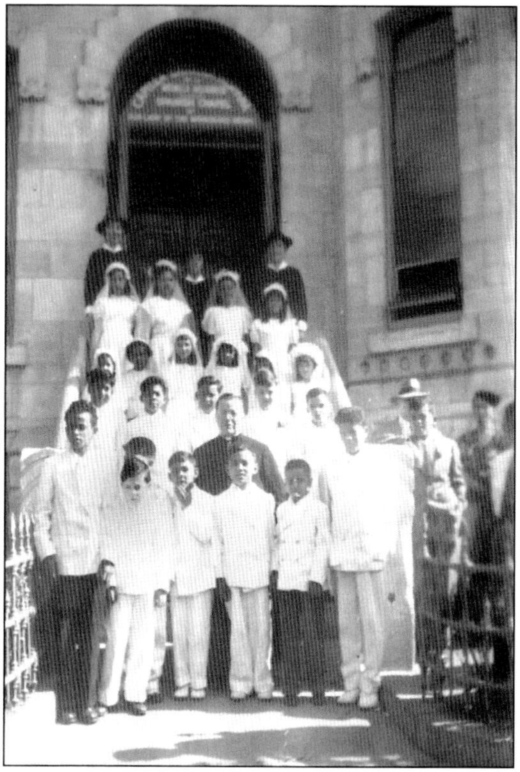

Mary Faustino receives her First Holy Communion at the Spanish chapel in Center City around the 1940s. The Our Lady of the Miraculous Medal Chapel welcomed the Spanish-speaking residents of the city and included the pioneering generation of Filipino Philadelphians. According to the 1910 *First Annual Report of the Spanish-American Colony* by Antonio Casulleras, "The Spanish-American Colony of Philadelphia consists of about 2,000 Spanish-speaking people, dispersed all over the city, including Spaniards, South Americans, Mexicans, Cubans, Puerto Ricans and Filipinos." Under the auspices of the Most Reverend P.J. Ryan, archbishop of Philadelphia, a "Spanish Chapel"—Our Lady of the Miraculous Medal Chapel—was established in January 1912. (Courtesy of Mary Faustino.)

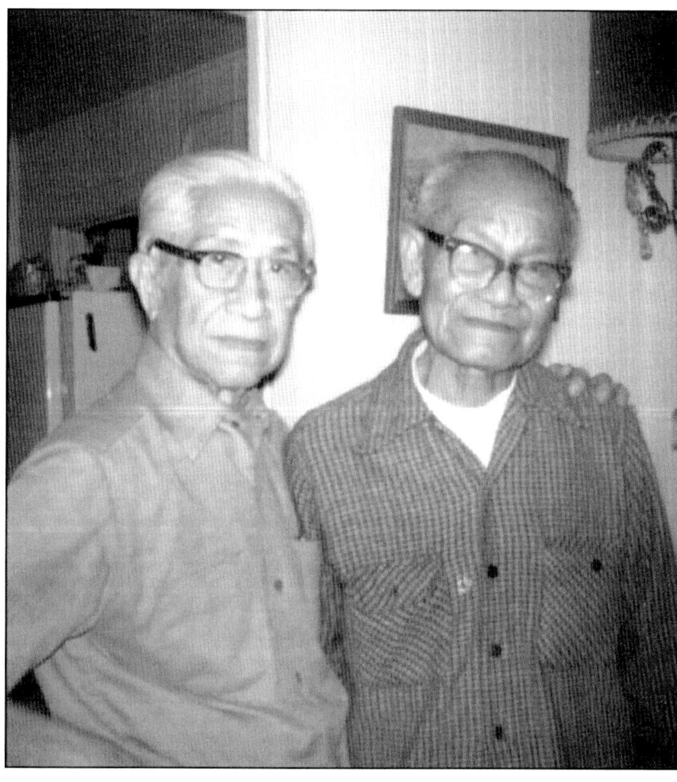

True to Philadelphia's renown as the "city of brotherly love," on January 14, 1966, the local paper covered the story of Jaucian reuniting with his long-lost brother after 59 years. The two were separated in 1907, when Jaucian's younger brother Juan ran away from home. Jaucian was always checking phone books whenever he could to find anyone with the same last name as his. This remarkable reunion also gave Jaucian the opportunity to experience air travel for the first time. (Courtesy of Darlene Ragucci.)

Mary Faustino is shown with her brother George after their First Communion at the Spanish chapel in the 1940s. As a child, Mary met the Bayanihan dancers backstage after their performance at the Academy of Music in Philadelphia. She has a long history of service to Pennsylvania's Filipino and Asian communities. Mary served as the director of constituent services for the Philadelphia office of former Pennsylvania senator Rick Santorum. In 1998, she was honored with an award given by the Susan B. Komen Foundation. (Courtesy of Mary Faustino.)

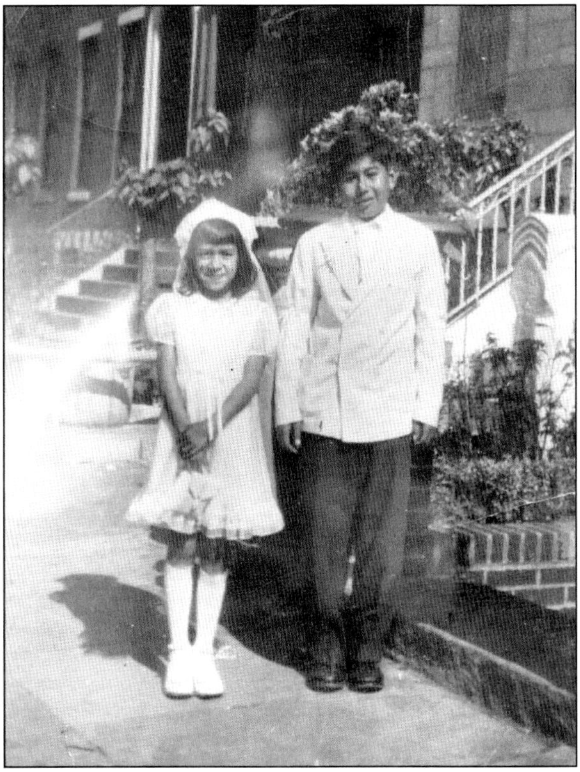

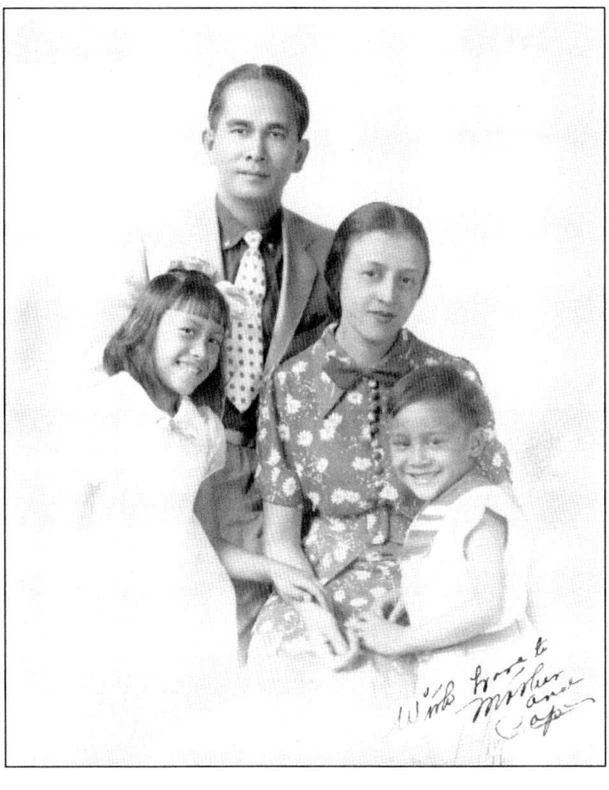

Voluntad family members included (clockwise from left) Flora, Pioquinto Sr., Francisca, and Pioquinto "Skip" Jr. Born in 1930 in Philadelphia, Skip recalls that there were Filipino barbershops and a restaurant in Chinatown. Tommy's was located at 116 North Tenth Street, and Ancheta's was at 934 Race Street. His family flew back to the Philippines in 1936 and came back in 1941. He finished his studies at Northeast High School and went on to attend Penn State University. In 1952, Skip served in the Marine Corps during the Korean War. (Courtesy of Skip Voluntad.)

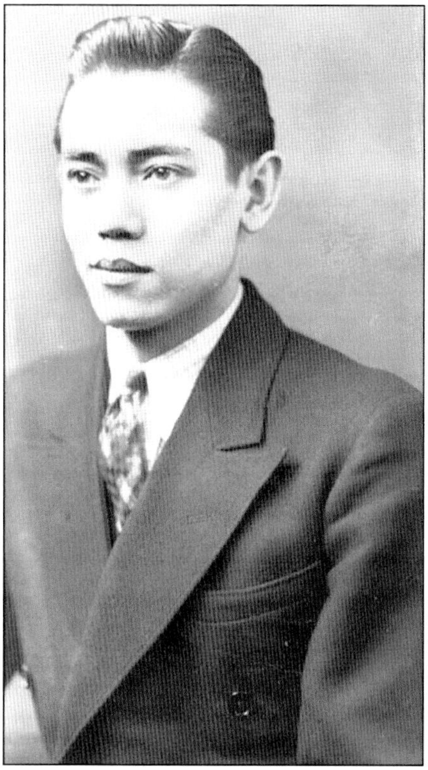

Theodore Roosevelt Carino was very close to his *Tito* (Uncle) Pete and *Tita* (Aunt) Catherine. His lifelong friendship with another Filipino American, Clifford Jarin, began in Philadelphia, and Ted brought his Southern wife, Jean, to Philadelphia the day after they were married. Catherine's two sisters, one of whom was Ted's mother, Florence, also married Filipinos. Family life was one of music, laughter, hard work, and large close-knit gatherings. (Courtesy of Patricia Carino Pasick.)

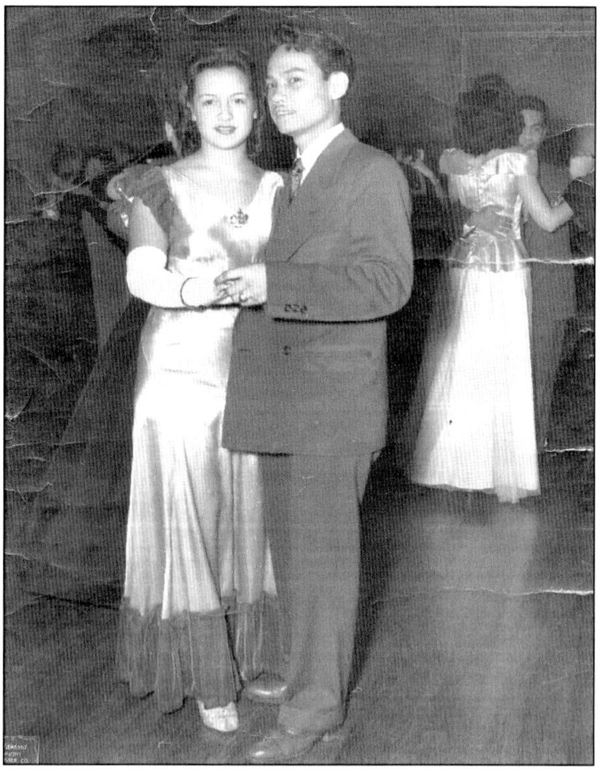

Tony Hermano and Audrey Carbonel are at the Rizal Ball on December 26, 1947, held at the Broadwood Hotel in Philadelphia and sponsored by FAAPI. Audrey is the daughter of Marciano and Laura Nagele Carbonel, seen on page 41 in their wedding picture. At around this time, approximately 1,000 Filipinos lived in Philadelphia, and about 34 of them were active FAAPI members. (Courtesy of Patricia Carino Pasick.)

Four

FROM NATIONALS TO CITIZENS

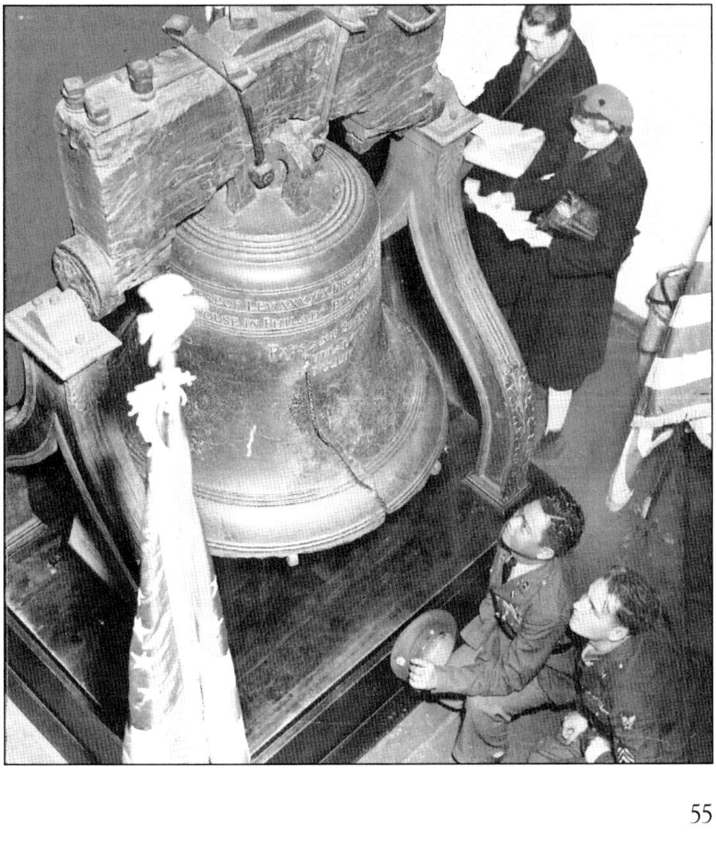

On February 10, 1945, Pvt. Nicholas Ragodes (bottom, left), who resided at 2536 North Bouvier Street, and Sgt. Joseph F. St. John, of 2940 South Sydenham Street, both wounded in the Philippine campaign, kneeled at the Liberty Bell as Filipino residents of the city observed MacArthur's victory in the Philippines. Thirty-five FAAPI members contributed $625 toward the war chest. (Courtesy of Temple University Libraries, Urban Archives.)

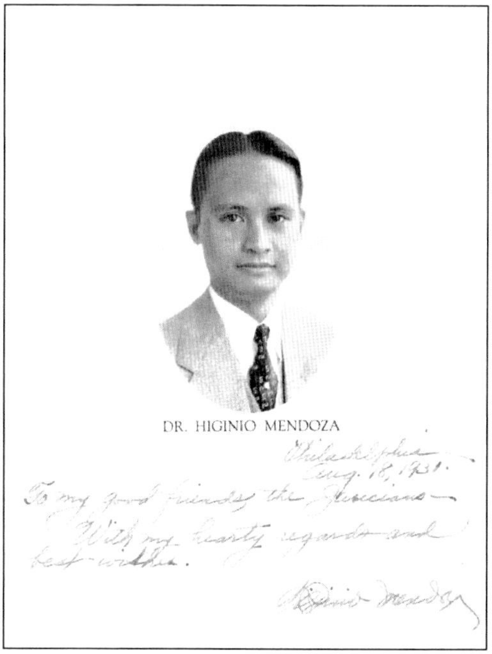

Dr. Higinio Mendoza Sr. was in Philadelphia on August 18, 1931, as a guest of Agripino M. Jaucian. Dr. Mendoza was the governor of Palawan, Philippines, from 1931 to 1937. Later, he led his province in guerilla activities against the Japanese during World War II. He was eventually captured and executed on January 24, 1944, at Canigaran Beach. He is recognized as Palawan's greatest World War II hero. The provincial park Mendoza Park was named in his honor. (Courtesy of FAAPI.)

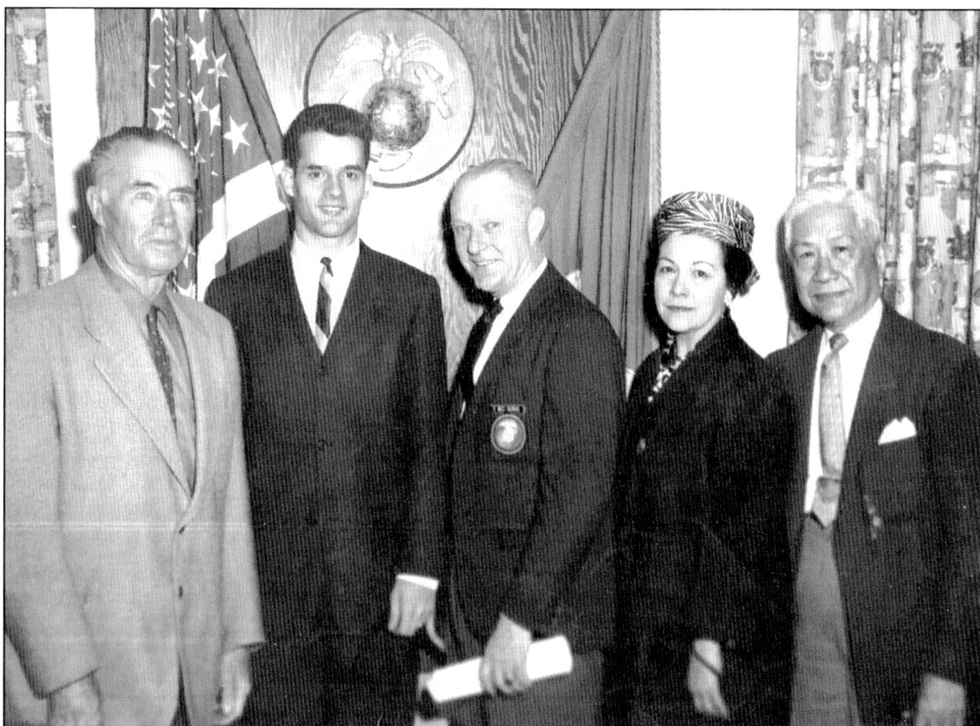

Around the 1960s, Agripino Jaucian, with members of his family, visits Lt. Gen. Lewis Burwell "Chesty" Puller, the most decorated U.S. Marine in history, and the only Marine to be awarded five Navy Crosses. The Marine Corps mascot is named "Chesty Pullerton" in his honor. From left to right are Puller, Donald Burns, Charles Burns, Florence Jaucian Burns, and Agripino Jaucian. (Courtesy of FAAPI.)

The Battle of Manila cost millions of lives, and Manila was the second-most devastated city after Warsaw, Germany. US bombs targeting Japanese positions destroyed the *intramuros* (city walls). Built to protect Spanish inhabitants starting in 1590, this priceless heritage site contained the national library/archives, national museum, the governor's and archbishop's palaces, nine convents and colleges, eight churches, and thousands of 18th-century houses. A centerpiece of the "Pearl of the Orient" was lost due to the tragedy. (Courtesy of Dnvzs Zjzllg.)

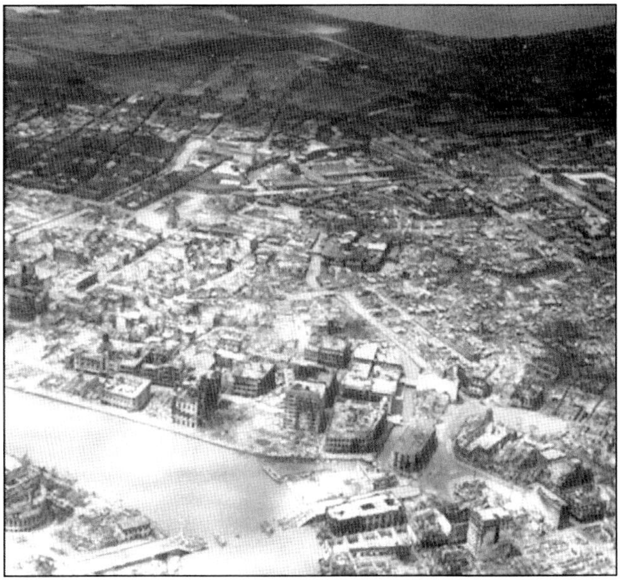

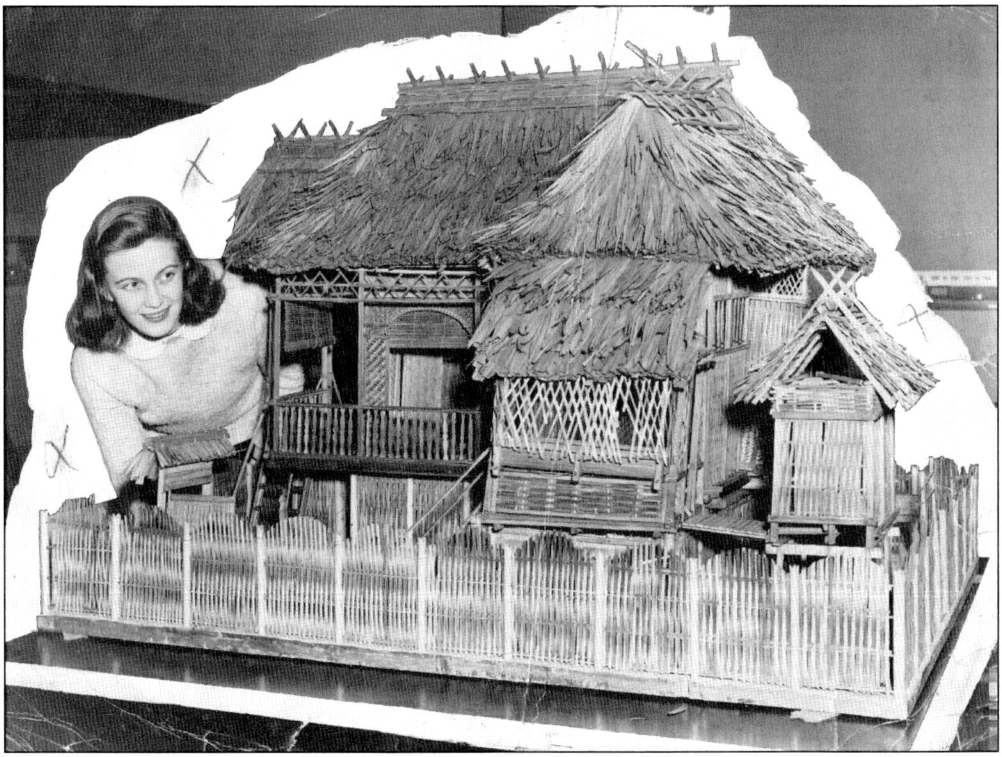

The *bahay kubo* (nipa nut) replica at the University Museum intrigues Mrs. Laird Myers, a museum staff assistant, in 1946. This artifact was a part of the Philippine Exhibit showcased during the Philippine Independence Day celebrations at Philadelphia's Memorial Hall. Also displayed at the same venue 70 years earlier was the Philippines' award-winning *Orchestra in the Provincial Town of Pampanga* by Simon Flores, which debuted during the 1876 Philadelphia Exposition celebrating the centennial of US independence. (Courtesy of Temple University Libraries, Urban Archives.)

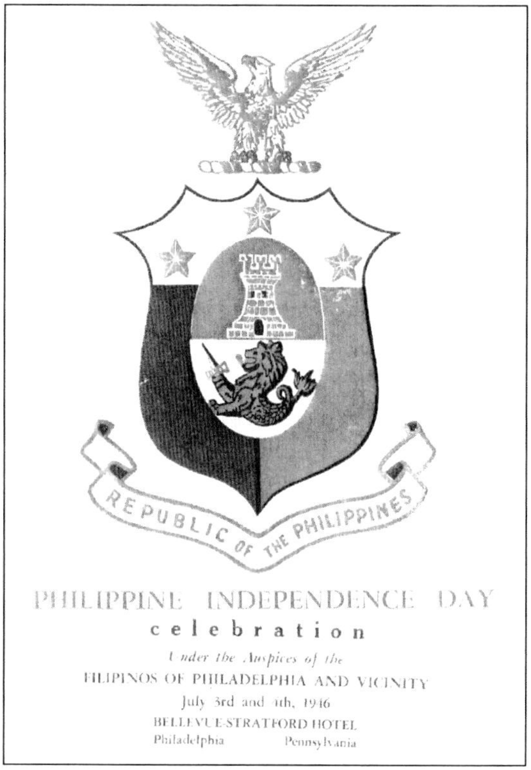

The Allied forces' victory in World War II changed the status of Filipinos in America from colonial subjects to citizens. Their voice was soon heard through the writings of Carlos Bulosan, a poet and novelist celebrated for providing an Asian perspective on the American labor movement. In *America is in the Heart*, Bulosan wrote: "We in America understand the many imperfections of democracy and the malignant disease corroding its very heart. We must be united in the effort to make an America in which our people can find happiness. It is a great wrong that anyone in America, whether he be brown or white, should be illiterate or hungry or miserable." (Courtesy of FAAPI.)

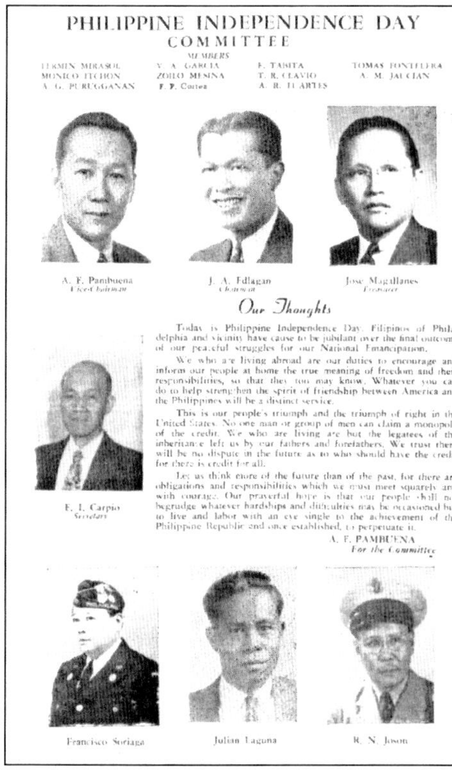

PHILIPPINE INDEPENDENCE DAY COMMITTEE

MEMBERS

FERMIN MIRASOL, MONICO ITCHON, A. G. PURUGGANAN, V. A. GARCIA, ZOILO MESINA, F. P. Cortez, F. TABITA, T. R. CLAVIO, A. R. ILARTES, TOMAS FONTELERA, A. M. JAUCIAN

A. F. Pambuena, *Vice-Chairman* — J. A. Edlagan, *Chairman* — Jose Magallanes, *Treasurer*

Our Thoughts

Today is Philippine Independence Day. Filipinos of Philadelphia and vicinity have cause to be jubilant over the final outcome of our peaceful struggles for our National Emancipation.

We who are living abroad are our duties to encourage and inform our people at home the true meaning of freedom and their responsibilities, so that they too may know. Whatever you can do to help strengthen the spirit of friendship between America and the Philippines will be a distinct service.

This is our people's triumph and the triumph of right in the United States. No one man or group of men can claim a monopoly of the credit. We who are living are but the legatees of the inheritance left us by our fathers and forefathers. We trust there will be no dispute in the future as to who should have the credit for there is credit for all.

Let us think more of the future than of the past, for there are obligations and responsibilities which we must meet squarely and with courage. Our prayerful hope is that our people shall not begrudge whatever hardships and difficulties may be occasioned but to live and labor with an eye single to the achievement of the Philippine Republic and once established, to perpetuate it.

A. F. PAMBUENA
For the Committee

F. I. Carpio, *Secretary*

Francisco Soriaga — Julian Laguna — R. N. Joson

The Filipino residents of Philadelphia celebrated in the streets upon hearing of MacArthur's victory in Manila, and their jubilation was manifested in full force on July 4, 1946, when Independence Day coincided with the US recognition of Philippine independence. J.A. Edlagan, who chaired the Philippine Independence Day Committee, was also the president of FAAPI before and after World War II. A significant contribution of the Philippines was when Pres. Manuel Quezon saved 1,200 Jews from the holocaust, providing them refuge in the Philippines. (Courtesy of FAAPI.)

The committee designed a program that included a grand military parade from Reyburn Plaza to Independence Hall, a Mass at St. John's Catholic Church, Filipino *rondalla* music and Philippine exhibits in Memorial Hall, and a grand ball at the Bellevue-Stratford Hotel. Dr. Jose Imperial of the Philippine Commissioner's Office received a scroll of the 13 original colonies from the City of Philadelphia. In 1945, FAAPI, together with the Tomas Claudio Post 1063, organized a Mass with a Filipino priest at Our Lady of Mercy Church on Broad Street to honor the war dead. (Courtesy of FAAPI.)

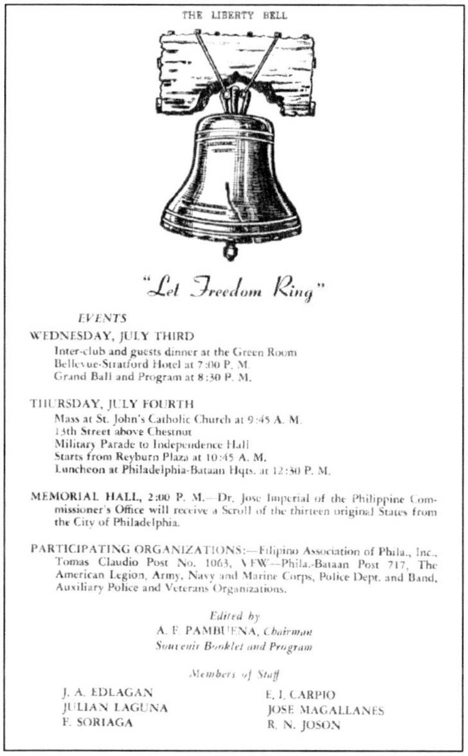
THE LIBERTY BELL

"Let Freedom Ring"

EVENTS

WEDNESDAY, JULY THIRD
Inter-club and guests dinner at the Green Room
Bellevue-Stratford Hotel at 7:00 P. M.
Grand Ball and Program at 8:30 P. M.

THURSDAY, JULY FOURTH
Mass at St. John's Catholic Church at 9:45 A. M.
13th Street above Chestnut
Military Parade to Independence Hall
Starts from Reyburn Plaza at 10:45 A. M.
Luncheon at Philadelphia-Bataan Hqts. at 12:30 P. M.

MEMORIAL HALL, 2:00 P. M.—Dr. Jose Imperial of the Philippine Commissioner's Office will receive a Scroll of the thirteen original States from the City of Philadelphia.

PARTICIPATING ORGANIZATIONS:—Filipino Association of Phila., Inc., Tomas Claudio Post No. 1063, VFW—Phila.-Bataan Post 717, The American Legion, Army, Navy and Marine Corps, Police Dept. and Band, Auxiliary Police and Veterans Organizations.

Edited by
A. F. PAMBUENA, *Chairman*
Souvenir Booklet and Program

Members of Staff

J. A. EDLAGAN
JULIAN LAGUNA
F. SORIAGA
E. I. CARPIO
JOSE MAGALLANES
R. N. JOSON

FAAPI president Florence J. Burns is surrounded by Filipino American World War II veterans after an event honoring Lt. Col. John Draniese. Burns followed in her father's footsteps and served as FAAPI president from 1942 to 1971. Mr. and Mrs. Jaucian had four daughters, all born during the Great Depression. (Courtesy of FAAPI.)

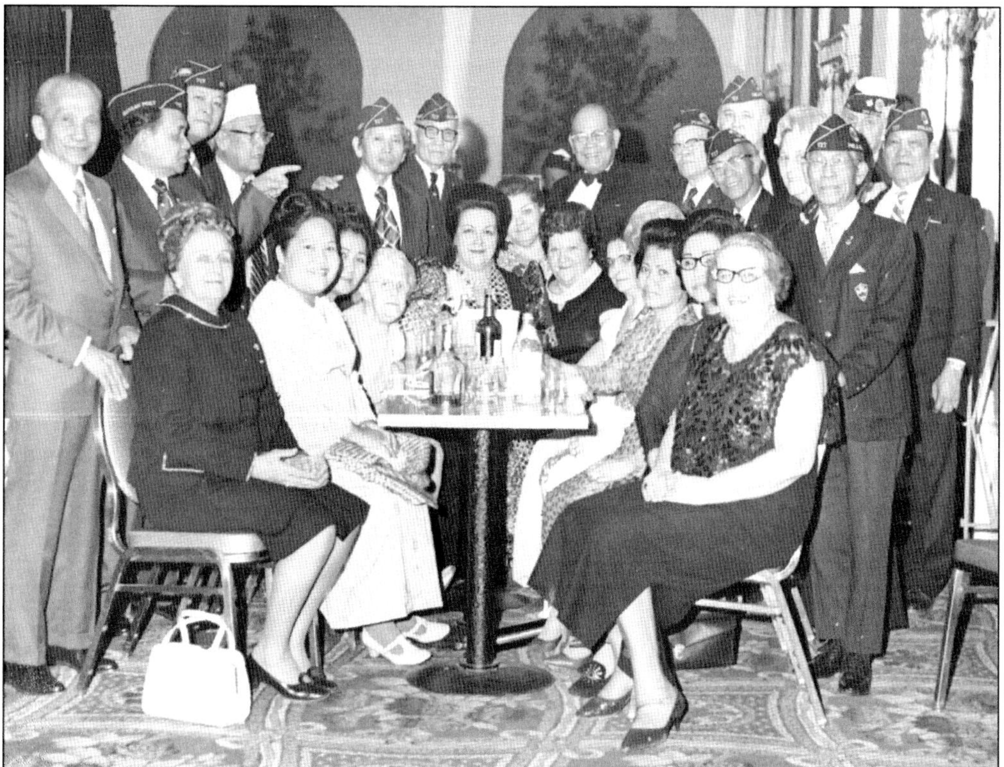

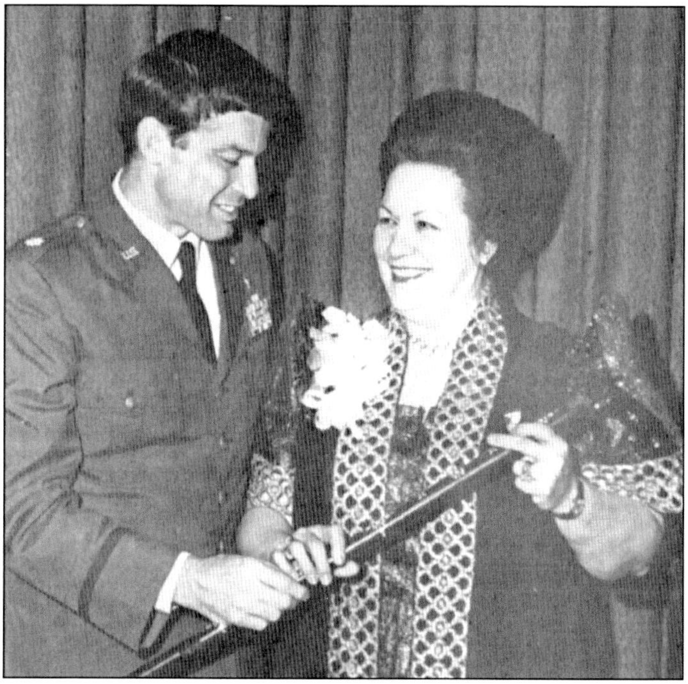

Lt. Col. John Draniese, who made an American flag while imprisoned by Japanese forces in the Philippines, receives a gift from FAAPI president Florence J. Burns. Many imprisoned American soldiers felt abandoned by their government for three years. An estimated 30,000 did not make it; if it weren't for Philippine guerillas who risked their lives providing them with stolen medicine and food, many more of the 76,000 POWs would not have survived. Those who did named themselves the "Battling Bastards of Bataan: No Mama, No Papa, No Uncle Sam." (Courtesy of FAAPI.)

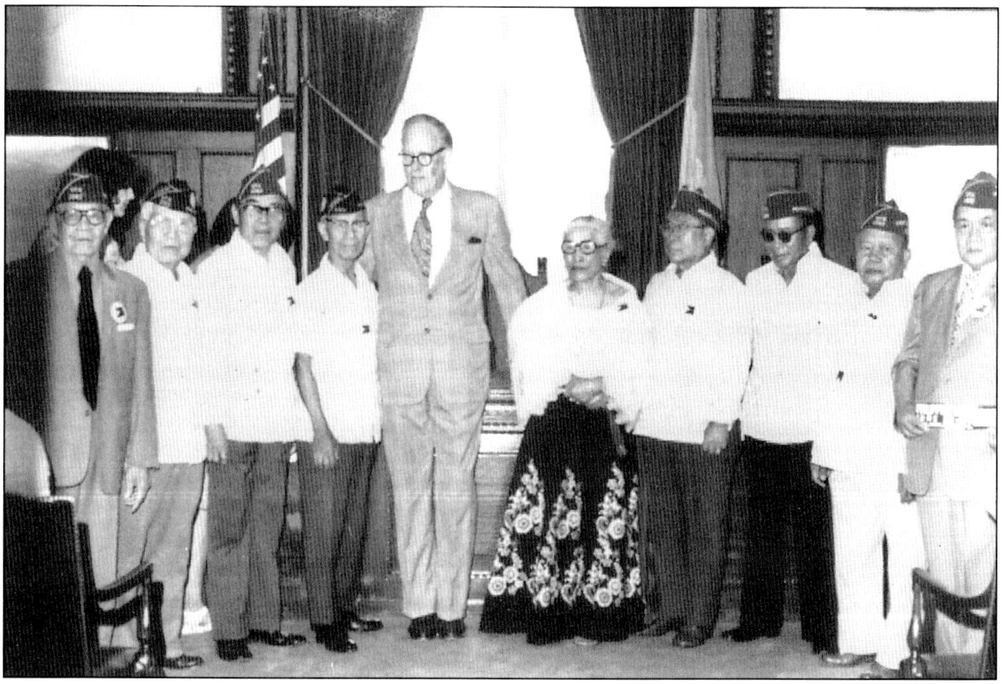

Filipino Day is celebrated in June 1978. Of note is Mrs. Expectacion Adriano Olivar representing her husband since there was no ladies auxiliary yet. The plight of Filipino veterans is the equivalent to the social injustice inflicted upon Japanese Americans forced into concentration camps. The Rescission Act, signed by Pres. Harry Truman on February 18, 1946, stripped Filipinos of the benefits they were promised. Of the 66 countries allied with the United States, only Filipinos were denied benefits. (Courtesy of Virginia Luz.)

Gen. Emilio Aguinaldo leads the July 4, 1946, parade at the Luneta, celebrating US recognition of Philippine independence, carrying the same flag he designed and unfurled in Kawit, Cavite, on June 12, 1898, after he proclaimed the independence of the Philippines. The same flag that Aguinaldo designed and the anthem that he commissioned in 1898 were raised and sung by a joyous and grateful nation in 1946. Journalist and historian Hilarion Henares wrote in 1991, "Diosdado Macapagal is the third greatest Filipino president with Emilio Aguinaldo and Manuel Quezon as greatest and second greatest respectively." (Courtesy of Dnvzs Zjzllg.)

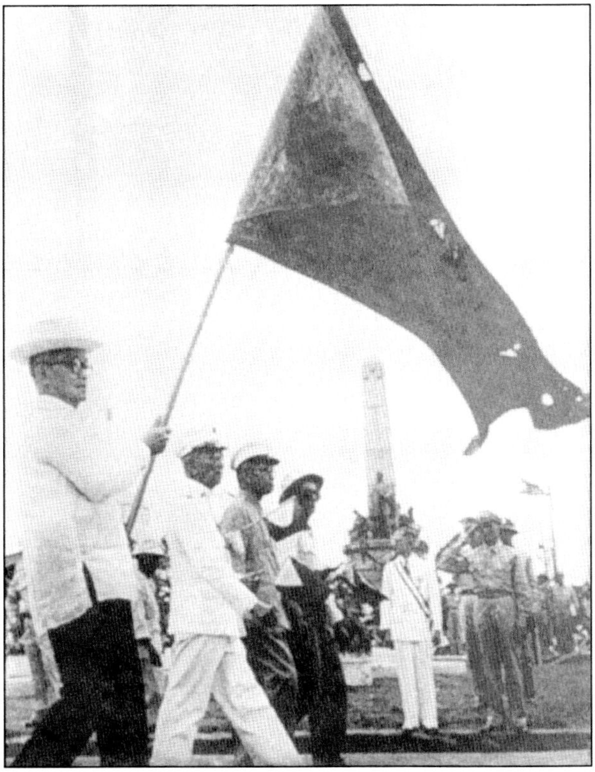

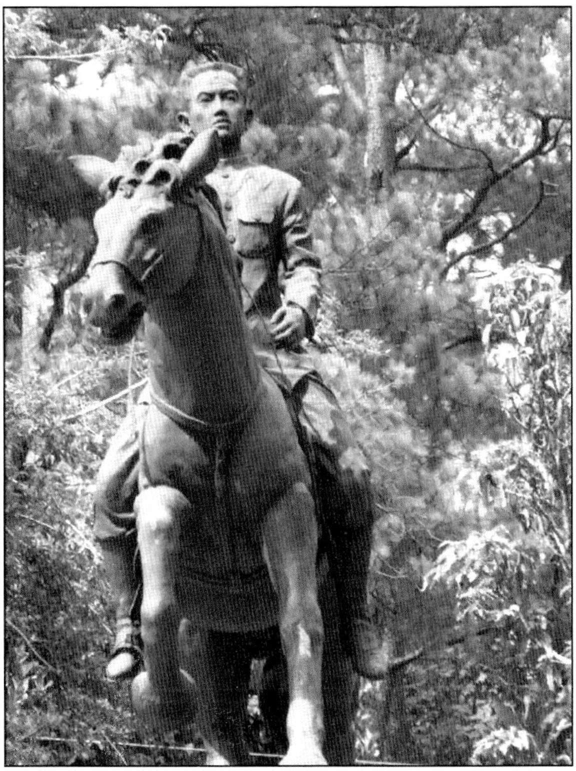

Emilio Aguinaldo's revolution antedated the Chinese Revolution of 1911 and launched Asia's first guerilla warfare, preceding Mao Tse Tung's campaign from 1927 to 1949. Aguinaldo's legacy helps to downplay the American father-figure image and transform Filipinos into dynamic, dignified citizens of their country. According to Raul Manglapus, "The powerful shadow of America remains cast over our land, the Americans solved their problem by crawling away from the British shadow, thus speeding their growth. But the long, fixed shadow of the United States stretches over the land and mind of the Filipino." (Courtesy of Emilio Aguinaldo Museum.)

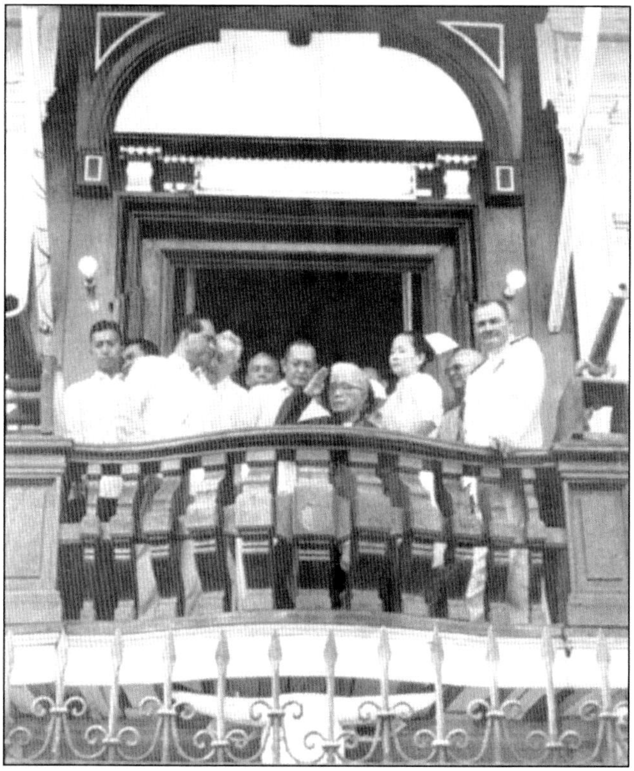

The United States recognized Philippine independence on July 4, 1946. In the 1950s, Alejandro Roces became an exponent of changing the national day to June 12, which Pres. Diosdado Macapagal made a reality. Even the United States celebrates the day it declared its right to be independent, and not the day governance was turned over to the governed. On June 12, 1962, on the same spot where he declared independence 64 years earlier, the nation joined Emilio Aguinaldo to celebrate June 12 as the birthday of the Philippines. (Courtesy of Edward de los Santos.)

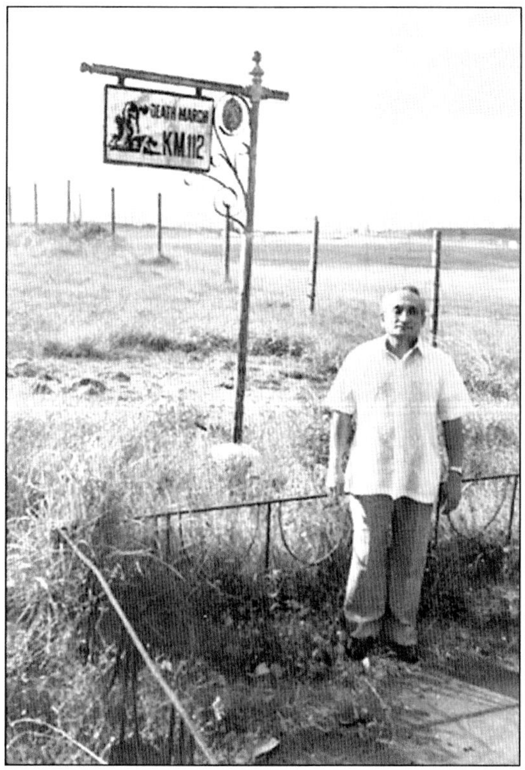

Dr. Adriano S. Olivar Jr. went back to Bataan to commemorate the 50th anniversary of the Death March. It was difficult for him to be on the same grounds where he was forced at gunpoint to march 150 miles from Bataan to San Fernando, Pampanga, Philippines, where he lost a leg at 17 from a bomb. During this march, 10,000 Filipino and 1,000 American soldiers died out of 70,000 Filipinos and 20,000 Americans. (Courtesy of Virgina Luz.)

Five

Bridging Generations

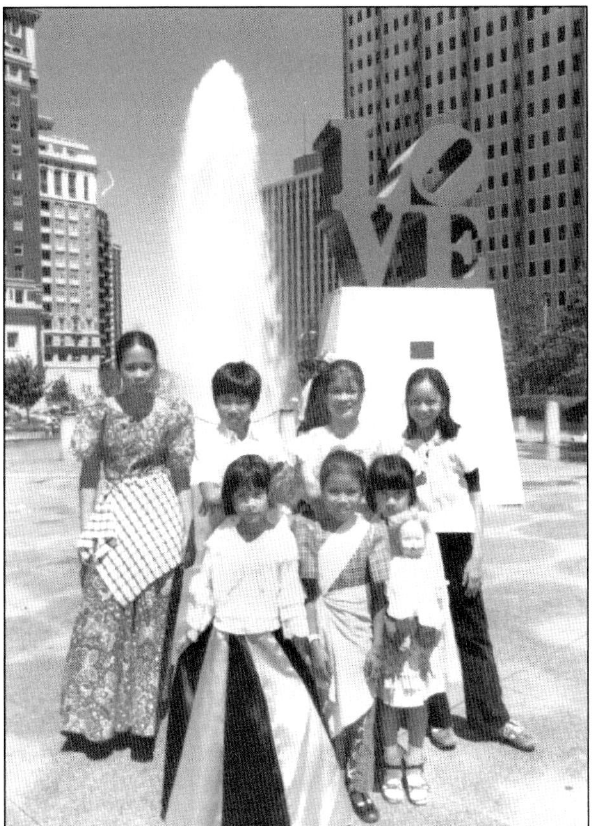

Here is a Philippine Independence Day celebration at Love Park in Philadelphia in June 1978. A FAAPI Youth Dance Troupe is in front of the iconic Robert Indiana *Love* sculpture at JFK Plaza. This period is known as "the great migration," when thousands of Filipino professionals left their homeland as fresh graduates to work in the United States as nurses, doctors, and other skilled laborers. (Courtesy of Virgina Luz.)

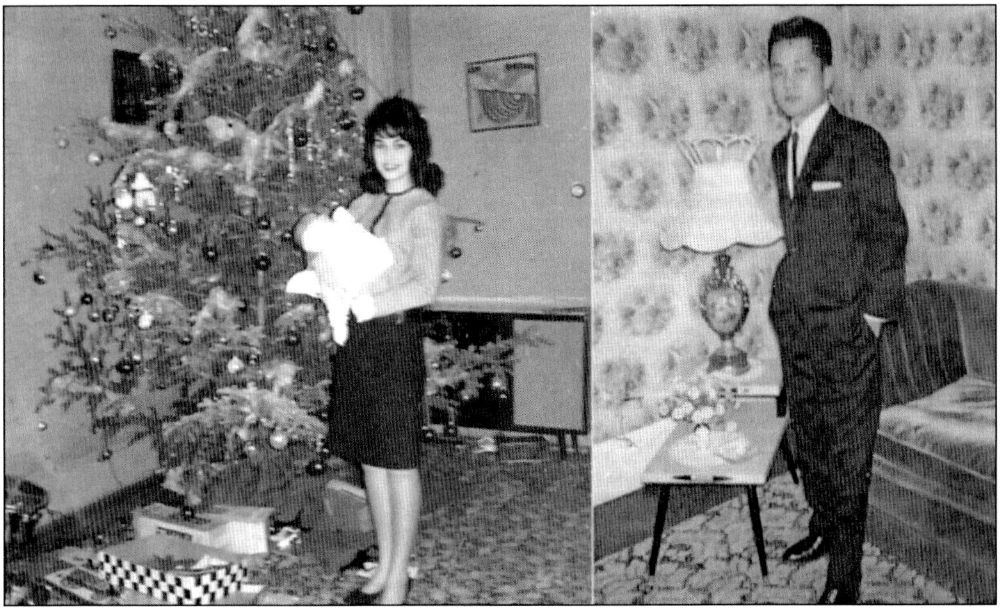

On the left is Barbara Magallanes, who was born in Philadelphia to a Filipino father and a Scottish/Welsh mother. She was Dick Clark's principal dancer on *American Bandstand* and was the first Philly "Pinay" on American television. On the right is Ray Burdeos, a native of Butuan, Philippines, who joined the US Coast Guard to "see the world." He chronicled his years in Philadelphia from 1956 to 1962 in *Flips in Philadelphia*. (Courtesy of Ray L. Burdeos.)

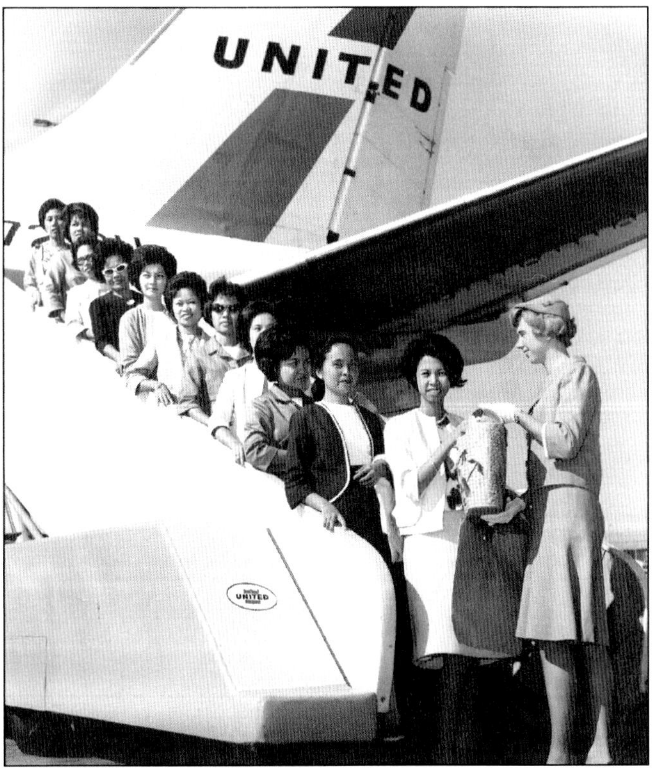

Eleven nurses from the Philippines arrive at International Airport for a one-year training program at Presbyterian Hospital. United Airlines stewardess Mancy Saffell escorts the nurses off the jet. (Courtesy of Temple University Libraries, Urban Archives.)

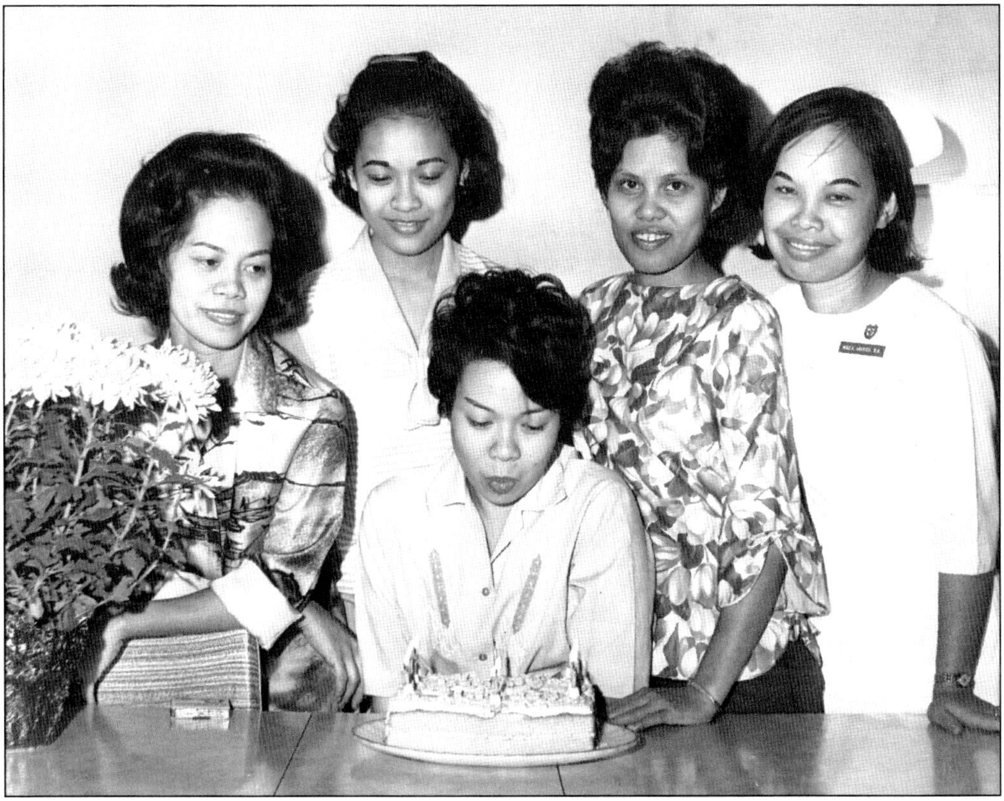

Filipina nurses stand around a seated Consuelo C. Aguilar while she blows candles out on a cake during her birthday celebration on December 22, 1966. Incidentally, as the 100th photograph in this book, this is a symbolic gesture to celebrate 100 years of Filipino presence in Philadelphia. (Courtesy of Temple University Libraries, Urban Archives.)

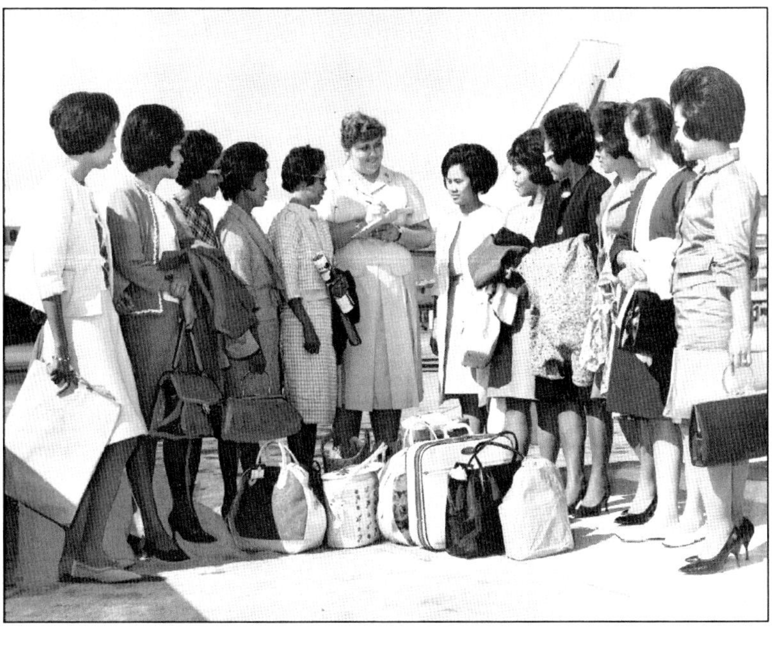

Mary Louise Burk (center), associate director of nurses, greets the newly arrived nurses from the Philippines on September 2, 1965. (Courtesy of Temple University Libraries, Urban Archives.)

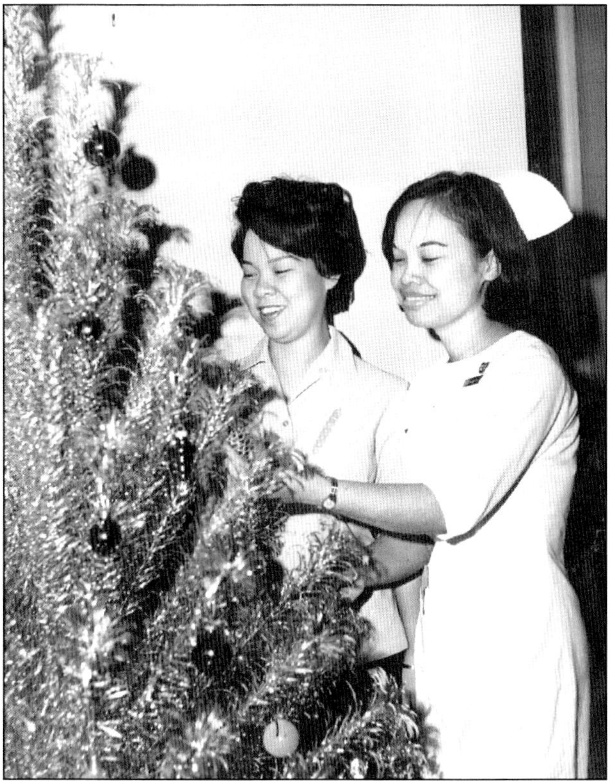

Philippine nurses Consuelo C. Aguilar (left) and America M. Abarico are trimming a Christmas tree. (Courtesy of Temple University Libraries, Urban Archives.)

A family from the Philippines visits Independence Hall for the first time in July 1975. The adults are, from left to right, Greg Estrella, an engineer from Lipa City; Eleanor Lao-Estrella, RN, from Manila; Virgie O. Luz; and Zosing U. Luz. The children are, from left to right, Michael Estrella (carried by his father), Andrew Estrella, Melissa Estrella, Tricia Luz, Cecilia Luz, and Mimi Luz. (Courtesy of Virginia Luz.)

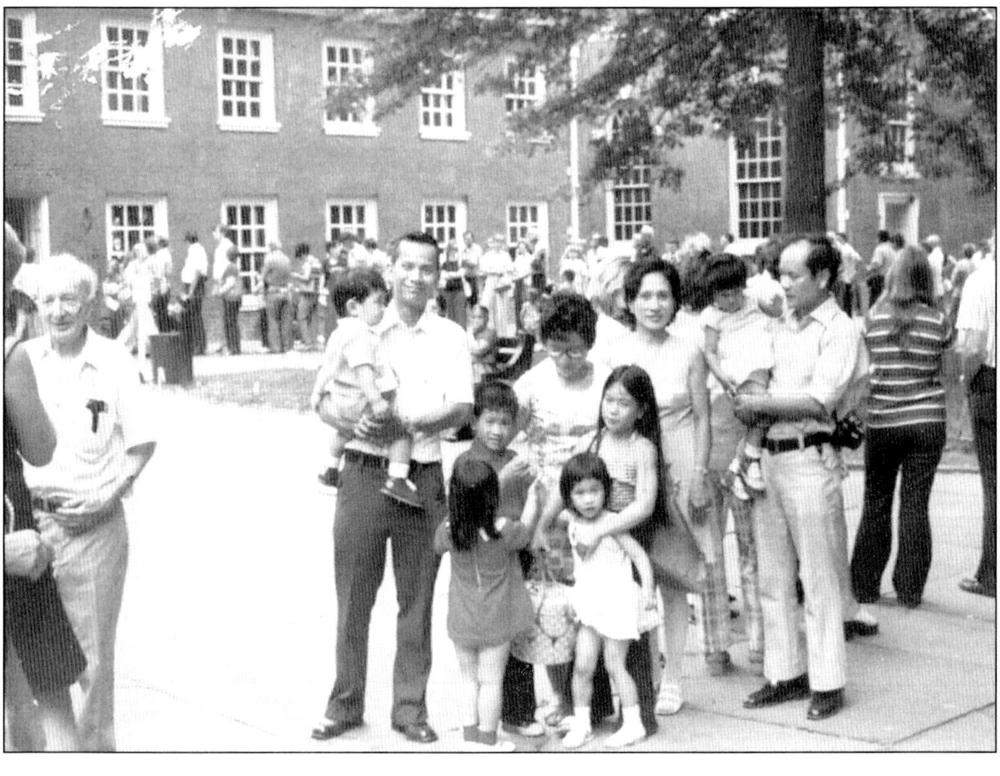

From left to right are Dr. Juan Mandanas Umali, Ben Velez, Maria Umali-Velez, and son Jimmy Velez in Philadelphia. (Courtesy of Noel Abejo.)

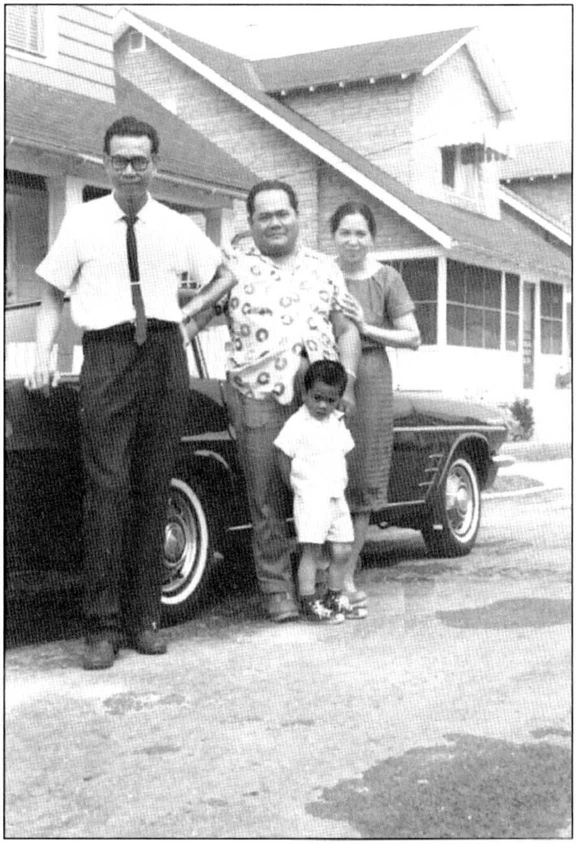

Maria Velez-Umali is pictured inside her home during a birthday party on September 2, 1960. Considered by many as the matriarch of the Filipino community, Maria ran a boardinghouse for Filipino nurses, provided newly arrived Filipino immigrants with initial housing arrangements, babysat their children, and offered meals. She bought and sold television sets and household appliances while running mahjong parlor games. (Courtesy of Noel Abejo.)

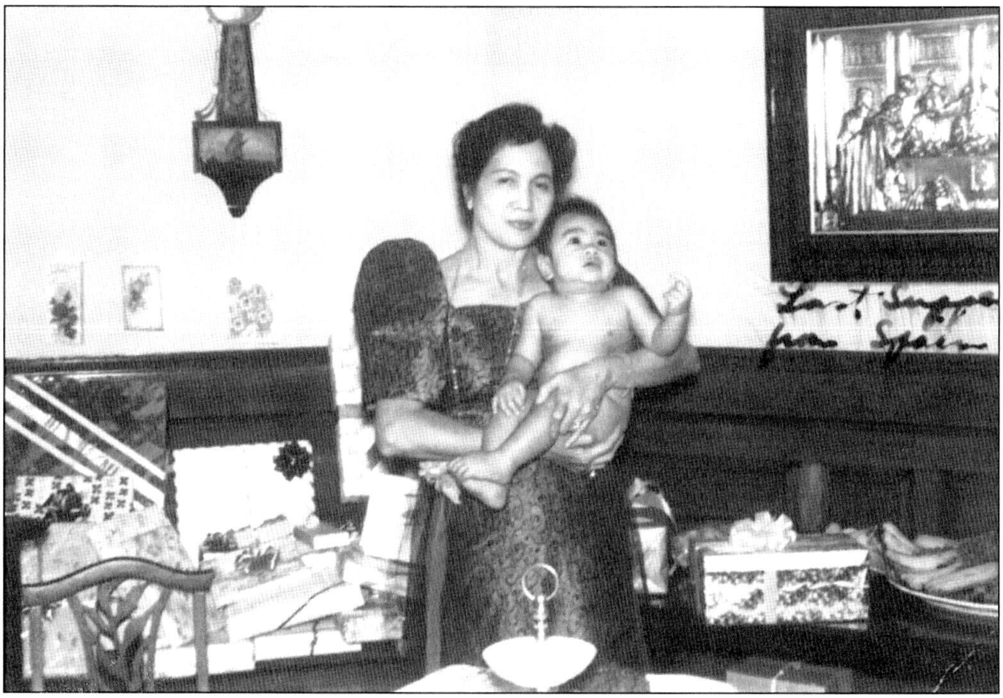

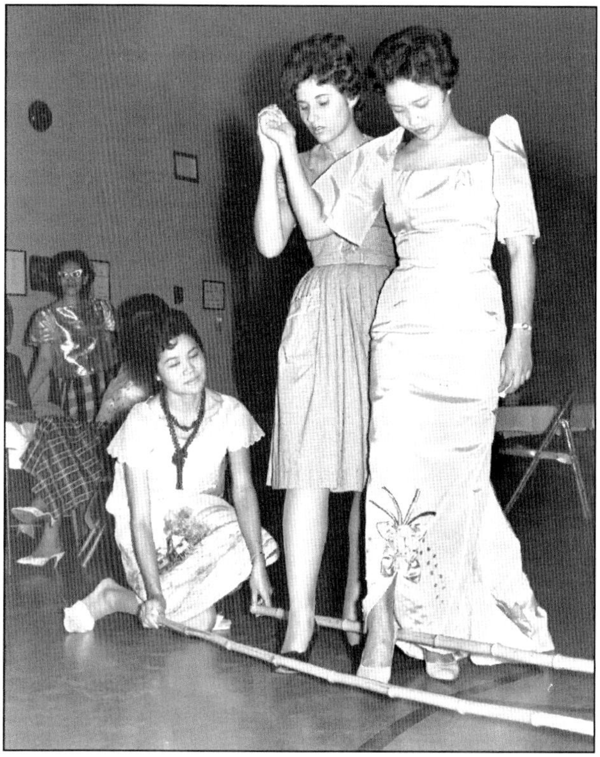

Luz Baldin (standing, left) and Ninfa A. Tirol (standing, right) show Joyce Kantor how to do a Filipino dance at the Albert Einstein Medical Center in 1961. This photograph was titled "Nurses stage Filipino Bandstand," referencing the popular dance craze in America at that time. *American Bandstand* began as a local program on WFIL-TV, present-day WPVI, in Philadelphia on October 7, 1952, and featured teenagers dancing to Top 40 music introduced by Dick Clark. (Courtesy of Temple University Libraries, Urban Archives.)

Philippine student nurses Lydia Pabilando (left) and Zenaida Vibar dance with candles (*pandanggo sa ilaw*) in Albert Einstein Medical Center on February 10, 1969. (Courtesy of Temple University Libraries, Urban Archives.)

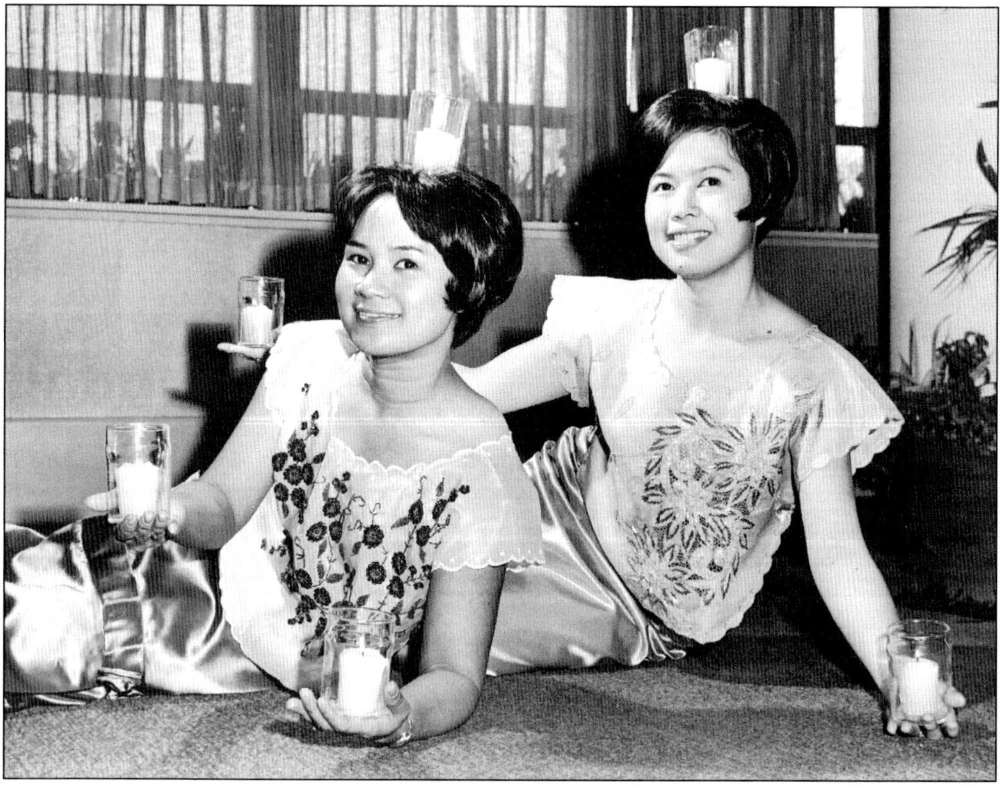

Zosing U. Luz, an engineer from Lipa, Batangas, takes a bride (Virginia Olivar) from Philadelphia. The two ladies sitting are the bride's aunt Jesusa Dalisay and sister-in-law Elvira Olivar from Vancouver, Canada. During most of the 1960s and 1970s, Filipino men were drawn to Philadelphia to find their future wives. The great migration of professionals came to the United States through the 1960 Exchange Visitor Program (EVP) Act, bringing hundreds of skilled laborers to the Keystone State. (Courtesy of Virginia Luz.)

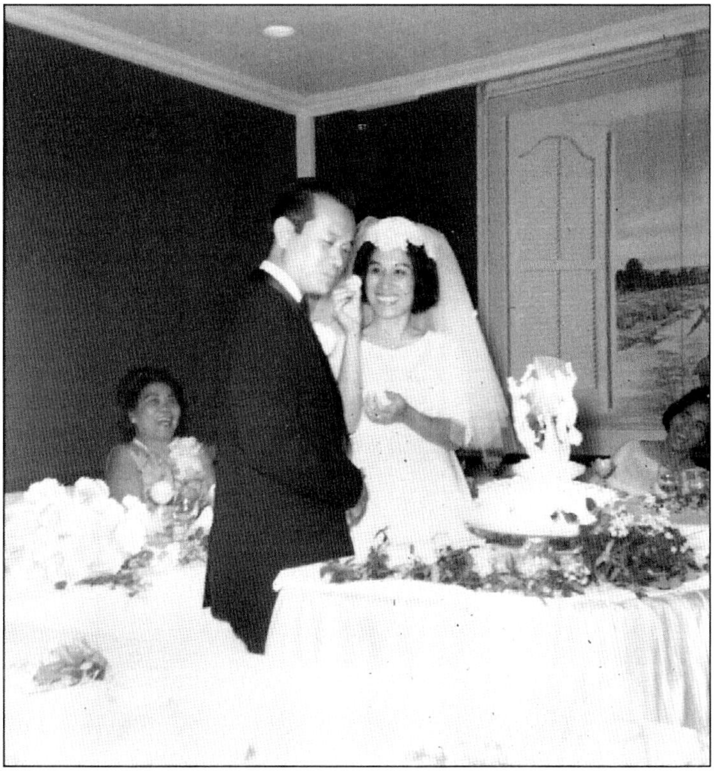

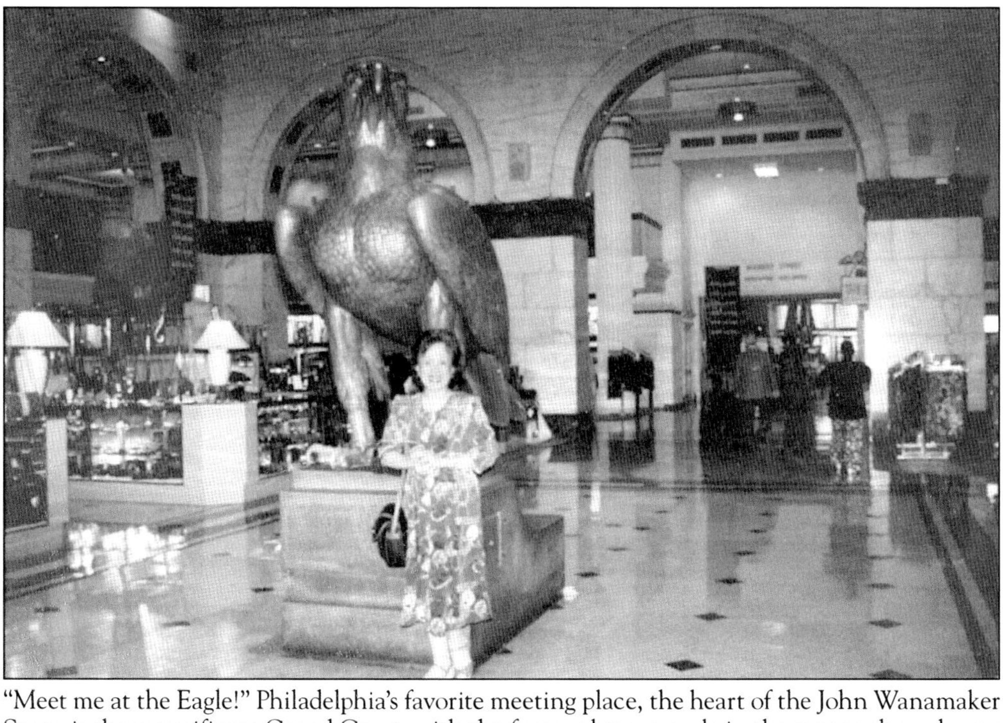

"Meet me at the Eagle!" Philadelphia's favorite meeting place, the heart of the John Wanamaker Store, is the magnificent Grand Court, with the famous bronze eagle in the center, the only one of its kind in the world. (Courtesy of Virginia Luz.)

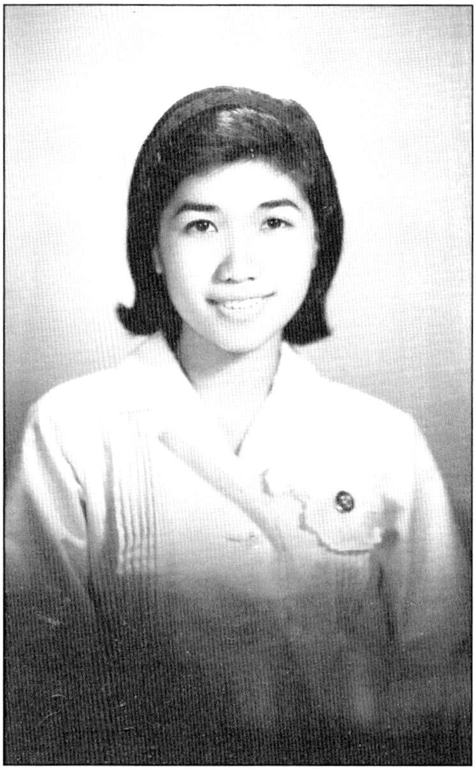

Norma Arevalo graduated from the University of the Philippines with her bachelor of science in nursing in 1969 and immigrated to the United States the same year through the Exchange Nurse Visitor Program at Temple University Hospital. It was her father's dream for her to work in America, and he encouraged her to take up nursing. She is thankful for fulfilling her father's wish. (Courtesy of Norma Arevalo Yabut.)

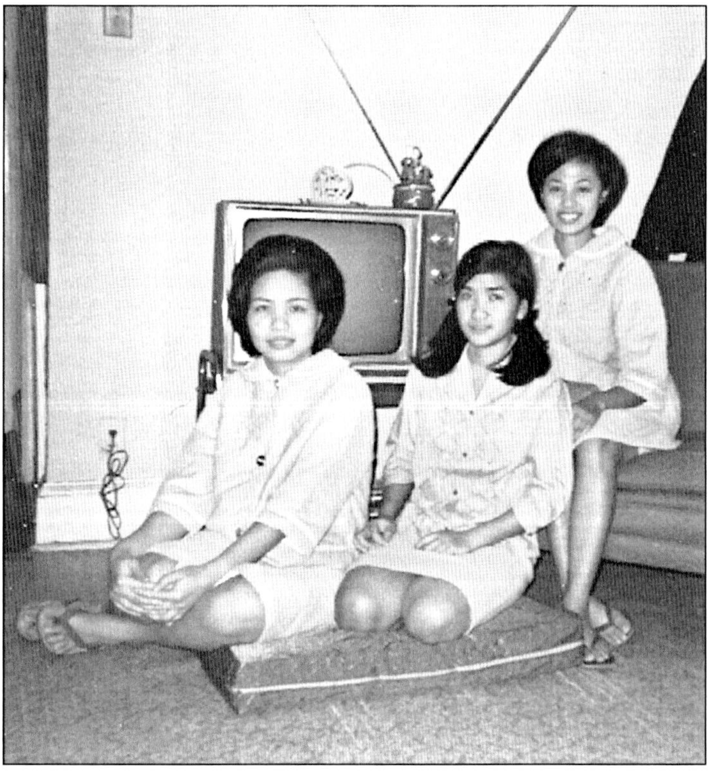

Norma Arevalo (center) is seen with roommates Sally (left) and Judy Laroco (right) in their first apartment in Philadelphia at 3518 North Broad Street, just across the street from Temple Hospital. Many exchange nurses could only stay in the United States for two years; Filipino men who were allowed to stay legally in the country as long as they were in service with the US Navy or Coast Guard were a perfect match. (Courtesy of Norma Arevalo Yabut.)

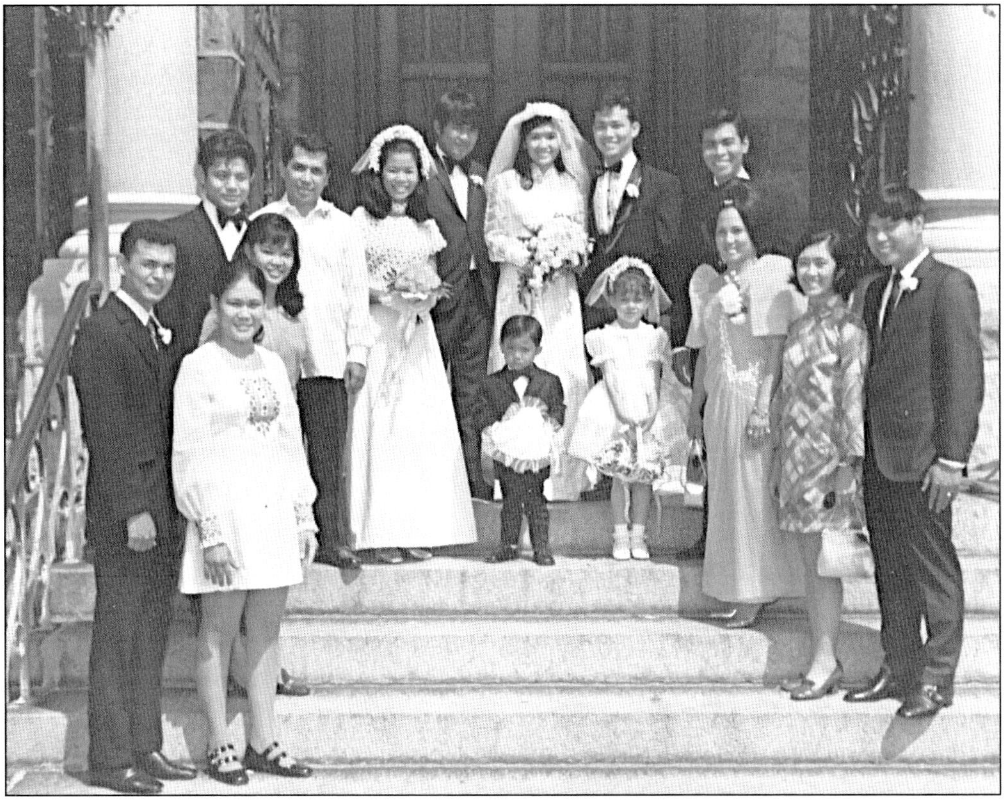

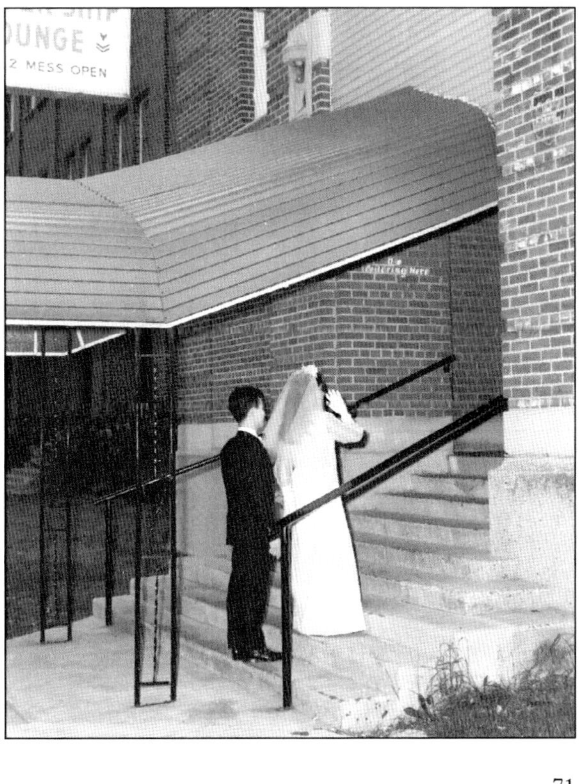

Norma Arevalo and Rick Yabut embodied the popular practice of matchmaking between US Navy personnel and Filipina nurses among Philadelphia Filipinos. On June 5, 1971, at Stephen's Church (now Calvary Church) on North Broad Street, the couple tied the knot as Mr. and Mrs. Yabut. The bride and groom's entourage includes Lilia Relova, Lod Relova, Crosita Gomez, Joey Gomez, Rick Riel, Susan Palis, Romy Arevalo, Tony Yabut, Susan Pacifico, Daisy Reyes, Alex Reyes, Michael Pacifico (ringbearer), and Pamela Marinas (flowergirl). The newly married couple's reception was held at the Clipper Ship Lounge at the US Navy base on South Broad Street (right). (Both, courtesy of Norma Arevalo Yabut.)

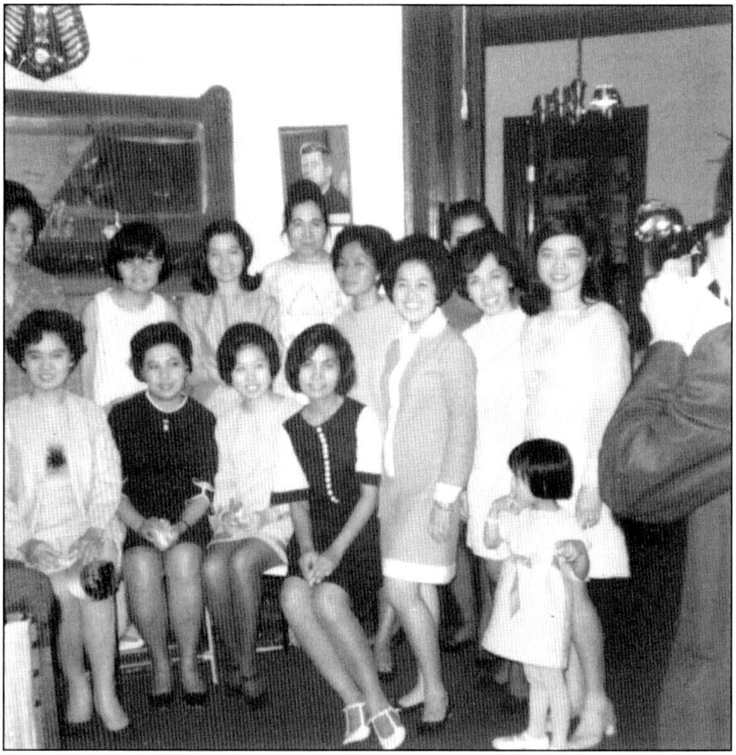

Pictured in March 1968 is the inside of the home of Maria Umali-Velez (standing fourth from left), located near the University of Pennsylvania. Ben Velez took the photograph. Newly arrived Filipina nurses, lodging at her boardinghouse, surround Maria Umali-Velez. (Courtesy of Noel Abejo.)

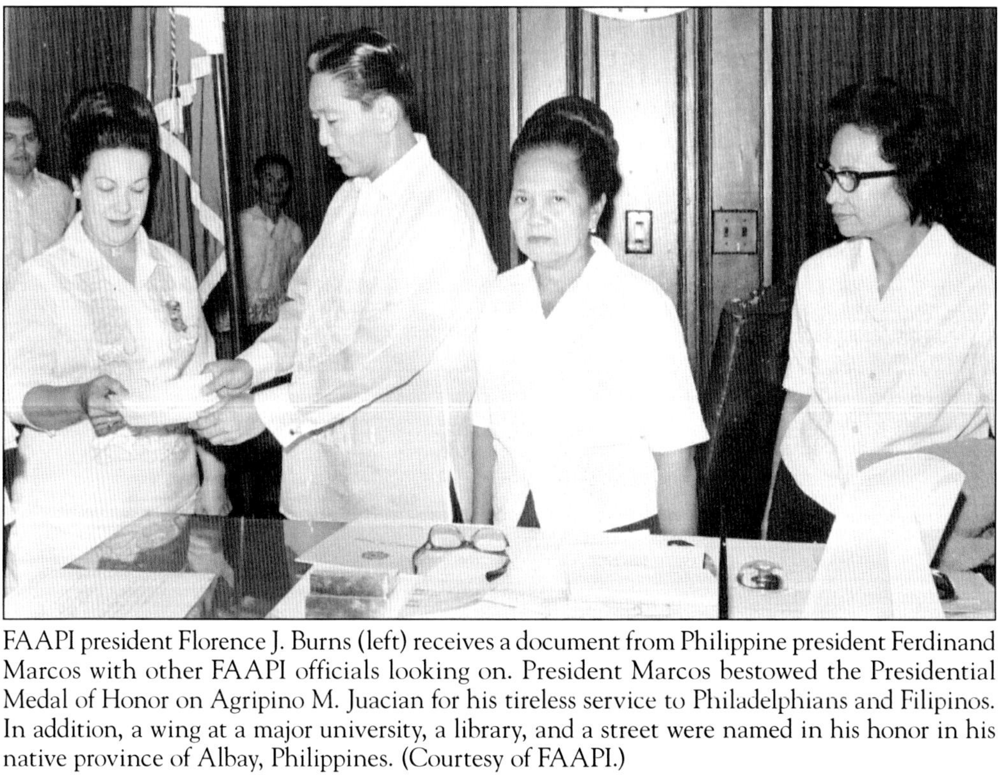

FAAPI president Florence J. Burns (left) receives a document from Philippine president Ferdinand Marcos with other FAAPI officials looking on. President Marcos bestowed the Presidential Medal of Honor on Agripino M. Juacian for his tireless service to Philadelphians and Filipinos. In addition, a wing at a major university, a library, and a street were named in his honor in his native province of Albay, Philippines. (Courtesy of FAAPI.)

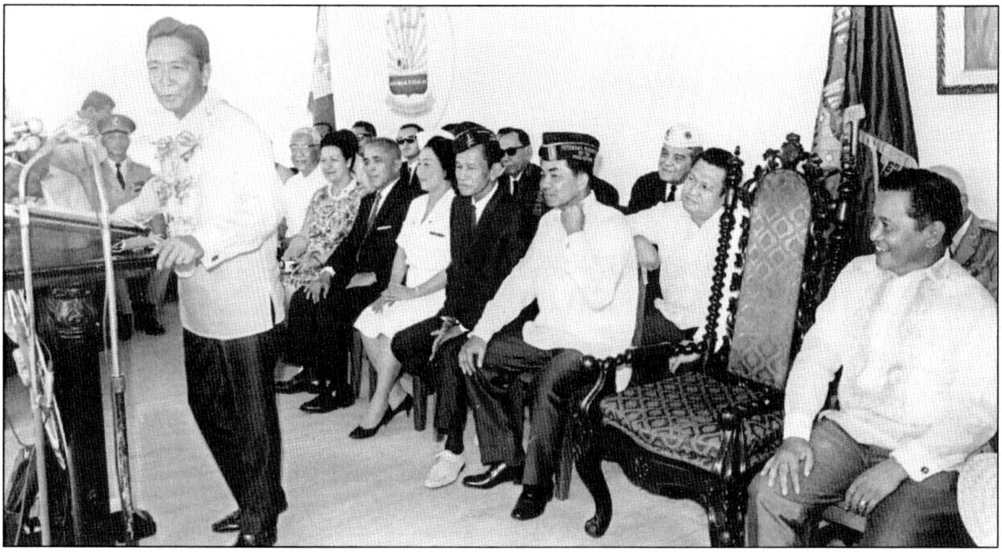

With Filipino American veterans and FAAPI officials behind him, President Marcos delivers a message to Philadelphians in the mid-1970s. This was around the time of the "Thrilla in Manila," the much-awaited epic fight between Philadelphia-based Joe Frazier and Muhammad Ali. (Courtesy of FAAPI.)

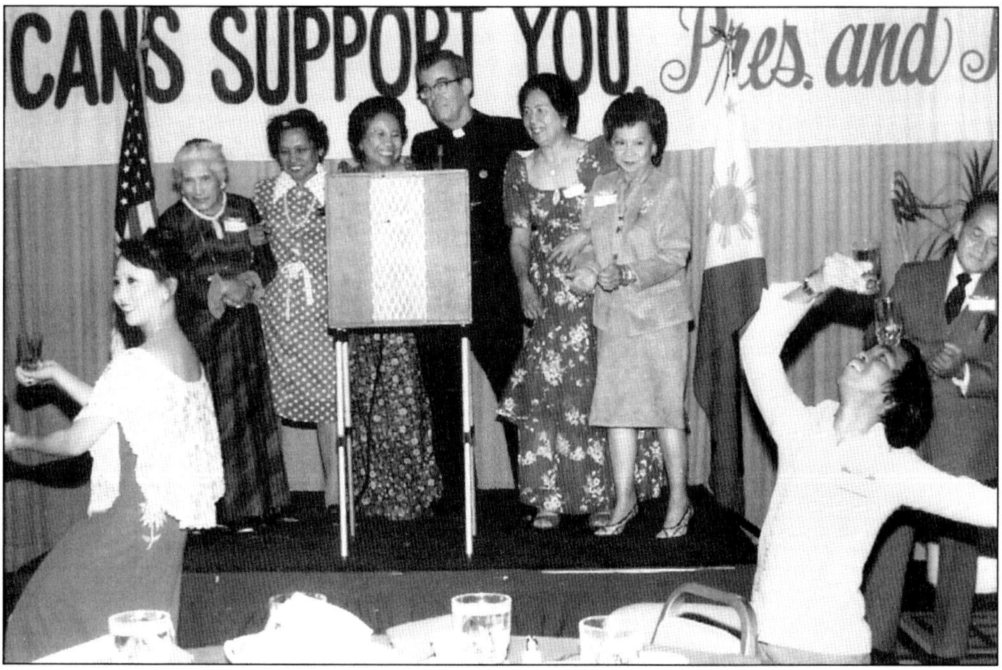

Here is a community celebration welcoming President Marcos and his wife, Imelda, at the Marriot Hotel in 1977. Their daughter Imee was a student at Princeton University at that time. Dancing *wasiwas* and *tinikling* were Mariel Ruelan and Mel Ninobla. Standing at the back are, from left to right, Mrs. Expectacion Salazar-Olivar, Lita Mendoza, Vicky Peralta, an unidentified American priest, Maria U. Velez, an unidentified Filipina pharmacist, and Jesus Ventura, applauding the performance. (Courtesy of Virginia Luz.)

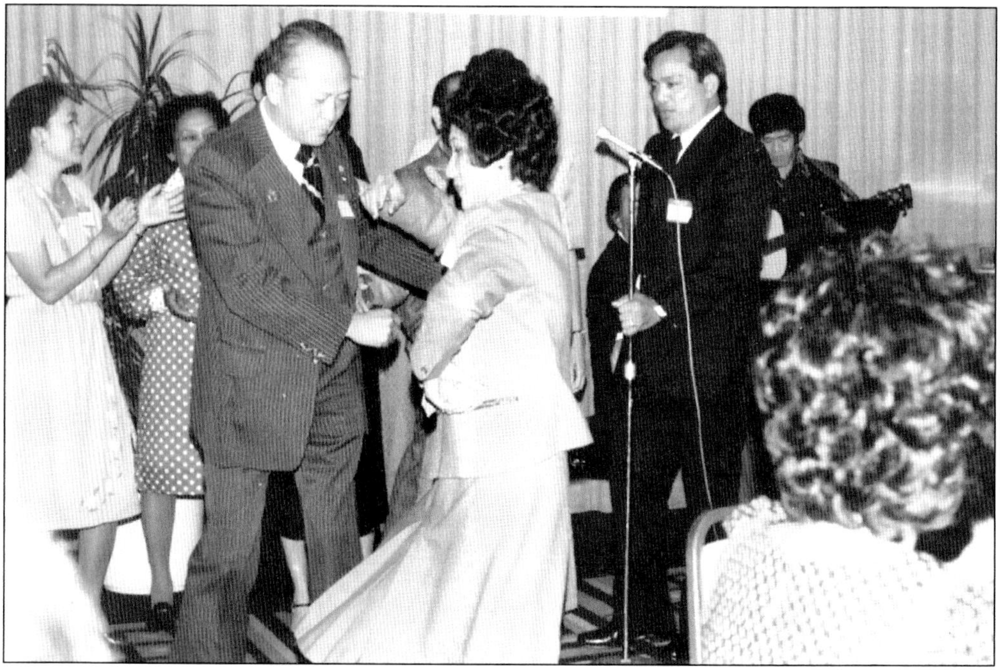

Manong "Pete" Supelana and *Tita* Virgie Luz dance the night away, while Ely Dungca leads the singing complete with a live band during the party welcoming the president of the Philippines and his first lady. Manong Pete served in the US Navy, where most Filipinos were once called "Flip," a racial slur. As a courtesy to the dedicated service of Filipino sailors, the word was permanently removed from use, including such terms as "flip-chart." (Courtesy of Virginia Luz.)

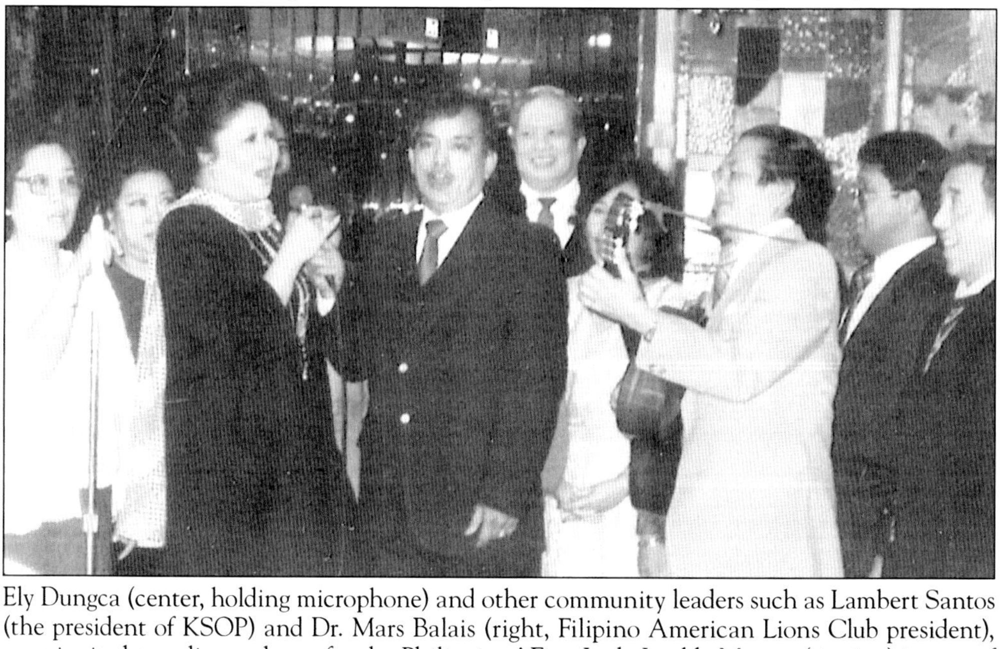

Ely Dungca (center, holding microphone) and other community leaders such as Lambert Santos (the president of KSOP) and Dr. Mars Balais (right, Filipino American Lions Club president), were invited to a dinner-dance for the Philippines' First Lady Imelda Marcos (singing) in one of the hotels in Philadelphia. Filipino community leaders introduced Dungca as "Philadelphia's best Filipino tenor." (Courtesy of Maria E. Dungca-Agkoz.)

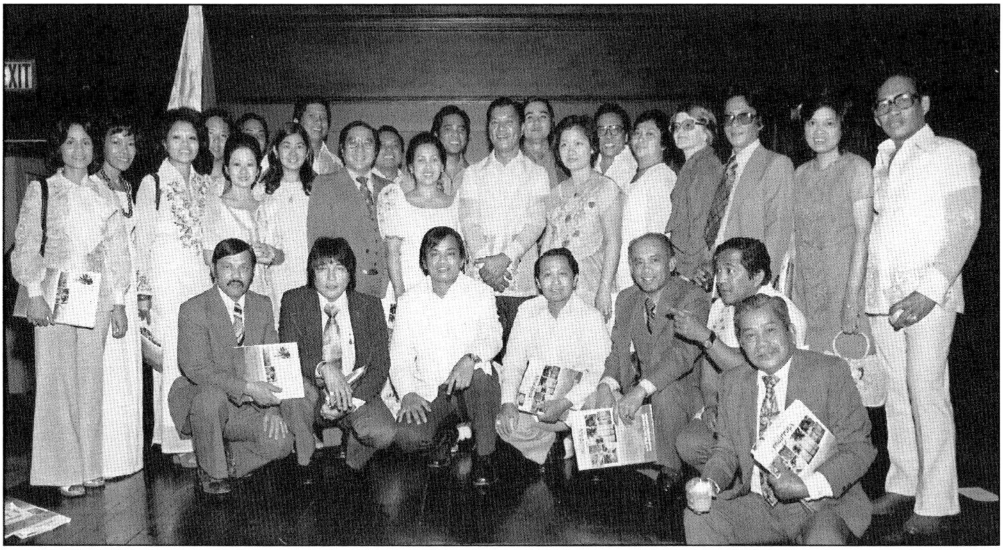

The Philadelphia delegation meets the incoming Philippine consul general in New York, the Honorable Ernesto C. Pineda, in 1970. Pictured are, from left to right, (first row) Dr. Ray Soriano, Dick Velasco, Ely Dungca, Mike Ruelan, Ben Macanas, Jimmy Peralta, and Dr. Venerando Jaurigue; (second row) Virgie Magana, Bernie Aguilar, Rose Spadaro, unidentified, Lina Santos, unidentified, Gloria Ruelan, Ernesto Pineda, Auring Dungca, Dr. Angelina Jaurigue, unidentified, Joe Magana, and unidentified; (third row) Ramon Supelana, Jimmy Soriano, Lambert Santos, unidentified, and attorney Rolly Burgos (Courtesy of Virginia Luz.)

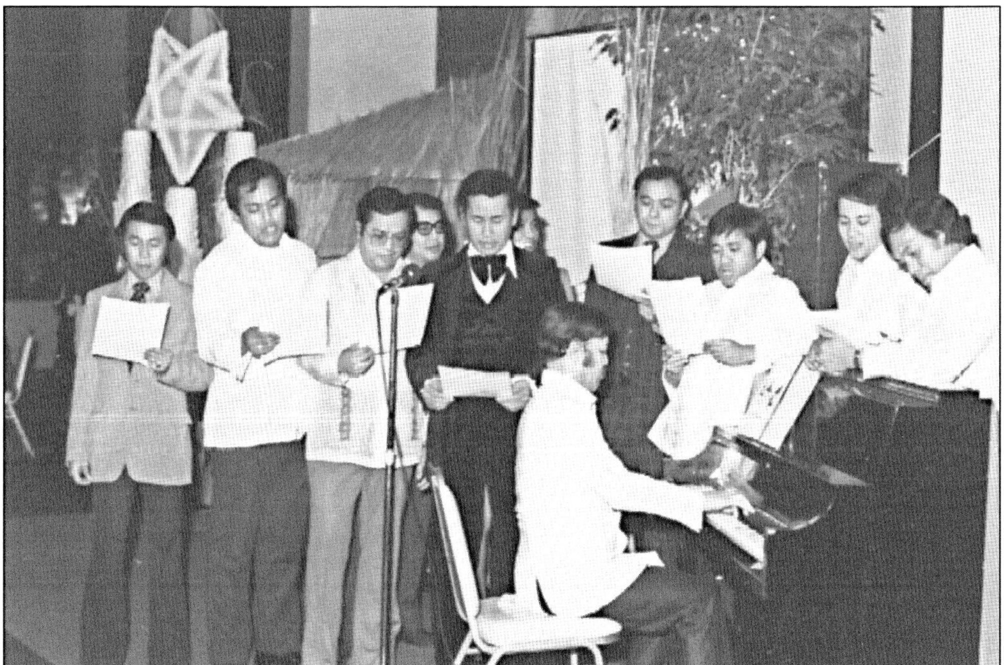

Dr. Raymond Soriano (on piano) leads the singing of Filipino Christmas songs at the Pista Sa Nayon Christmas party, sponsored by the Filipino American Association of Bucks County, Inc. (FAABCI). (Courtesy of Norma Arevalo Yabut.)

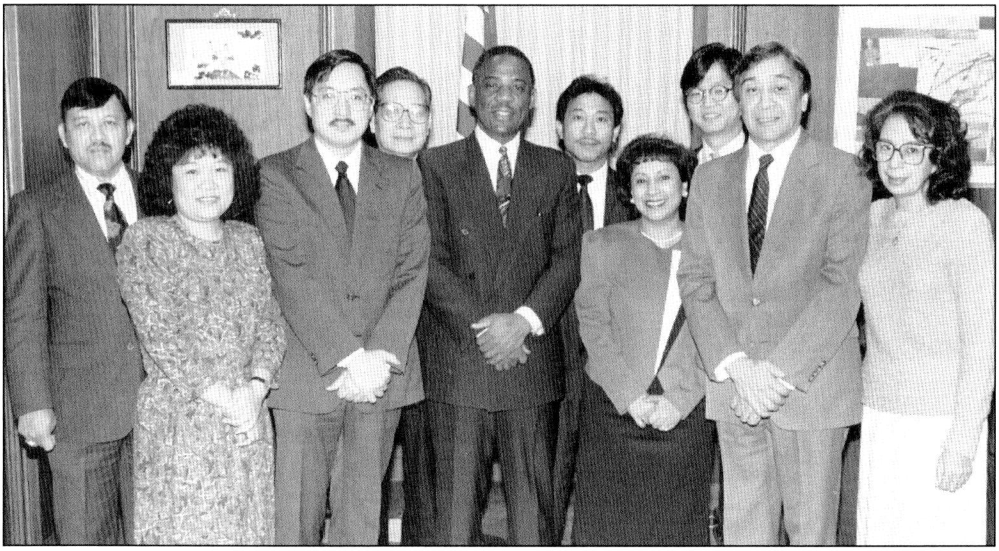

Here, Mayor Wilson Goode establishes Philadelphia's first Mayor's Commission of Asian Pacific American Affairs. From left to right, those identified are Dr. Raymond Soriano, Mayor Goode (5th), Skip Voluntad (9th), and Mary Faustino (10th). Mayor Michael A. Nutter re-established this commission on January 8, 2009, as an important link between city government and the Asian American communities. The 2009 Filipino Philadelphian appointees were Dr. Rommel Rivera and Brad Baldia. (Courtesy of Dr. Raymond Soriano.)

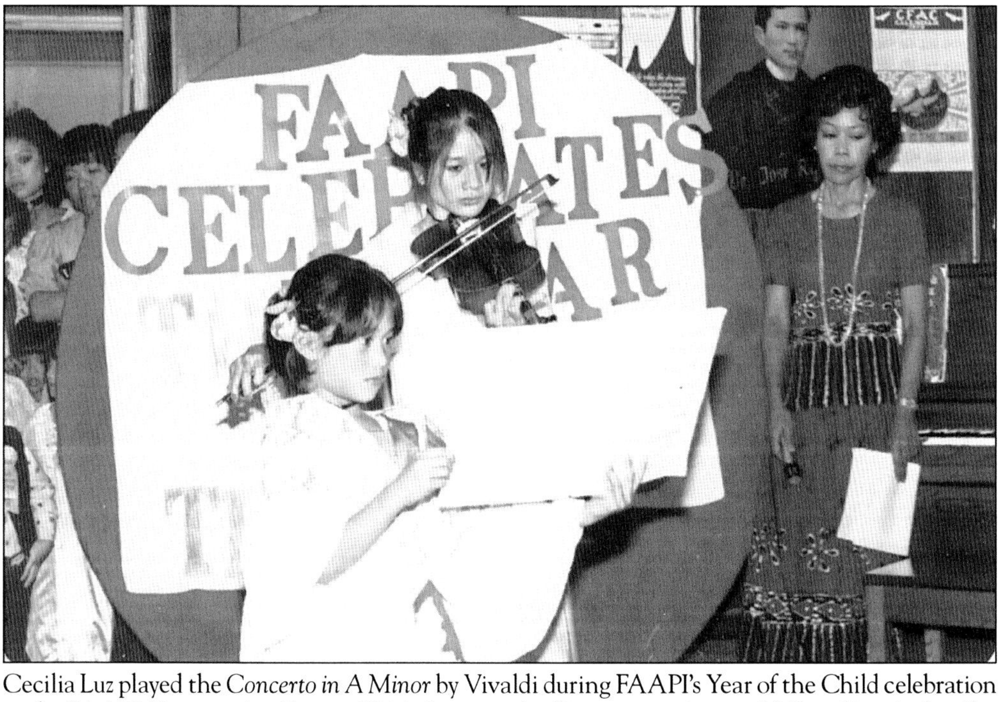

Cecilia Luz played the *Concerto in A Minor* by Vivaldi during FAAPI's Year of the Child celebration at the FAAPI Community Center. Tricia Luz was the "human music stand." Pres. Bernie Aguilar looks on, while the rest of the FAAPI youth dancers await their turn. A well-attended event, community leaders and children from other organizations were invited. The show focused on them, the shining stars of the community. (Courtesy of Virginia Luz.)

In 1978, FAAPI celebrated the Year of the Child at the FAAPI Center. These two young members of the FAAPI Youth Dance Troupe received trophies for participating. (Courtesy of Virginia Luz.)

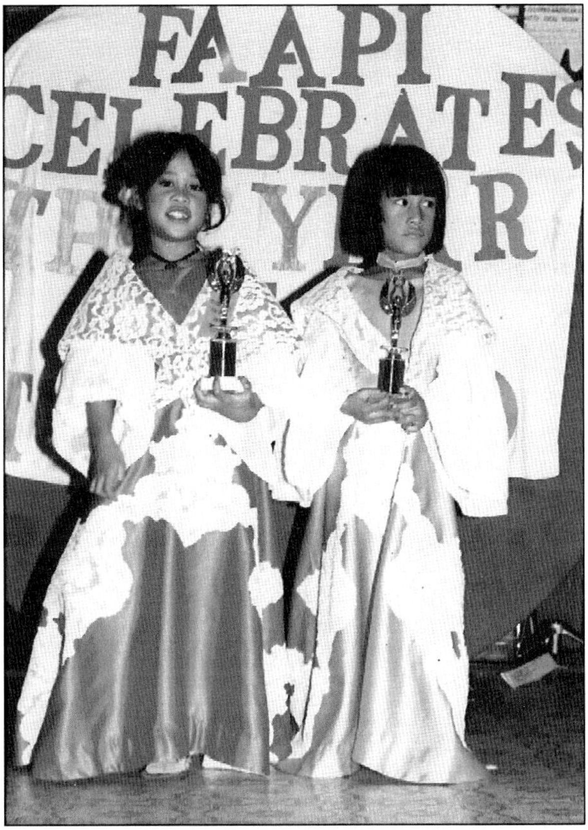

Shown is the curtain call for the FAAPI Youth Dance Troupe's United Nation's celebration of the Year of the Child, held at the Kravitz Auditorium in New York. Filipino children and young adult members from different organizations in the tri-state area were invited. Pictured are, from left to right, Tricia Luz, Vivian Ouano, Arnold Dungca, unidentified, Mimi Luz, Maria Ellen Dungca, and Elizabeth Dungca. (Courtesy of Virginia Luz.)

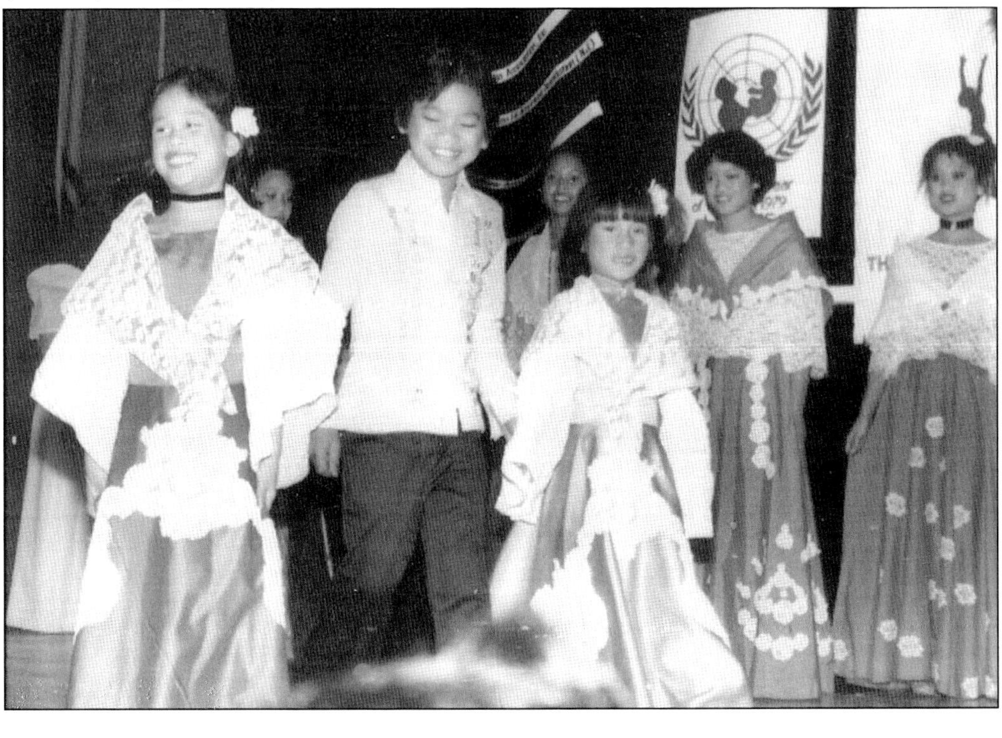

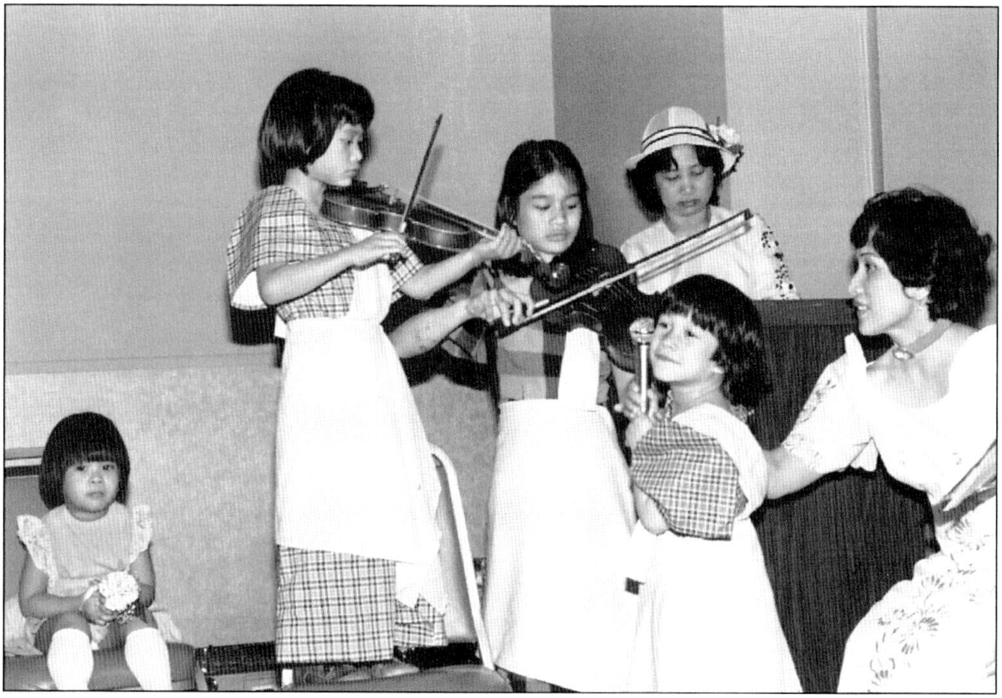

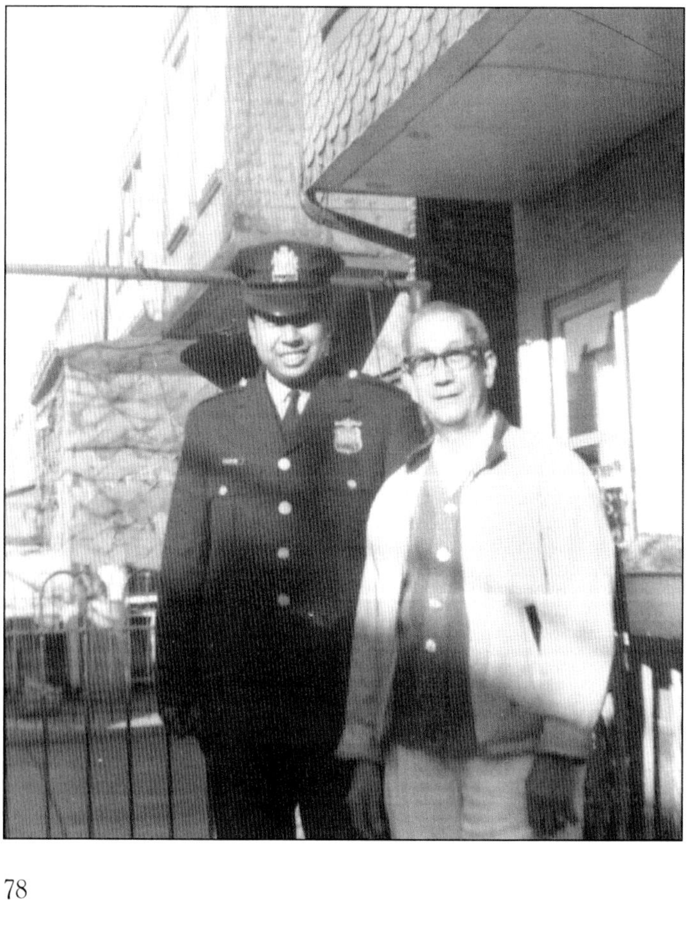

Pictured at a 1978 Mother's Day celebration are, from left to right, Tricia Luz-Holgado, Cecilia Luz-Cariaga, Puring Macanas-Acosta at the podium, Mimi Luz-Royall, and Virgie O. Luz. They played "Dandansoy," a Visayan love song. (Courtesy of Virginia Luz.)

The first Filipino American police officer in Philadelphia, George Faustino started out at the traffic department in 1963 and was eventually promoted to sergeant at the 24th District of the Philadelphia Police, serving Philadelphia for 15 years. He is pictured with his father, Jose Faustino, in North Philadelphia in the 1980s. (Courtesy of Mary Faustino.)

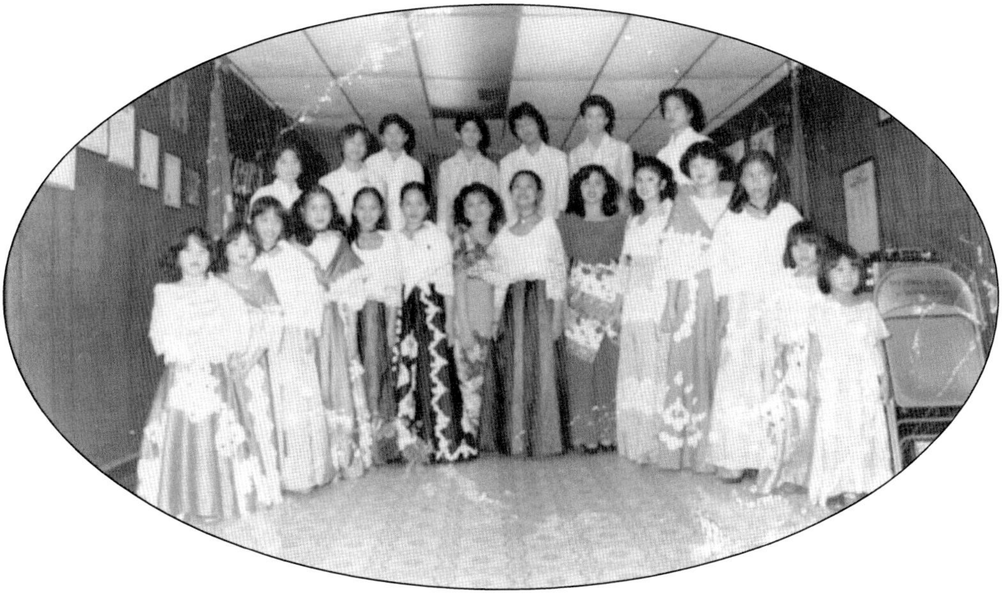

Twenty-one members of the FAAPI Youth Dance Troupe, the largest membership the group ever had, are getting ready to perform for the 1979 United Nation's Year of the Child celebration at the FAAPI Center. Although FAAPI was the main Filipino organization in the Delaware Valley, other groups started organizing after the great migration of Filipinos in the 1960s and 1970s. FAAPI, the "mother of all Filipino organizations of Greater Philadelphia," inspired other youth-centered Filipino groups such as Sinagtala Dance Troupe. (Courtesy of Virginia Luz.)

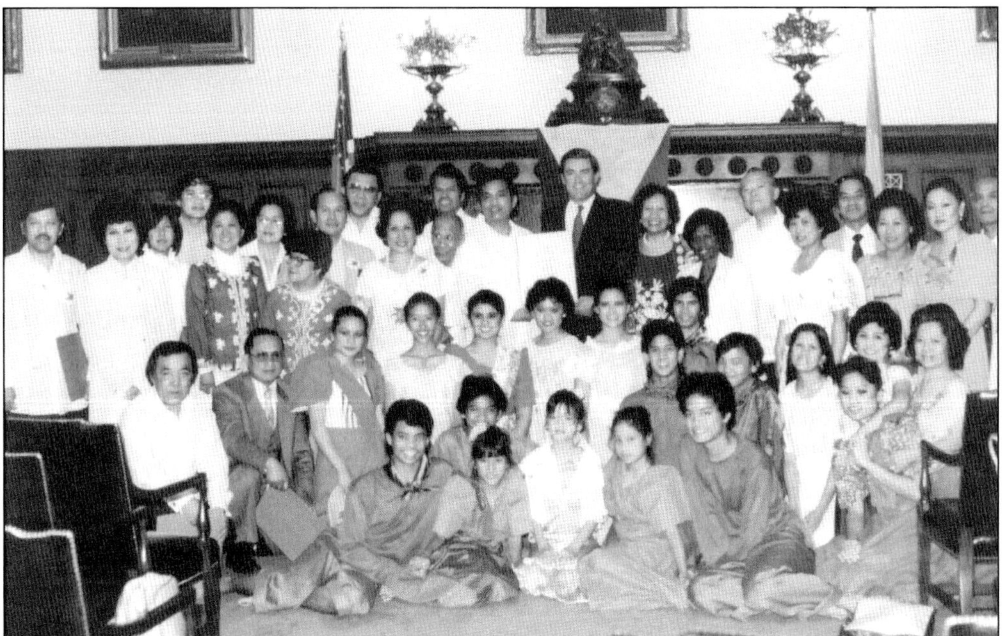

Philadelphia mayor William J. Green III invites FAAPI's dance troupe to perform at Philadelphia City Hall in June 1980. Ely Dungca, Filipino Executive Council of Greater Philadelphia (FECGP) president, receives a proclamation of Philippine Week in Philadelphia. (Courtesy of Virginia Luz.)

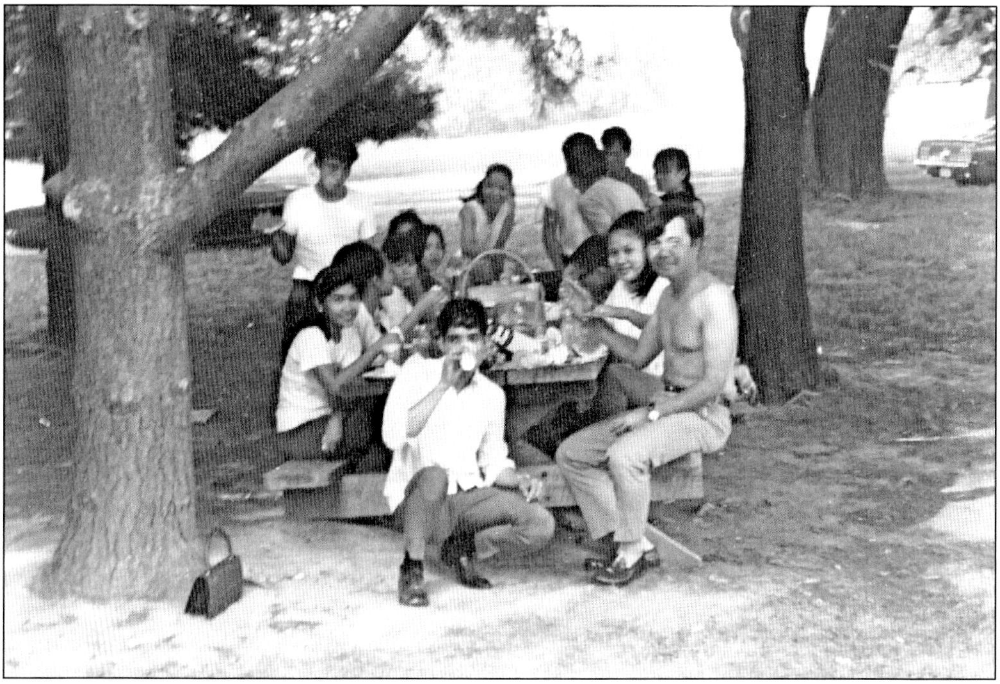

Here is a Filipino picnic at Valley Forge National Park around 1970. Norma Arevalo (left) is shown with future husband Rick Yabut standing behind her. The great migration of Filipino US Navy personnel and Filipina nurses during the 1960s and 1970s resulted in many such marriages, and this park continues to be a favorite place for social activities. (Courtesy of Norma Yabut.)

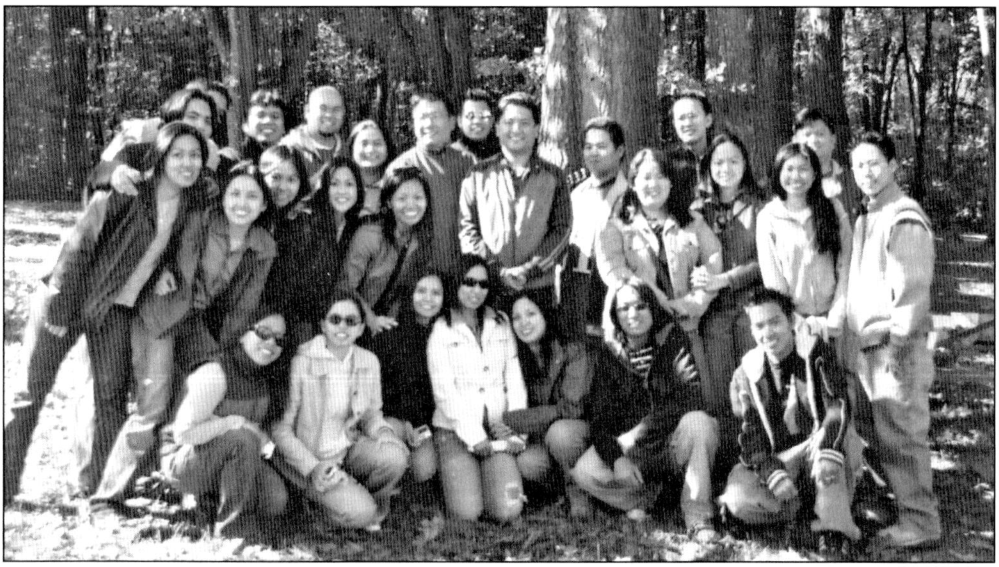

Shown around 2007 is a Singles for Christ (SFC) Pennsylvania picnic at Valley Forge National Park, with guests from SFC Delaware and SFC New Jersey. Eliseo Art Silva (center) served as SFC-PA household head from 2003 to 2009, when membership rose from five to fifty active members. Couples for Christ, with ministries like SFC, is the first Filipino-based organization in Pennsylvania to reach statewide membership, including Pittsburgh, Harrisburg, Reading, and the Poconos. (Courtesy of Eliseo Art Silva.)

Six

Martial Law Babies Come of Age

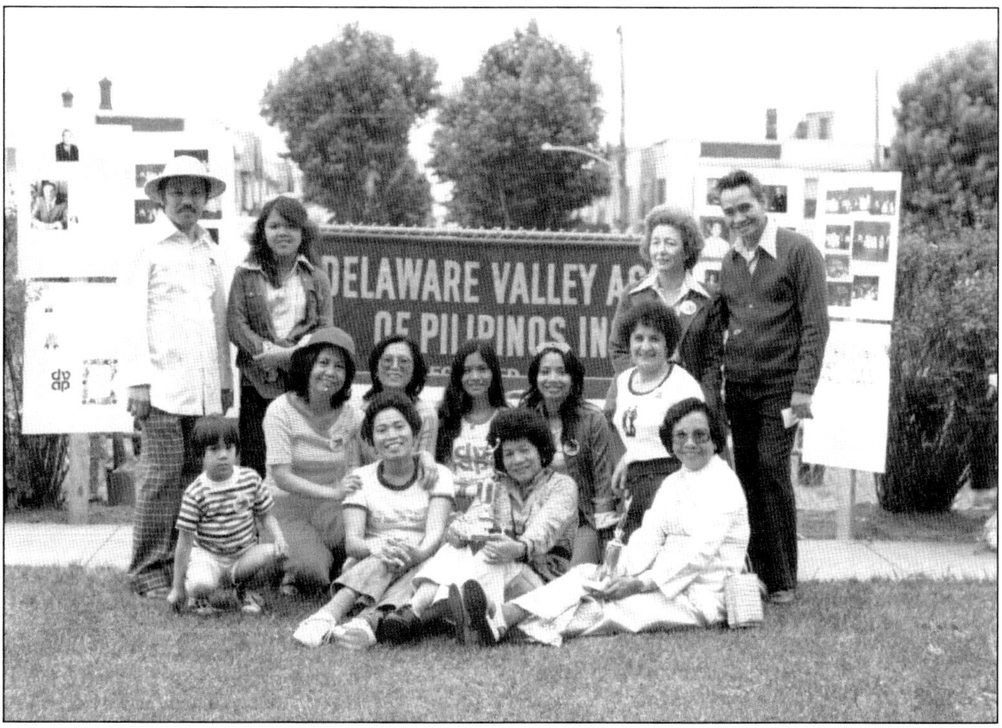

Delaware Valley Association of Pilipinos, Inc., (DEVAP) was the group that supported and advocated for the struggle for social justice and civil rights that defined the 1960s and 1970s. Although the community was deeply divided—for or against the Marcos regime—this movement ignited campaigns that benefited the community as a whole. On the other hand, martial law contributed to the exodus of professionals, contributing to a "brain drain" from the Philippines. (Courtesy of Dr. Raymond Soriano.)

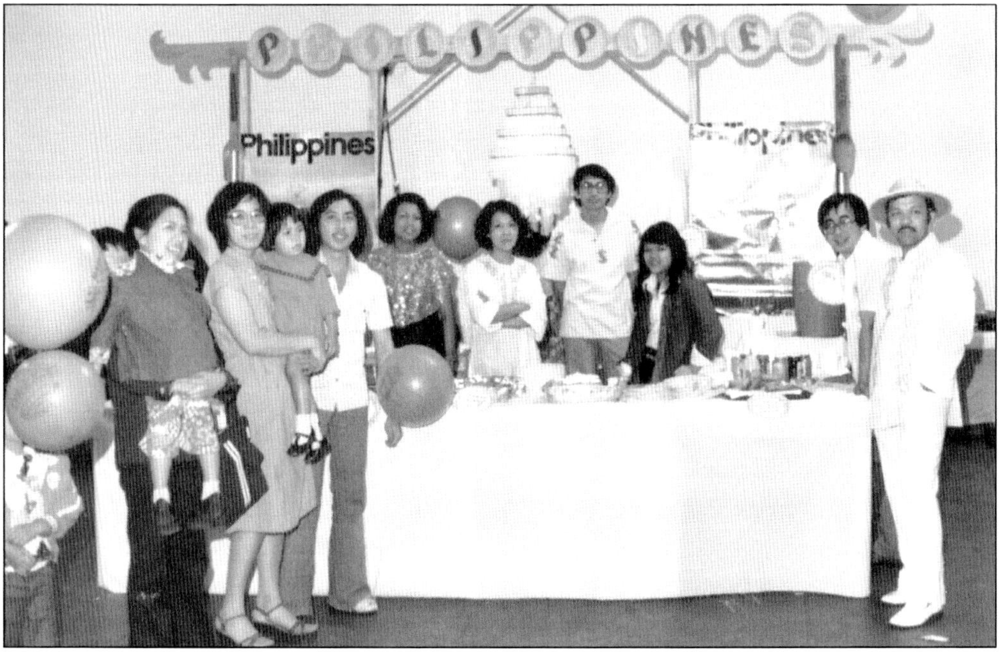

Here is the DEVAP booth at the International Folk Fair held at the Civic Center. In addition to an arts and crafts exhibit, Philadelphians can sample authentic Philippine cuisine and watch folk dances performed by Sinagtala DEVAP folk dance troupe. The annual event is a ball honoring outstanding Filipinos in the Delaware Valley while showcasing five to eight debutantes in the community in a traditional *rigodon de honor*. DEVAP also sponsored Tagalog classes conducted at the FAAPI center. (Courtesy of Dr. Raymond Soriano.)

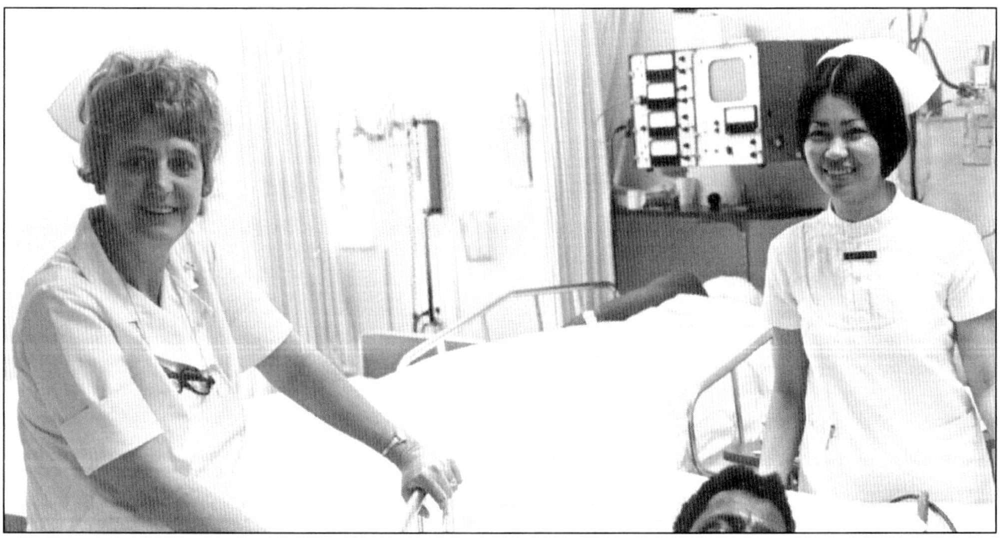

An unidentified nurse (left) is pictured with Elvie Castillo (right) at the Temple University Hospital around 1971. Harold Howland, US deputy assistant secretary of state, estimated in 1970 that the 100,000 foreign scientists and other highly skilled professionals constituted at least $4 billion in savings to the United States in educational costs. During this time, the Philippines was the number one Asian nation sending new immigrants and sent the highest number of foreign medical graduates to the United States. (Courtesy of Gregorio Santillan.)

Pictured here is a program from the first Maria Clara Coronation Night in 1972. Maria Clara is a fictional character in Jose Rizal's novel *Noli Me Tangere*. She is the epitome of the Filipina ideal of grace, nobility, beauty, and pure heart, a "muse" of Filipino nationalism. Although the gatherings often revolved around annual balls, the meetings also discussed social concerns such as housing and the needs of immigrants. The organization cut across social lines. (Courtesy of FAAPI.)

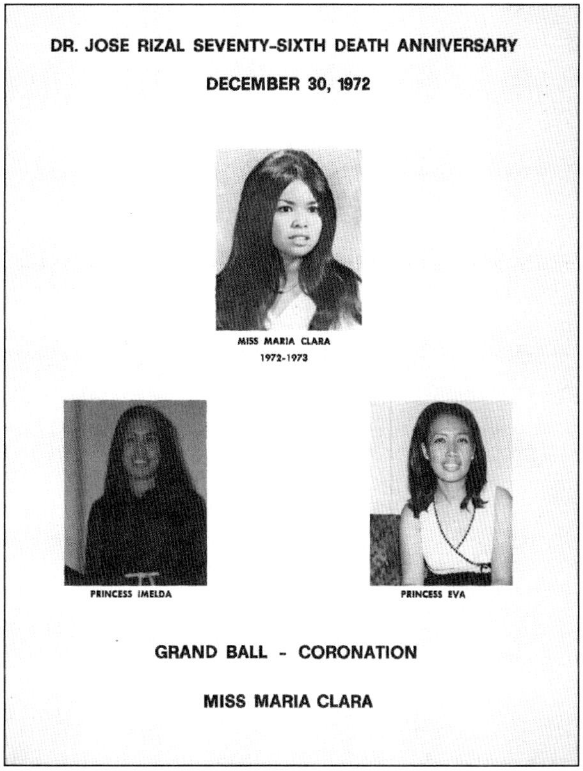

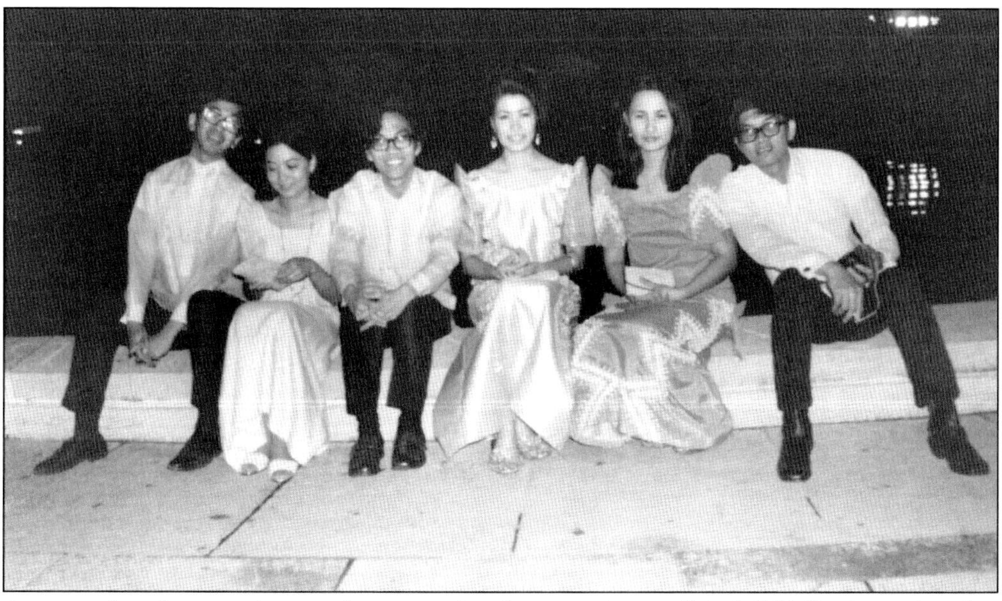

A group of graduate students and nurses enjoyed an evening stroll in full Philippine attire after the Hahnemann folk dancing program at the Philadelphia Art Museum. According to Greg Santillian, Hahnemann Hospital would later be the site of the first labor action by exchange Filipino nurses striking against deplorable working conditions and oppressive low pay in the early 1970s. From left to right are Eddie Chow, Eleonor Alviar, Greg Santillian, Elvie Castillo, Aster de la Cruz, and Rey Mariano around 1971. (Courtesy of Gregorio Santillan.)

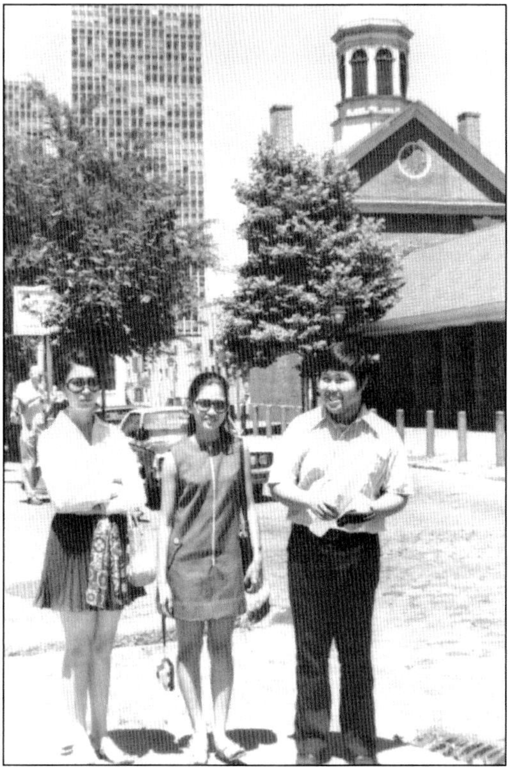

By 1971, there was a rising backdrop of political unrest in the Philippines. Filipino students in Philadelphia, including Lourdes Marzan and others, formed a group called the Philadelphia Committee of Concerned Filipinos (PCCF), which gathered regularly to discuss Philippine-related issues. On September 21, 1972, Greg Santillian received a call from a University of Pennsylvania student to protest the declaration of martial law. PCCF immediately organized a protest rally on October 2, 1972, in front of Independence Hall. (Courtesy of Gregorio Santillan.)

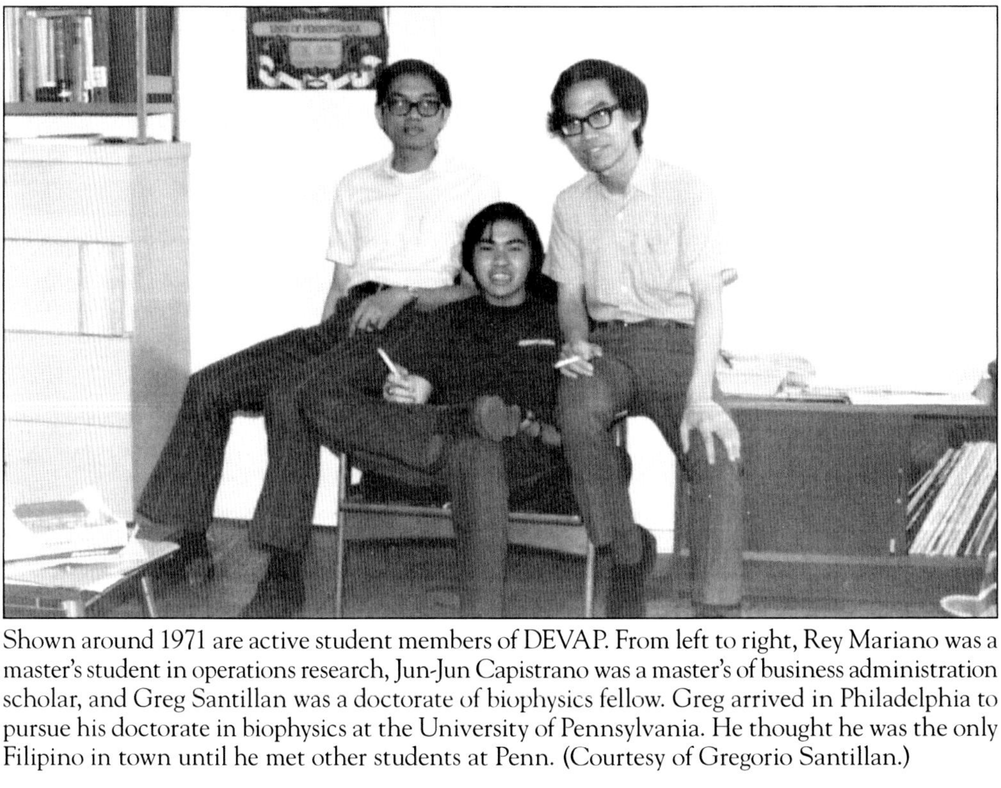

Shown around 1971 are active student members of DEVAP. From left to right, Rey Mariano was a master's student in operations research, Jun-Jun Capistrano was a master's of business administration scholar, and Greg Santillan was a doctorate of biophysics fellow. Greg arrived in Philadelphia to pursue his doctorate in biophysics at the University of Pennsylvania. He thought he was the only Filipino in town until he met other students at Penn. (Courtesy of Gregorio Santillan.)

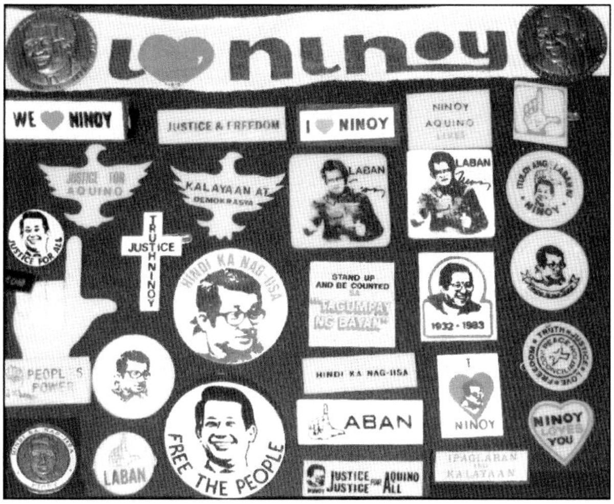

During the 1978 Batasang Pambansa elections, Benigno "Ninoy" Aquino created his own political party dubbed Lakas ng Bayan (People's Power) or LABAN. Later, a groundswell of support from the middle class emerged when, after his return from the United States, an assassin's bullet made him a martyr of the revolution that brought down Marcos. The dictatorship in the Philippines drew many young Filipinos into the community's political life. (Courtesy of Edward De Los Santos.)

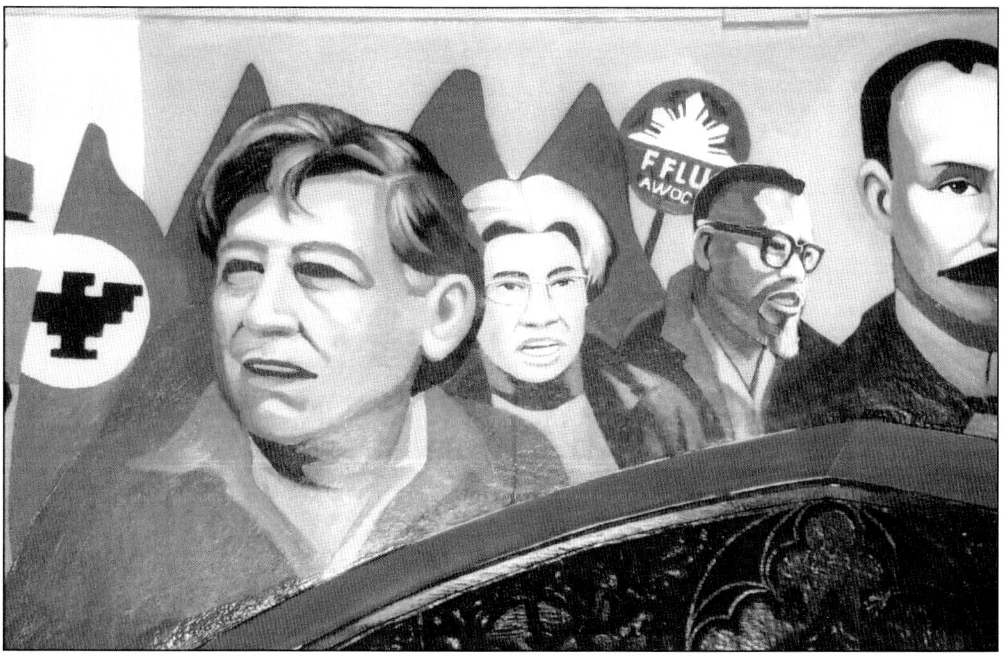

Seen here is the Wall of Inspiration mural by Eliseo Art Silva in Olney High, Philadelphia. This section features, from left to right, United Farm Workers Cesar Chavez, Philip Vera Cruz, and Larry Itliong. The Kilusan ng Democratikong Pilipino (KDP), Philadelphia chapter, was solidly supporting the grape boycott through the distribution *of Ang Katipunan*, the national newspaper of the KDP. Those who were involved were aware that Filipinos spearheaded the grape boycott and were very integral to the United Farm Workers. (Courtesy of Eliseo Art Silva.)

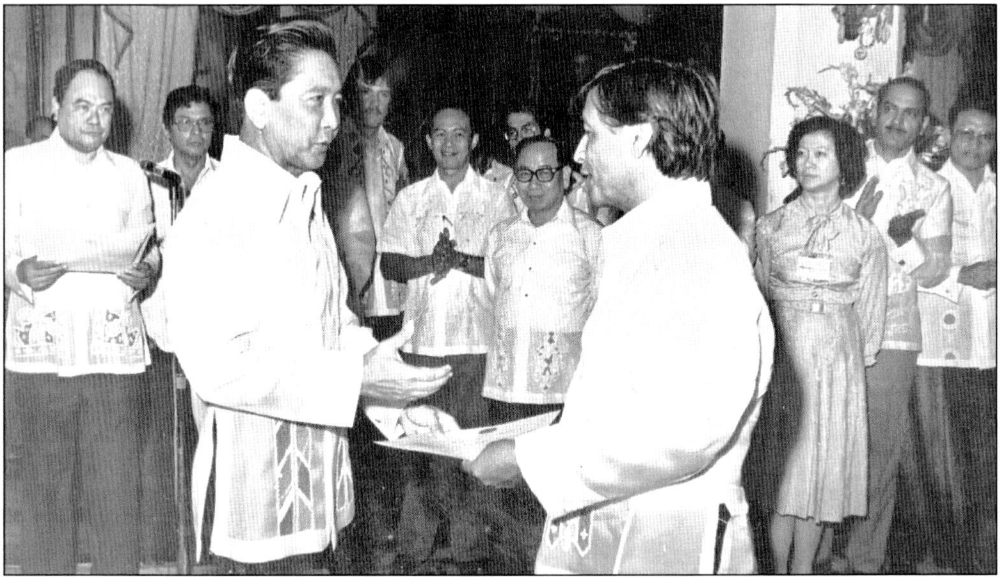

Philippine president Ferdinand Marcos (left) welcomes UFW director Cesar Chavez in Malacanang Palace during his trip to the country on August 26–28, 1977. This singular act by Chavez was viewed as a failed attempt to reach out to Filipino American farmworkers. Because Chavez endorsed Marcos during martial law, human rights advocates, religious leaders, and Filipino leaders in the UFW, such as Philip Vera Cruz (second vice president), openly broke away from the UFW, causing a deep rift within the union. (Courtesy of Walter P. Reuther Library.)

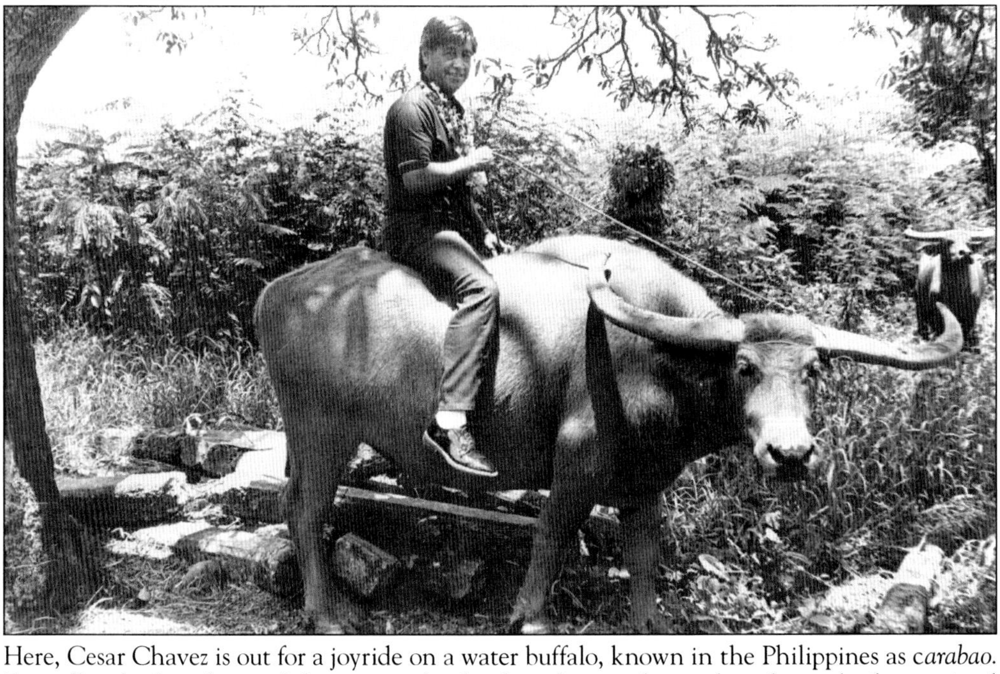

Here, Cesar Chavez is out for a joyride on a water buffalo, known in the Philippines as *carabao*. For pulling both a plow and the cart used to haul produce to the market, this is the farm animal of choice of Filipino farmers. While the Latino members of the UFW selected the Aztec Eagle as their symbol, the Filipino Americans prefer the *carabao* to symbolize their struggle for equality, civil rights, and social justice. (Courtesy of Walter P. Reuther Library.)

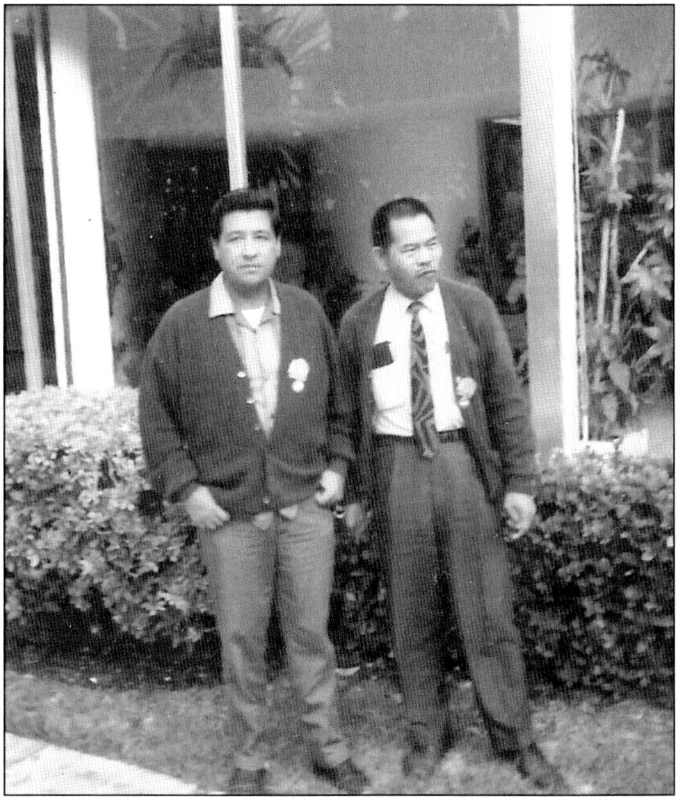

Cesar Chavez and Larry Itliong are pictured in Washington, D.C. Itliong resigned in 1971, due in part to disagreements with the leadership. With only three years of education, he taught himself nine Philippine dialects and three foreign languages, including Spanish, Portuguese, and English, making him the UFW's most effective organizer. Itliong was not only the catalyst of the 1965 grape boycott, he also had over 30 years of union organizing experience, in contrast to Chavez's two years, when Itliong's Agricultural Worker's Organizing Committee and Chavez's National Farmworker's Association merged to become the UFW. (Courtesy of Jonny Itliong.)

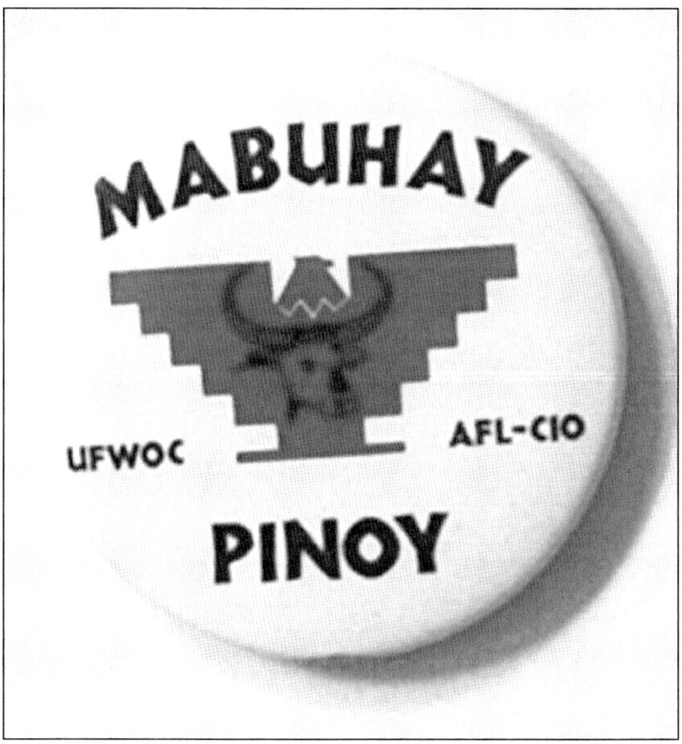

The UFW combined the Chicano Aztec eagle with the Filipino *carabao*. Since there were only 1,500 Filipino Americans and over 2,500 Latino members in the UFW, they were always out-voted. *Pinoy*, derived from Filipino, is the Filipino American equivalent of Chicano. *Mabuhay* is "long live" in Filipino. *Maboo-maboo-maboo-hay* was the chant conceived by Filipino farmworkers during the march from Delano to Sacramento in 1965. They also sang "Dahil sa Iyo" (Because of You) during the historic strike. (Courtesy of United Farm Workers of America.)

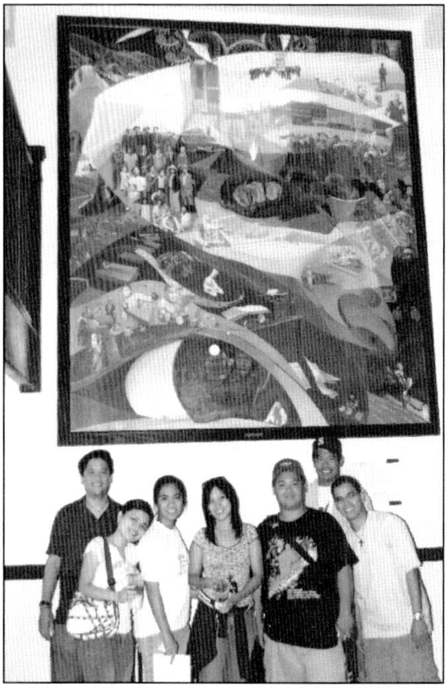

The Carlos Bulosan memorial mural entitled *Secrets of History*, by Eliseo Art Silva, is visited by Filipinos from Greater Philadelphia in the Eastern Hotel in the International District of Seattle, Washington. This 1999 acrylic on canvas depicts a portion of Bulosan's face. When viewed from afar, the details reveal images and narratives from his writings, most specifically his 1946 novel *America is in the Heart*. This is the first permanent American museum exhibit honoring a Filipino American. Larry Itliong and Bulosan worked together organizing labor unions in Seattle and Stockton, California's Little Manila during the 1930s and 1950s. (Courtesy of Eliseo Art Silva.)

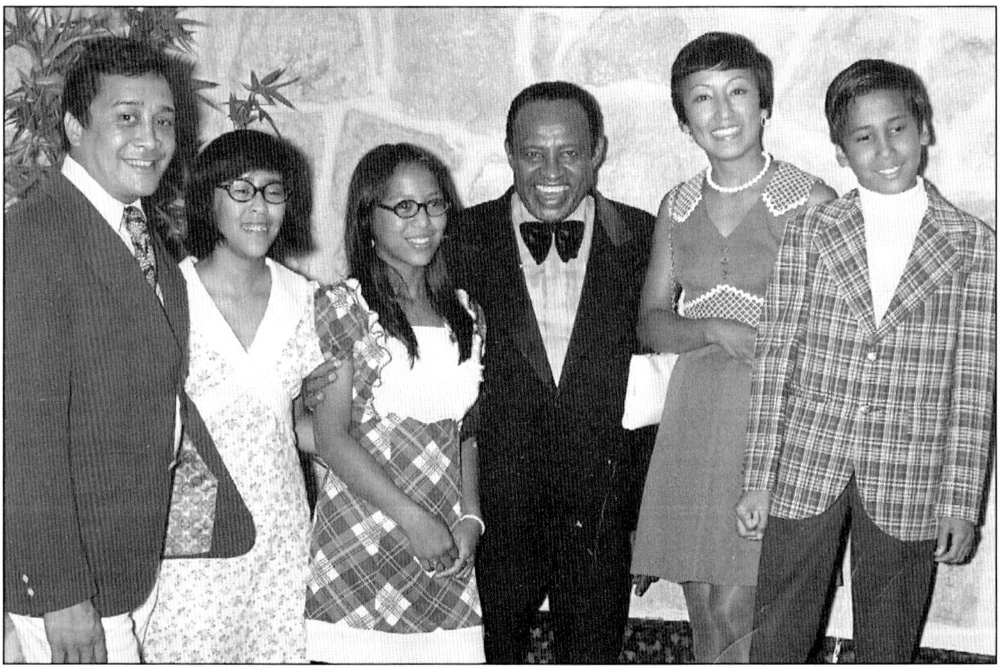

Pioquinto "Skip" Voluntad (left) is seen with his wife and kids after the concert of Lionel Leo Hampton (third from the right), a Jazz great and actor who filled the venue to capacity. Skip managed the popular Kona Kai in Philadelphia from 1976 to 1979. Among famous personalities who frequented the Polynesian-themed restaurant is Theodore Nam Sr., an architect with Filipino heritage who designed the African American Museum in Philadelphia. Skip also mentored Wilson and Cherrie Encarnation, who would later open up their own restaurants. (Courtesy of Skip Voluntad.)

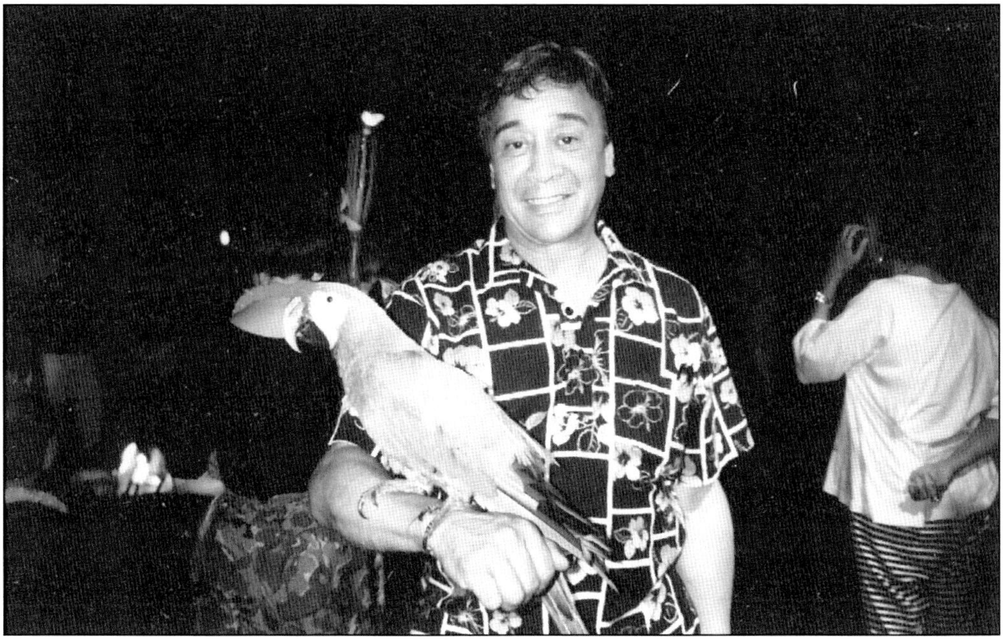

In 1980, Skip Voluntad became the first Asian to win an Equal Employment Opportunity Act case against a major hotel company for age discrimination and national origin. A nationally recognized Filipino Philadelphian activist, Voluntad served as the chairman of the Mayor's Commission for Asian Pacific American Affairs for three mayors and completed a six-year commitment as an executive board member of the United Way of Southeastern Pennsylvania. Skip received the Governor's Gold and Silver Awards for fostering diversity. (Courtesy of Skip Voluntad.)

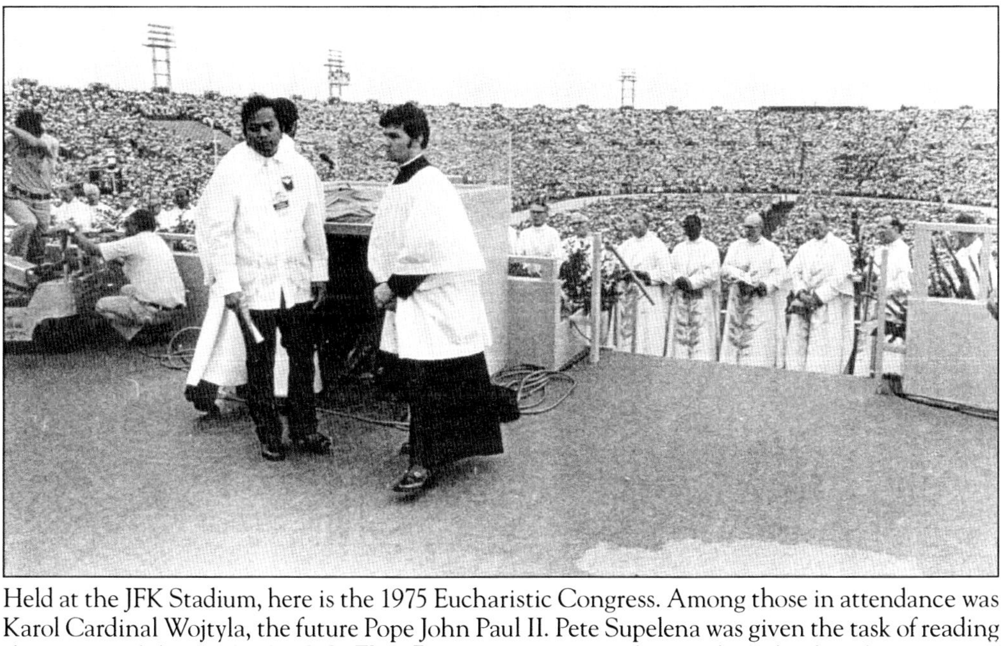

Held at the JFK Stadium, here is the 1975 Eucharistic Congress. Among those in attendance was Karol Cardinal Wojtyla, the future Pope John Paul II. Pete Supelena was given the task of reading the Prayer of the Faithful, while Elias Dungca was assigned to read out loud, in his signature booming voice, the Lord's Prayer in Tagalog, which was broadcast live to millions across the world. He later said that this had been the highlight of his life. (Courtesy of Auring Dungca.)

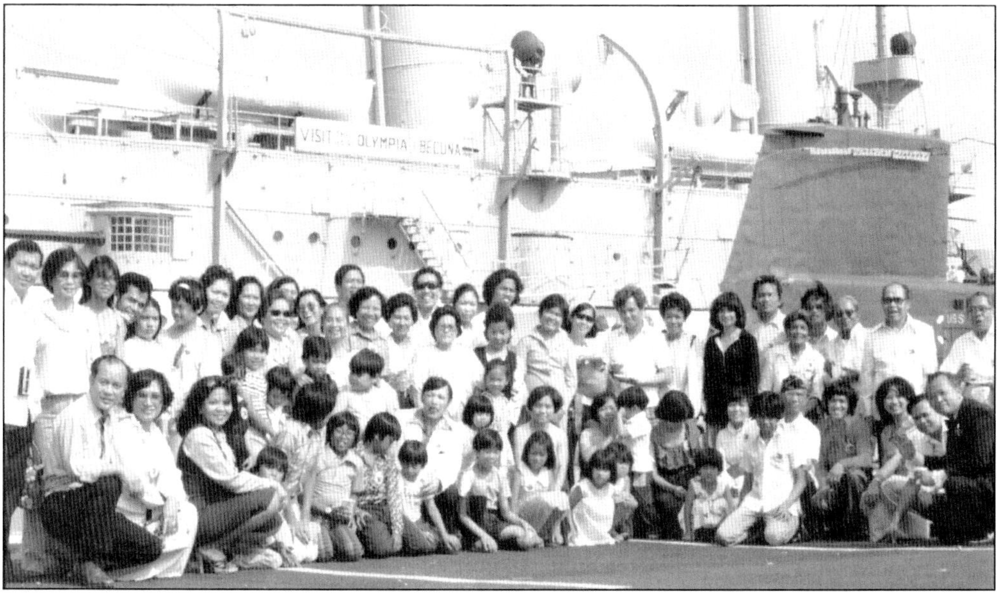

During the 1976 US Bicentennial, FAAPI was given a grant to organize cultural and social events. This started the annual raising of the Philippine flag at the USS *Olympia*. Highlights include Filipino-themed floats and costumes, including an authentic *kalesa*, or traditional Filipino horse-drawn carriage, leading the grand parade with over 500 Filipinos. After the *kalesa* reached its destination, it brought kids back to Roosevelt Park, where the celebration continued. (Courtesy of FAAPI.)

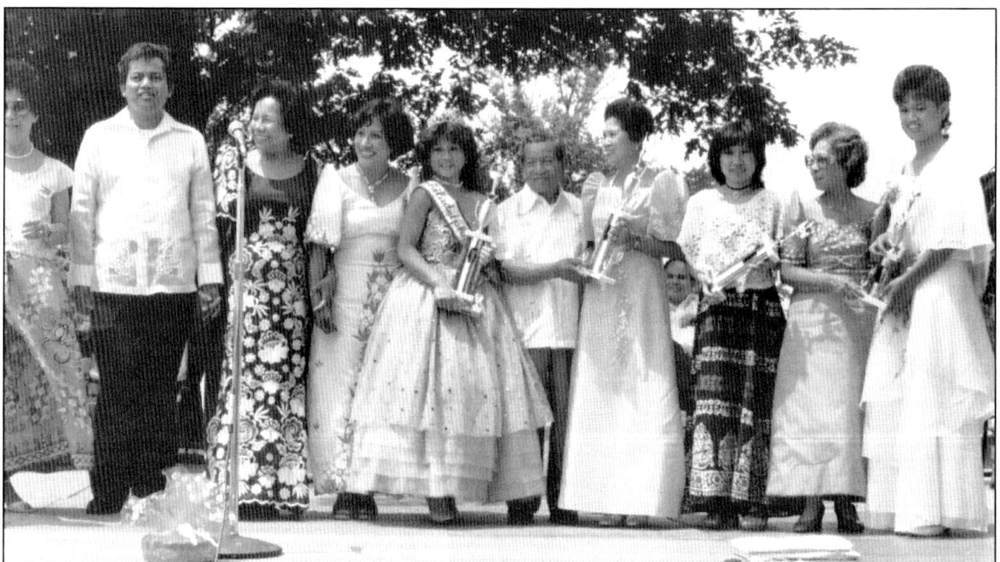

Following a parade through the main thoroughfare in downtown Philadelphia, this photograph was taken during the 1983 Philippine Independence Day program at Roosevelt Park in South Philadelphia. From left to right are Dr. Elsie Almario, Elias Dungca, Vicky Peralta, Virgie Luz, Cecilia Luz (winner of the Best Float award), Andy and Marina Lapinia, Mr. and Mrs. Pena (recipients of the FECGP award for service), unidentified, Mercedes Cava, and Ellen Dungca (recipient of the FAAPI Youth Dance Troupe award for "Most Significant & Most Historical Float"). (Courtesy of Vicky A. Peralta.)

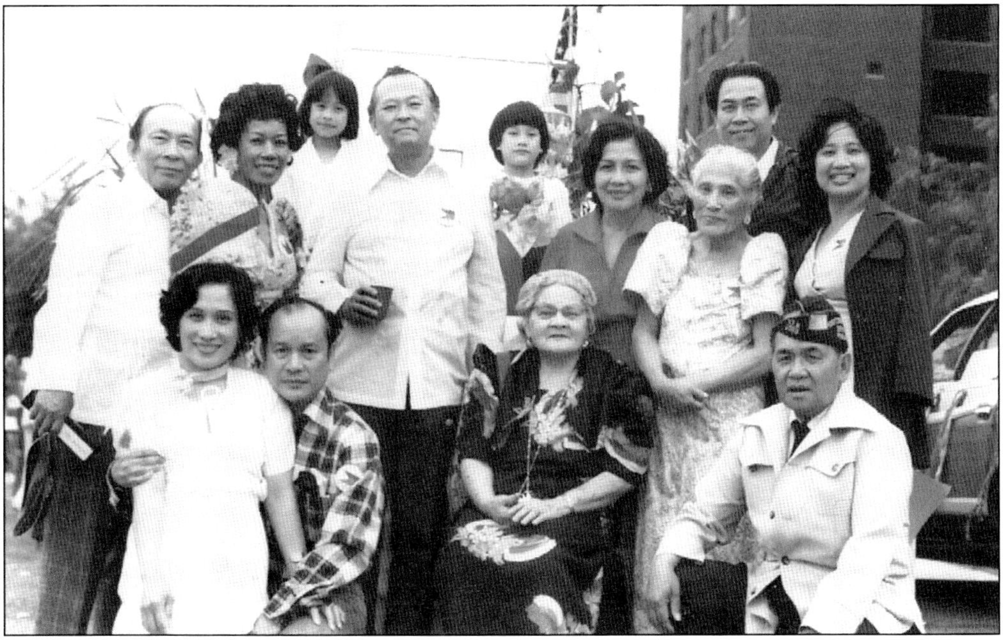

Pete Supelana (standing in the center) was president of the Filipino Executive Council of Greater Philadelphia (FECGP) during the June 1978 Independence Day celebration. During the 1970s, there were two instances when city officials excluded the Philippine flag. The first was along the motorcade route of the 1975 Eucharistic Congress, and the other was during the 1976 US Bicentennial's installation of the flag of nations along the Benjamin Franklin Parkway. Filipino leaders demanded inclusion. (Courtesy of Virginia Luz.)

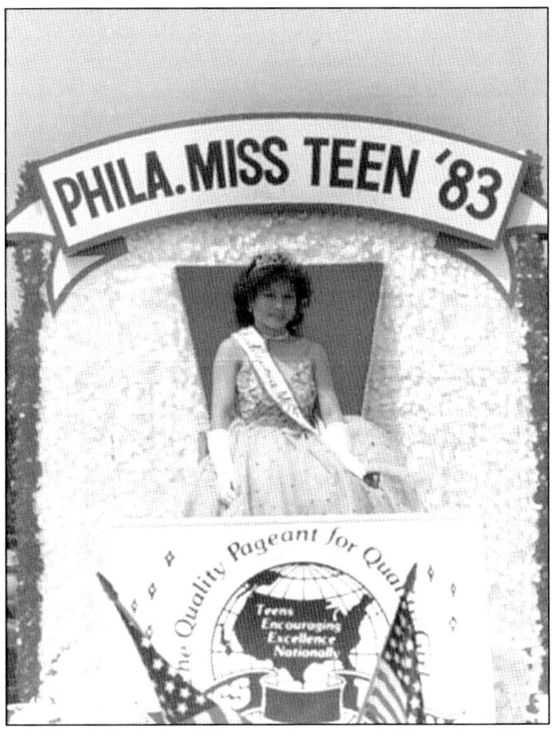

Cecilia Luz was the first Filipino to become Miss TEEN Philadelphia, which stands for Teens Encouraging Excellence Nationally. She bested 17 other contestants in five areas: scholastic achievement, volunteer service, talent, interview, and formal presentation at the Marriott Hotel on April 24, 1983. She earned a degree in chemical engineering from the University of Pennsylvania and her master's in business administration thereafter. She is currently the director of strategic sourcing at Johnson & Johnson. (Courtesy of Virgina Luz.)

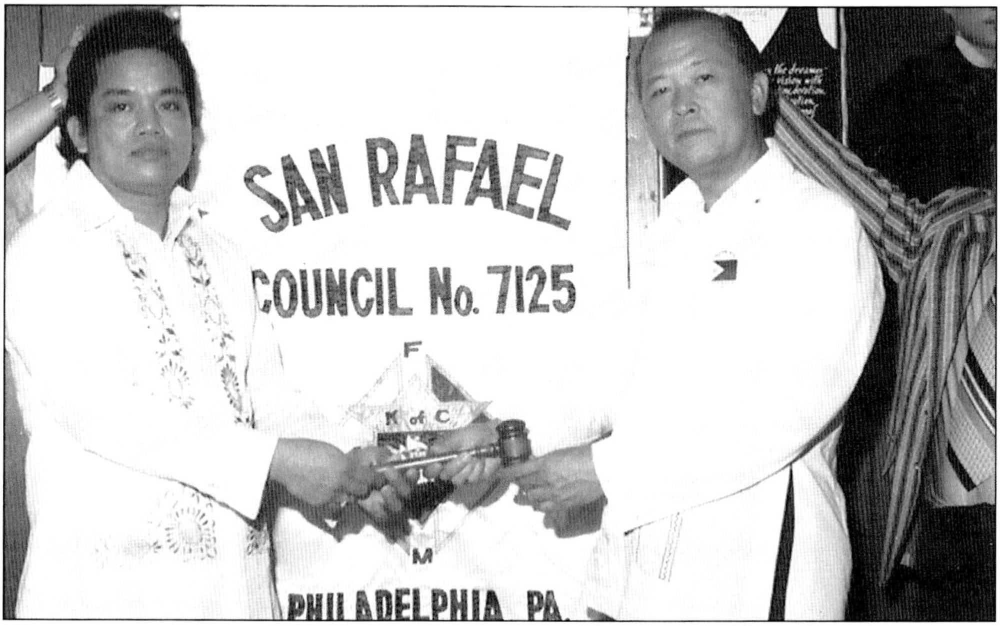

Here are the founding fathers, Ely Dungca (left) and *Manong* "Pete" Supelana (right), of the first Filipino Knights of Columbus in the 1970s. Pedro Supelana, or *Manong* "Pete," was a humble and soft-spoken gentleman, and his demeanor harkened back to a kinder and gentler time. He served as FAAPI president during the 1976 US Bicentennial and was the first president of FECGP. Heading the department of hiring and training for his company, he gave jobs to many Filipinos during the great migration of the 1960s–1970s. (Courtesy of Maria E. Dungca-Agkoz.)

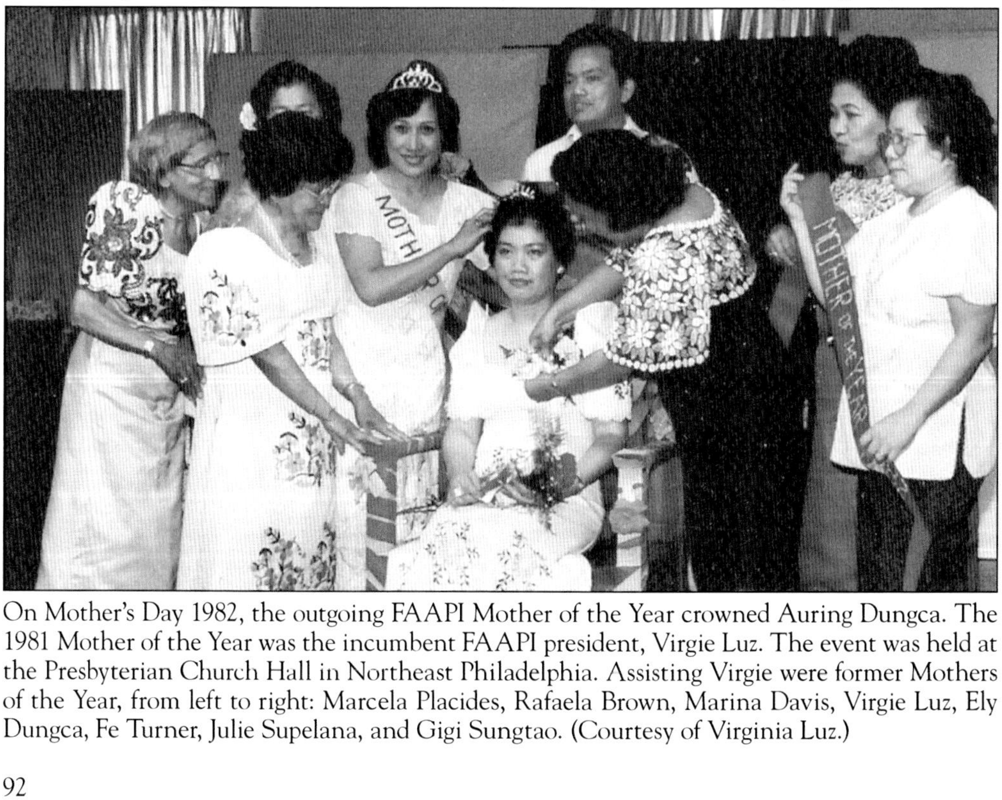

On Mother's Day 1982, the outgoing FAAPI Mother of the Year crowned Auring Dungca. The 1981 Mother of the Year was the incumbent FAAPI president, Virgie Luz. The event was held at the Presbyterian Church Hall in Northeast Philadelphia. Assisting Virgie were former Mothers of the Year, from left to right: Marcela Placides, Rafaela Brown, Marina Davis, Virgie Luz, Ely Dungca, Fe Turner, Julie Supelana, and Gigi Sungtao. (Courtesy of Virginia Luz.)

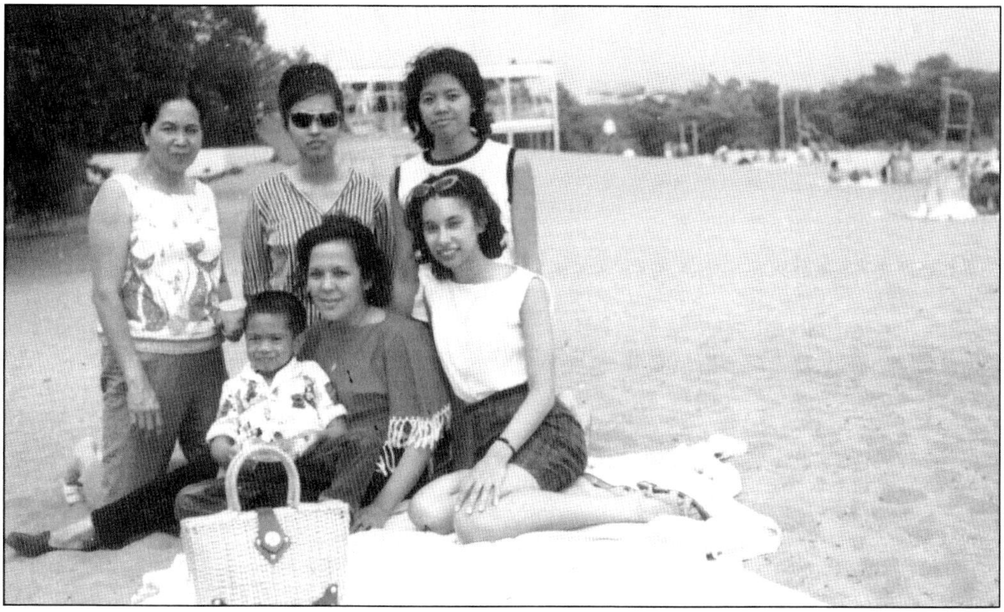

Here, Philadelphians have driven an hour and a half south toward Atlantic City for sun, sea, and sand in August 1964. Kneeling are Maria Velez (left) and Luz Grigg (right). (Courtesy of Noel Abejo.)

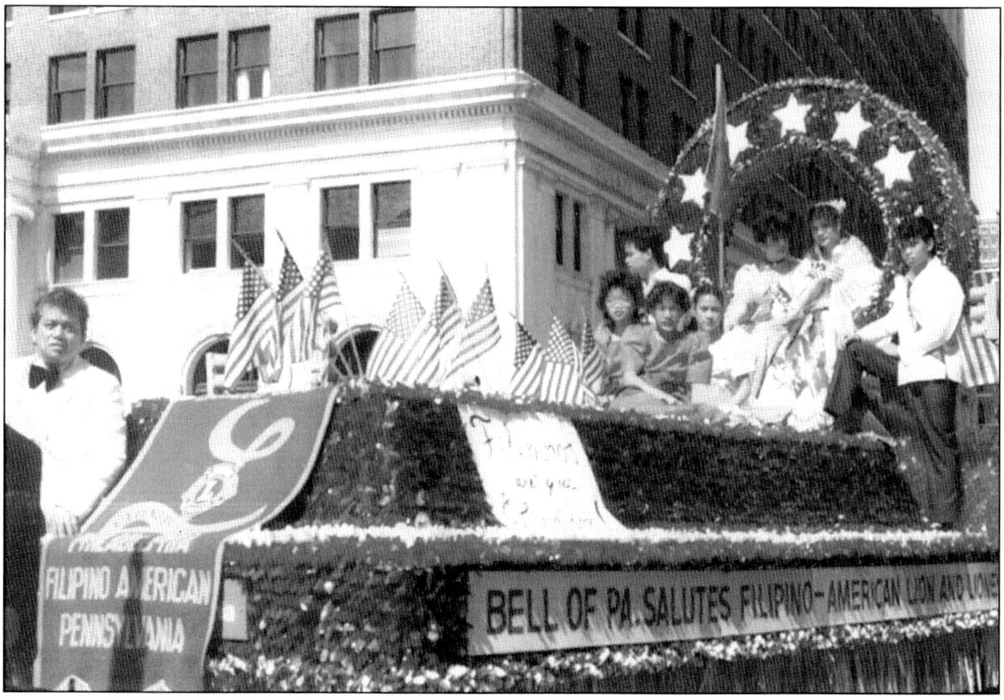

Elias Dungca, Lions Club president, is riding the Lions/Lionesses Club's float in the Philippine Independence Day Parade. On the float is the FAAPI Youth Dance Troupe. These parades contributed much to the visibility of the Filipinos in Philadelphia, earning them respect, goodwill, and recognition. Roosevelt Park and Love Park were popular venues. These famous parades celebrating Philippine Independence Day have ceased to exist after the completion of the Rizal Monument in Cherry Hill, Camden, New Jersey. (Courtesy of Virgina Luz.)

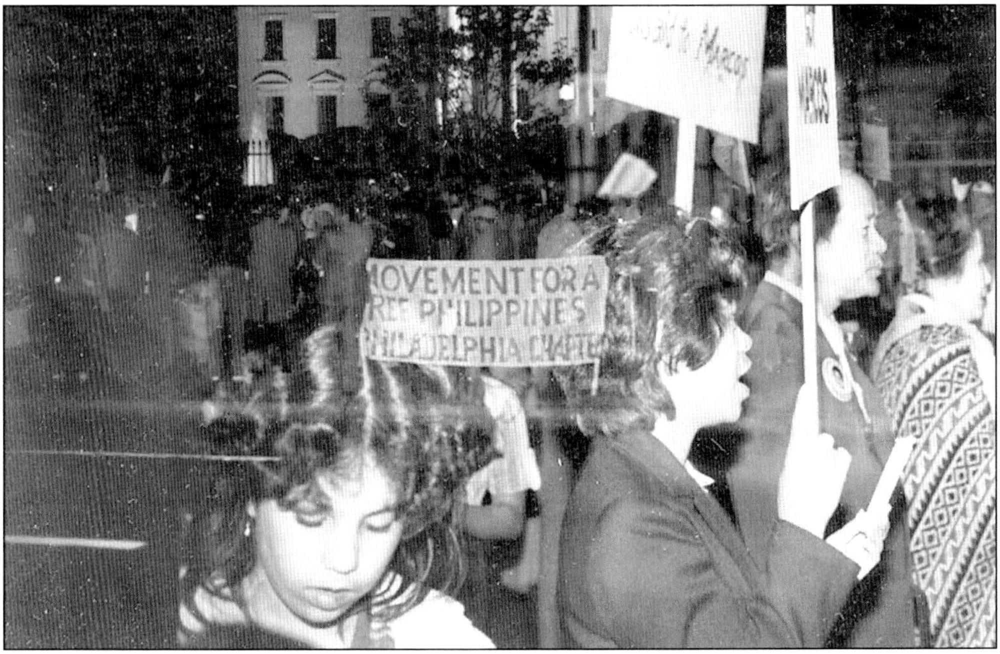

Philadelphia chapter protestors belonging to the Movement for a Free Philippines are seen in front of the White House. The PCCF became the Philadelphia Chapter of National Committee for the Restoration of Civil Liberties in the Philippines (NCRCLP), which was formed as an immediate response in opposition to the declaration of martial law. The Philadelphia chapter later became part of the nationwide effort, with local roots as well as nationwide contacts. (Courtesy of Virginia Luz.)

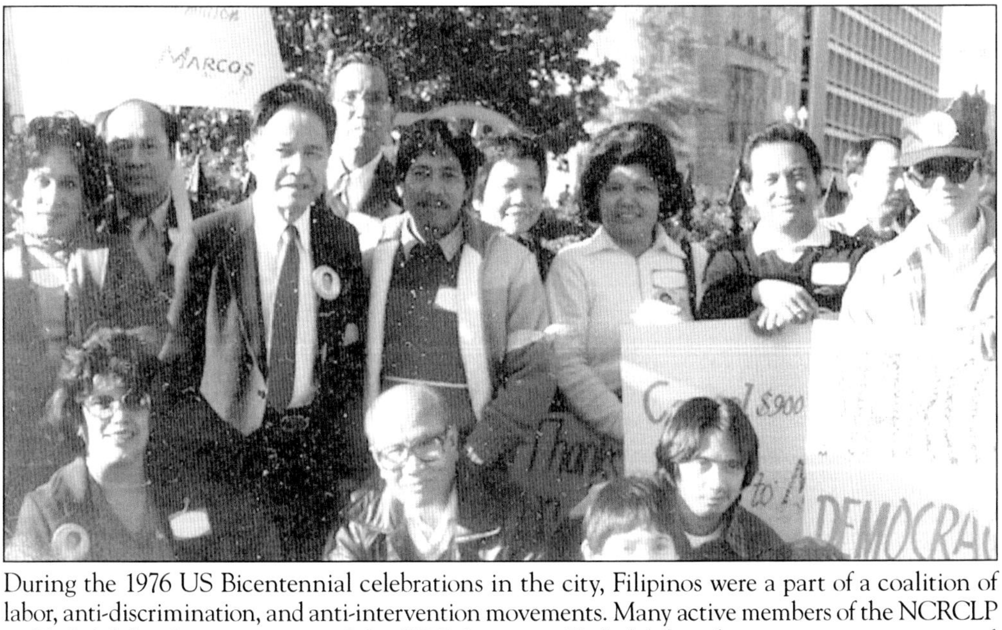

During the 1976 US Bicentennial celebrations in the city, Filipinos were a part of a coalition of labor, anti-discrimination, and anti-intervention movements. Many active members of the NCRCLP in Philadelphia became a part of the KDP. It was in Philadelphia that an important national organization of non-Filipinos, the Friends of the Filipino People (FFP), was founded in 1976. Friendly discussions, mutual support, and encouragement prevailed. (Courtesy of Virginia Luz.)

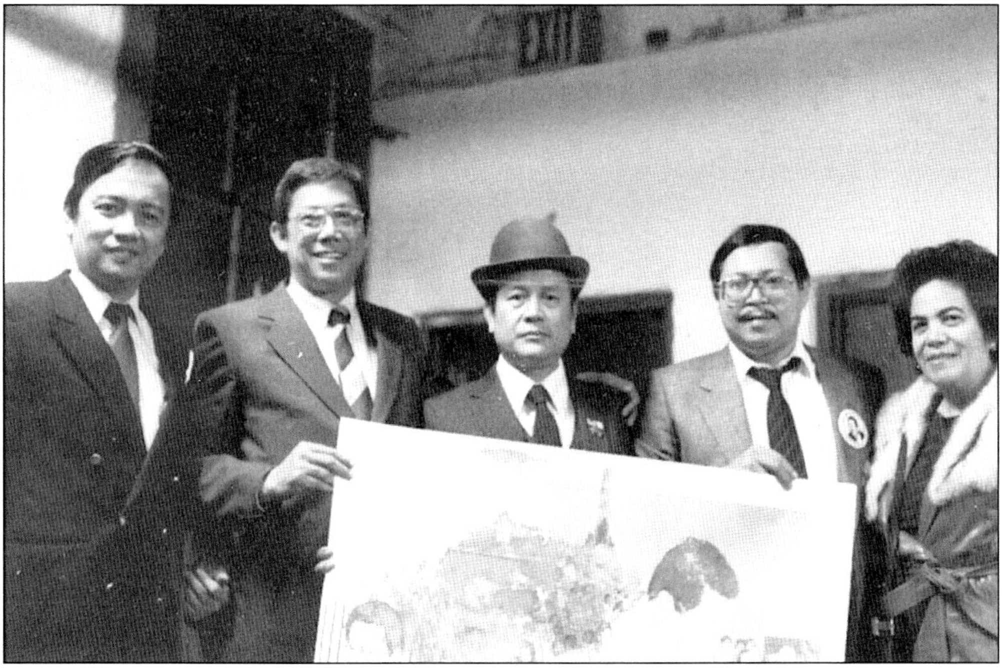

The KDP continued as part of the anti–martial law movement. The NCRCLP gradually changed its name into CAMDI, Campaign for Democracy and Independence, whose goals were the re-establishment of non-interference by the United States. It lobbied the US Congress against sending military aid to Marcos. By connecting with the nationwide movement, the active members of the Philadelphia Filipino American community became major players and integral parts of the national movement. (Courtesy of Virginia Luz.)

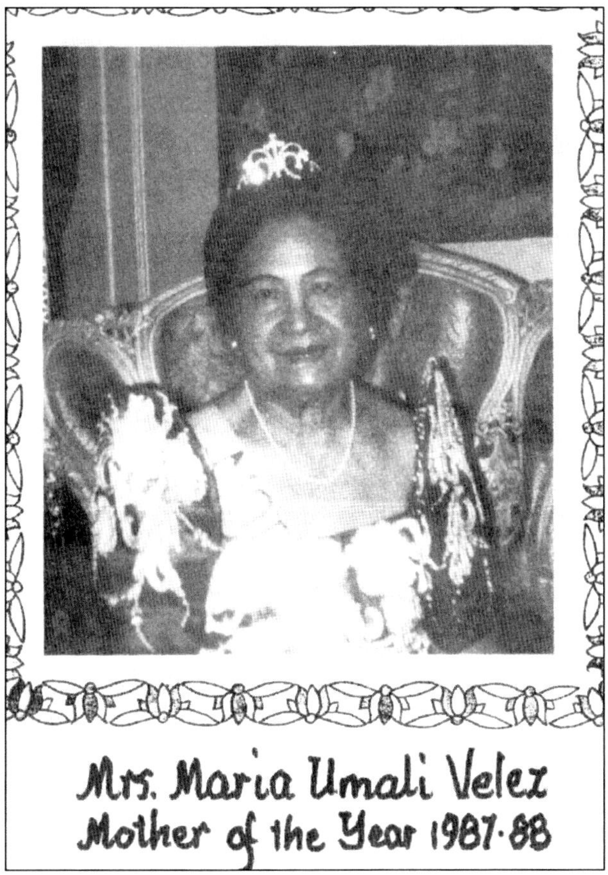

Maria Umali-Velez was FAAPI's Mother of the Year in 1987. After living 40 years in University City and upon retiring from accommodating guests and tenants in her boardinghouse, she involved herself with civic and social activities in the Filipino community that endeared her further as the matriarch of the Filipino community. (Courtesy of FAAPI.)

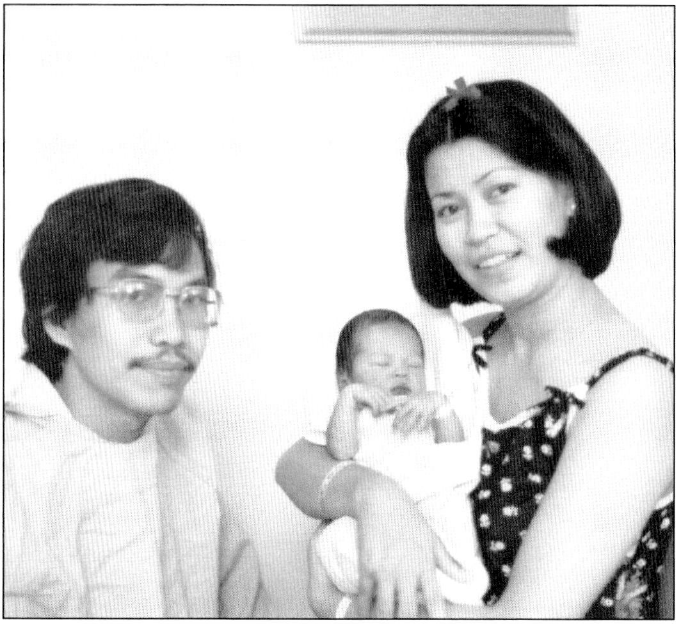

From left to right are Greg Santillan, Bicentennial baby Andres C. Santillan, and Elvie Castillo Santillan. Andres was born July 31, 1976, at the Pennsylvania Hospital, the nation's first hospital, during the 1976 Bicentennial celebrations. His parents, both active members of the KDP, named their Philly-Pinoy baby after Andres Bonifacio, a Filipino leader who came from a working-class background and armed the nation to strike the first major blow against Western imperialism during the 1896 Philippine Revolution. (Courtesy of Gregorio Santillan.)

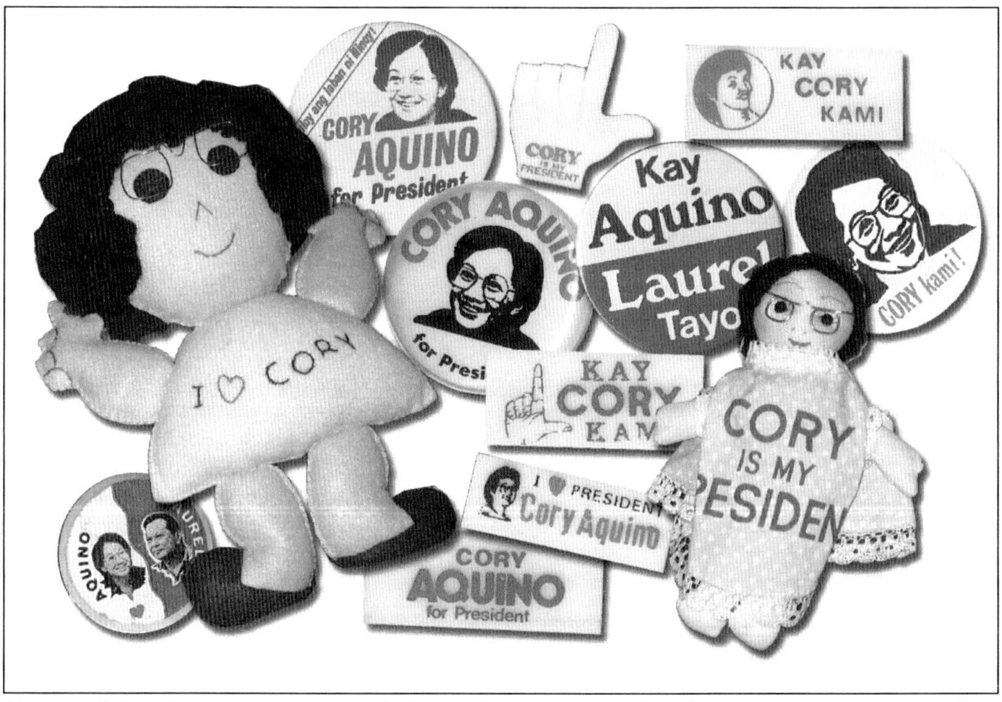

Corazon "Cory" Aquino was propelled into the limelight after the tragic assassination of her husband, Sen. Benigno "Ninoy" Aquino Jr., the most significant threat against Pres. Ferdinand Marcos. Her massive support was fueled by the Filipino middle class, centered in BF Homes Paranaque, Philippines, where her husband was laid to rest. Her eventual triumph captured the imagination of the world, igniting the rise of People Power, which inspired the dismantling of authoritarian rule on a global scale. (Courtesy of Edward De Los Santos.)

Freedom fighters, members of the Silva family of BF Homes, Paranaque, participated in the overthrow of Marcos in 1986. Arturo and Linda Silva owned Plaza Cinema, which was Aquino's campaign headquarters in BF, Paranaque. The mayor, a Marcos loyalist, padlocked their property. In defiance, the Silvas participated in the protest, mobilizing all their employees from their bakeries, restaurant, and movie theater, distributing food to rebel soldiers. From left to right are (first row) Carlo and Anabel Silva; (second row) Eliseo, Arthur, Linda with Kristine, and Arlene. Not pictured are Maria Luz and Alan Silva. (Courtesy of Arthur and Linda Silva.)

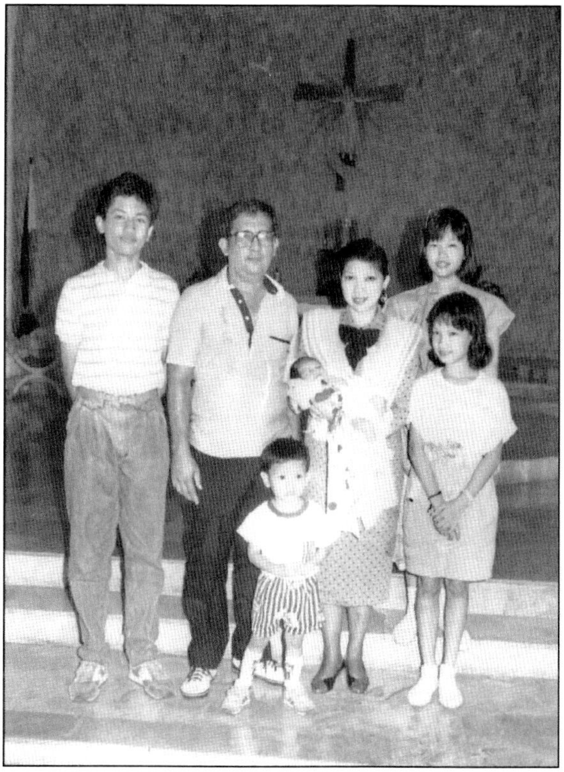

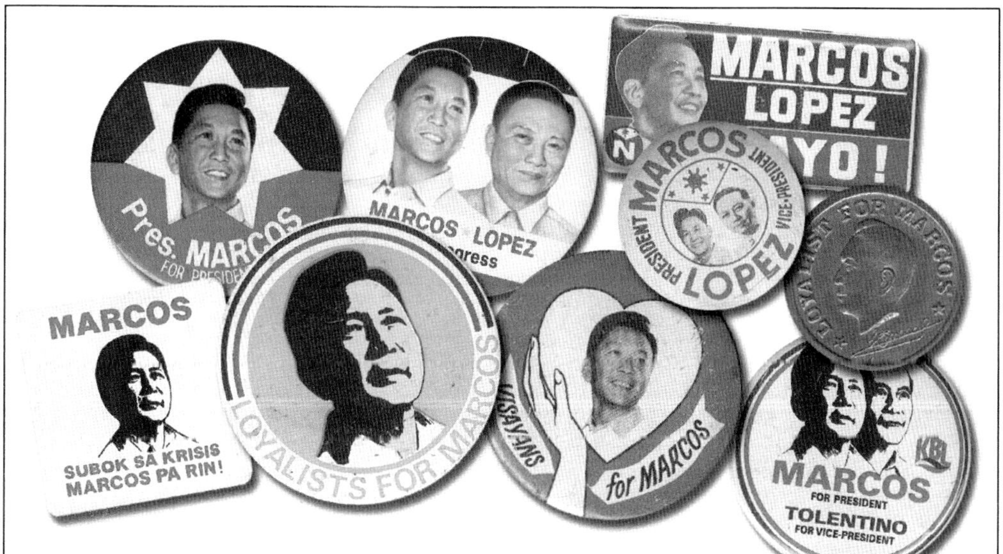

Marcos's administration was preceded by a gross domestic product per capita second only to Japan. What happened afterward was an unalterable state that succeeding leaders failed to resolve. In 1980, Ninoy stated: "I have carefully weighed the virtues and the faults of the Filipino and I have come to the conclusion that he is worth dying for because he is the nation's greatest untapped resource. He is not a coward. Given a good leader . . . the Filipino can attain great heights." (Courtesy of Edward De Los Santos.)

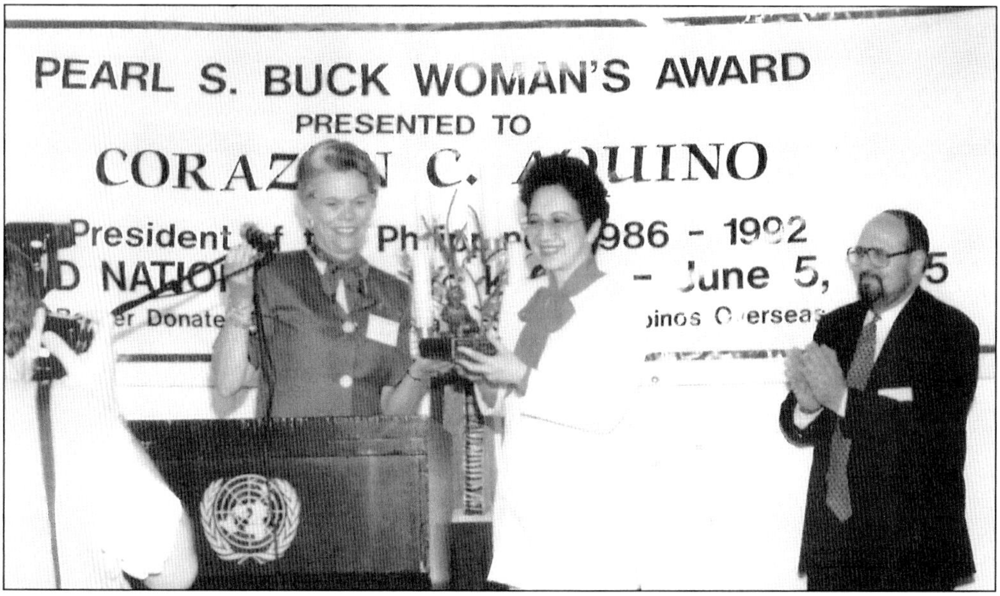

Here, Cory Aquino receives the Pearl S. Buck Woman's Award in Philadelphia on June 5, 1995. Long before she became Asia's first democratically elected head of state, Aquino was sent to the United States to study at the Assumption-run Ravenhill Academy in Philadelphia for her high school education. Only 13 years old, Cory was frail and thin from the ravages of the war. She spent seven years on the east coast finishing high school in New York. (Courtesy of Dr. Raymond Soriano.)

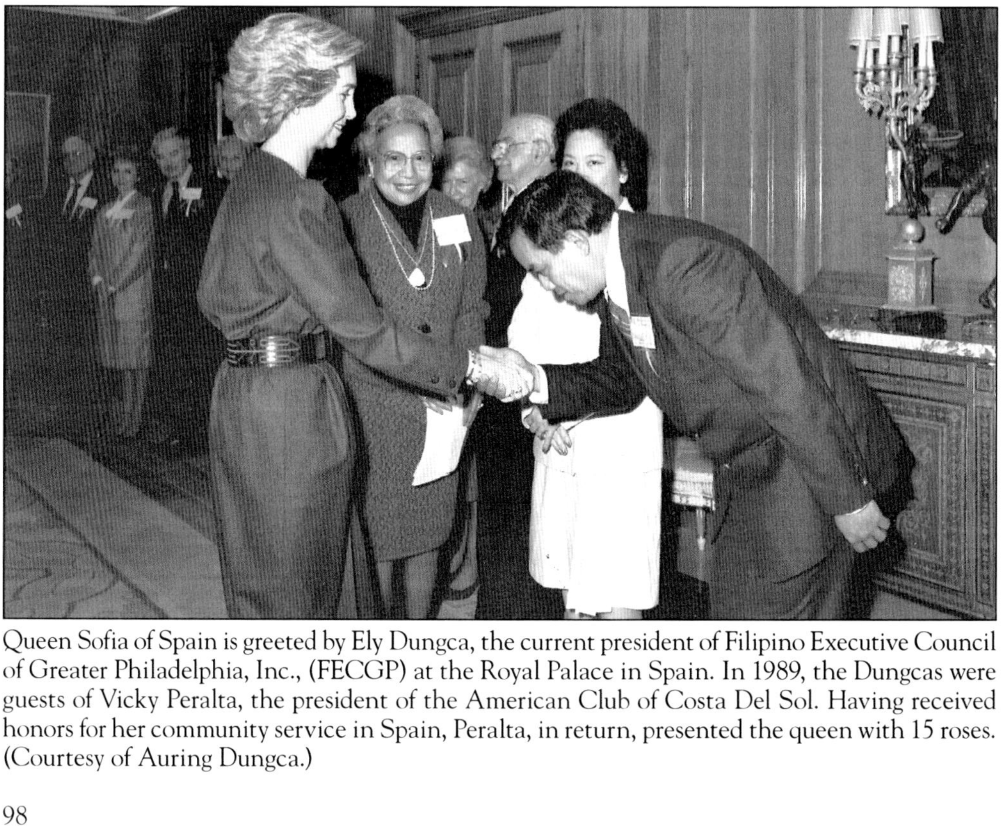

Queen Sofia of Spain is greeted by Ely Dungca, the current president of Filipino Executive Council of Greater Philadelphia, Inc., (FECGP) at the Royal Palace in Spain. In 1989, the Dungcas were guests of Vicky Peralta, the president of the American Club of Costa Del Sol. Having received honors for her community service in Spain, Peralta, in return, presented the queen with 15 roses. (Courtesy of Auring Dungca.)

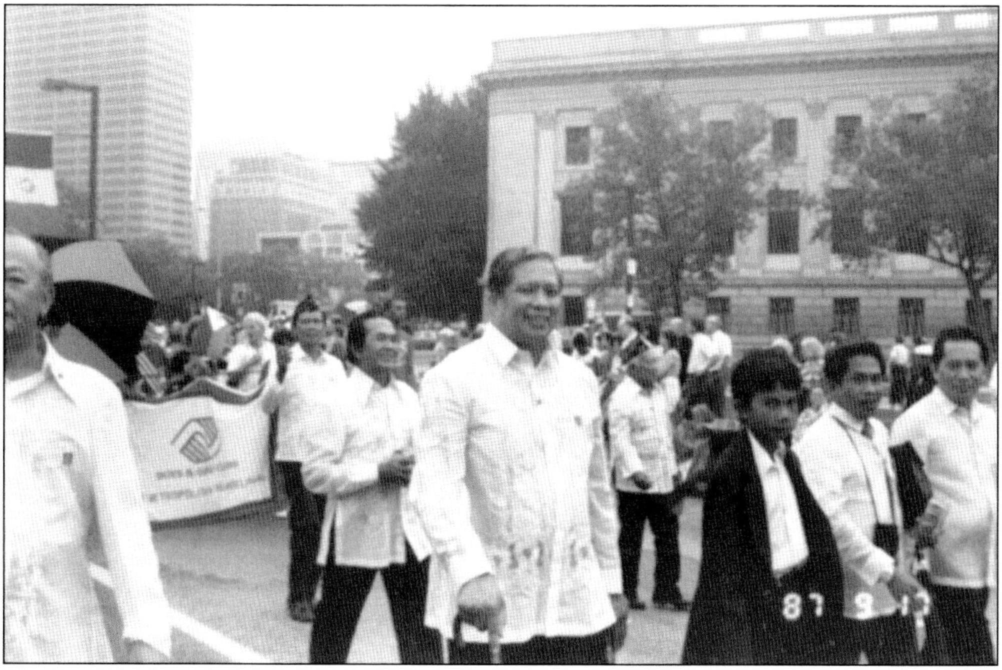

Shown is a male Filipino contingent of the US Constitution Bicentennial Parade in Philadelphia on September 17, 1987. Lamberto G. Santos (center) was most remembered for his civic and community contributions as well as his entrepreneurial legacy, Santos Travel and Tours. He believed that the Filipino community could move forward with a united effort to have an impact upon the mainstream. He served as a dedicated and inspirational president of KSOP, the Kayumanggi Society of Philadelphia. (Courtesy of Virgina Luz.)

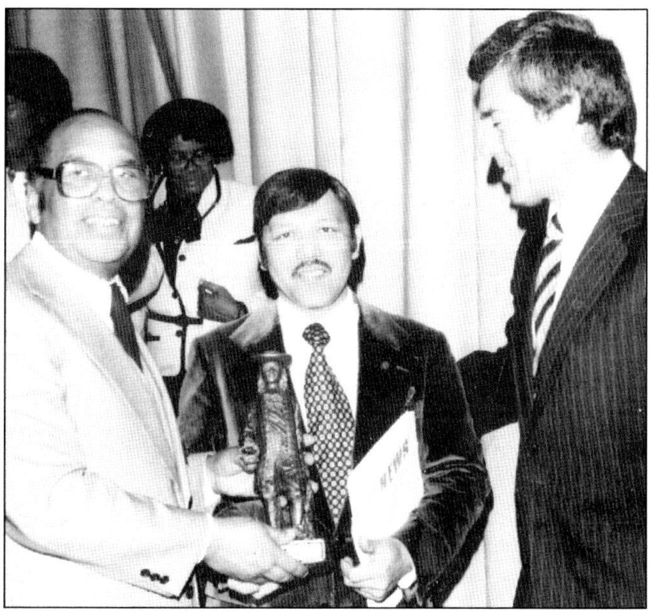

In 1982, Dr. Raymond Z. Soriano was the recipient of the prestigious William Penn Humanitarian Award from the Commission on Human Relations. Chairman Clarence Farmer is seen giving the award; looking on is guest speaker Dan Rather, CBS anchorman. Dr. Raymond Z. Soriano is a well-known leader, pianist, medical doctor, pathologist, and the acknowledged local historian of Filipino Philadelphians. The only other Filipino bestowed the same honor was *Manong* "Pete" Supelana. (Courtesy of Dr. Raymond Soriano.)

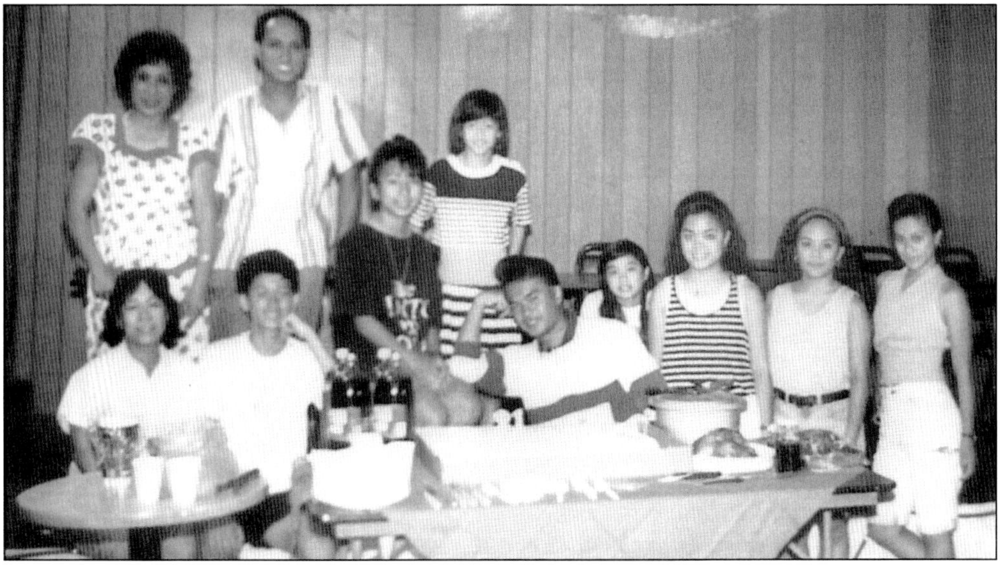

Original members of the Mutya Dance Company with artistic director Rey Borres are pictured during their summer rehearsal at La Tiffany Hall, Olney, Philadelphia, in 1990. The Mutya Dance Company was founded by Virginia Luz in April 1990 to satisfy the requests of her daughters to know their roots and to answer the general public's request. Today, Mutya has earned a reputation as one of the foremost dance troupes on the east coast. (Courtesy of Virgina Luz.)

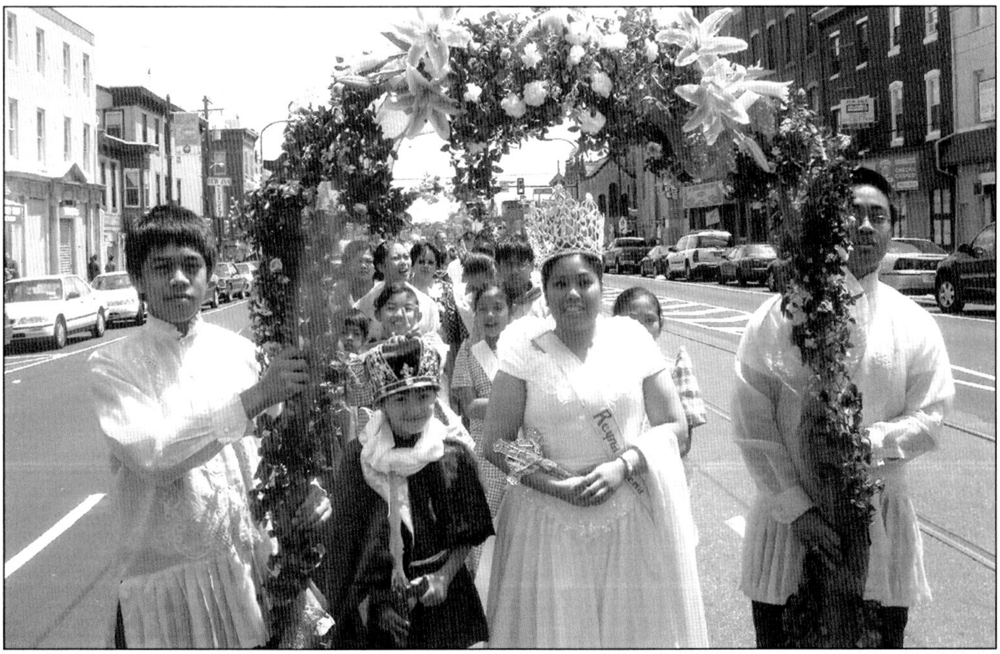

The *Santacruzan*, a novena procession celebrating the finding of the true cross of Jesus Christ by Saint Elena, is a Filipino tradition held annually in Philadelphia since the mid-1970s. It is organized by parishioners of St. Peter's Church under the auspices of Msgr. George Tomicheck, a priest of Polish background who was ordained in the Philippines and is a well-loved pastor within the Filipino community and beyond. The photograph shows Christina M. Rivera, the *reyna* Elena of the 2006 *Santacruzan*. (Courtesy of Dr. Rommel Rivera.)

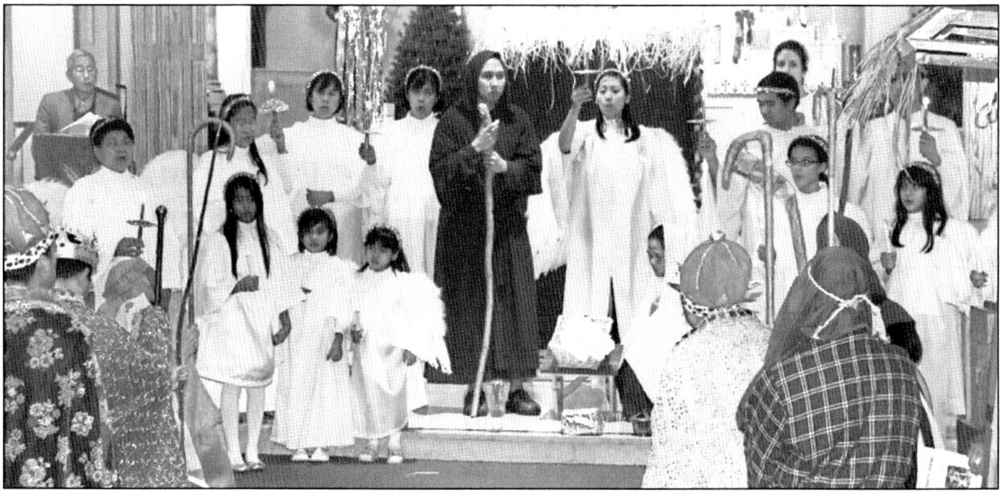

St. Peter's was designated for the Filipino Mass during the 1976 Eucharistic Congress in Philadelphia. Cardinal Rosales, along with other bishops, urged Father Tomichek to make St. Peter's a shrine for Filipinos in Philadelphia. A play of the Nativity was reenacted on December 21, 2011. From left to right are Ted Medrana, Judith Bellona, Teresita Banson, Delce Malaluan, Evelyn Mariano, Jan Warren Jalosjos, Minette Manalo, Marisol Jalosjos, Mark Casem, Lemuel Agustin, Angelique Casem, Patty Agustin, Ms. Jalosjos, Alma Canlas, Tati Jalosjos, and Maaliyah Jalosjos. (Courtesy of Minette Manalo.)

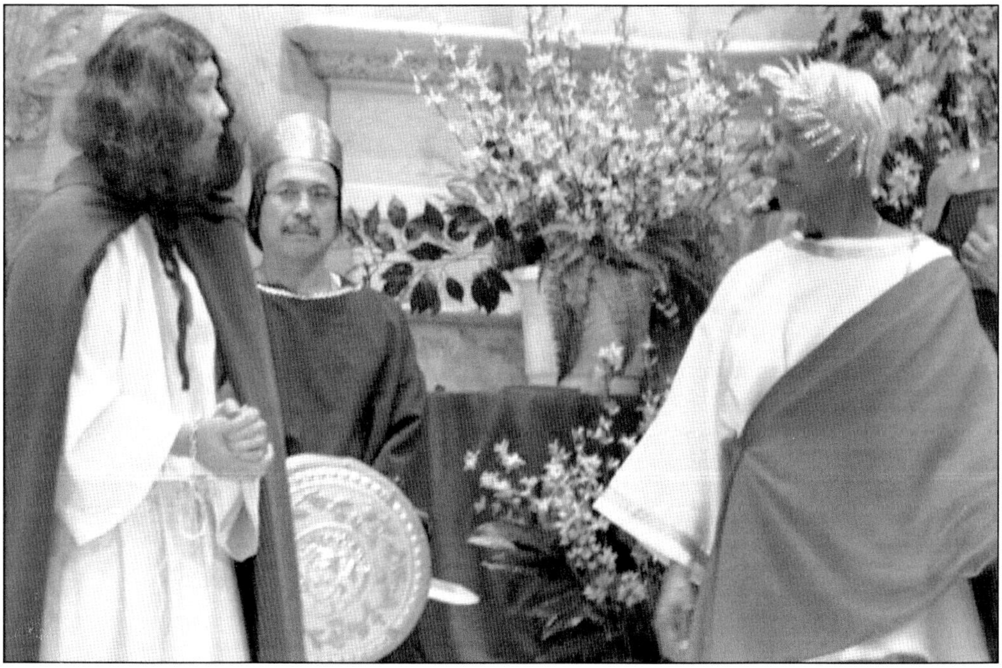

The Filipino parishioners of St. Peter's Church staged a play of the Passion on Palm Sunday, April 5, 2009. From left to right are Jan Jalosjos, Leo Patron, and Art Arana. St. Peter's was the first to hold novenas to the Mother of Perpetual Help in the area, and along with the *Pasyon*, the *Santaruzan*, and other religious activities, Filipinos are able to express their affection for remembered traditions, as well as concern for the preservation of their culture here. (Courtesy of Minette Manalo.)

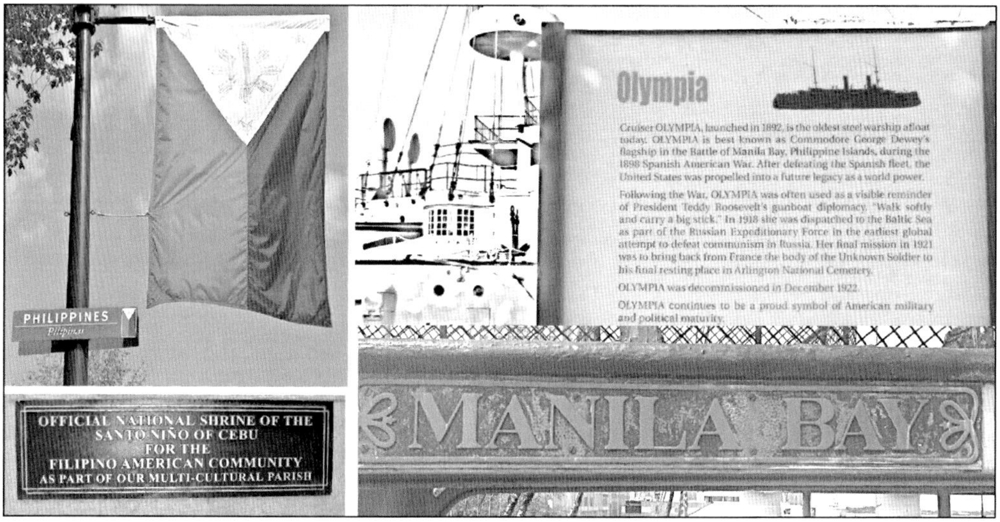

Counterclockwise from top left are the Philippine flag along the Parkway, St. Augustine's entrance plaque, and the USS *Olympia*. Identity gives purpose, transforming resource-driven individuals into a mission-driven citizenry. No Filipino masters are included in US museums, unlike in Singapore and Japan. When the United States invests in Filipino-themed modern art, and Filipinos visualize the magnificence of Luna's paintings and the boldness of Rizalian ideas, perhaps the American Filipino will become more visible. (Philippine flag photograph by Dania Schmidt; all others courtesy of Eliseo Art Silva.)

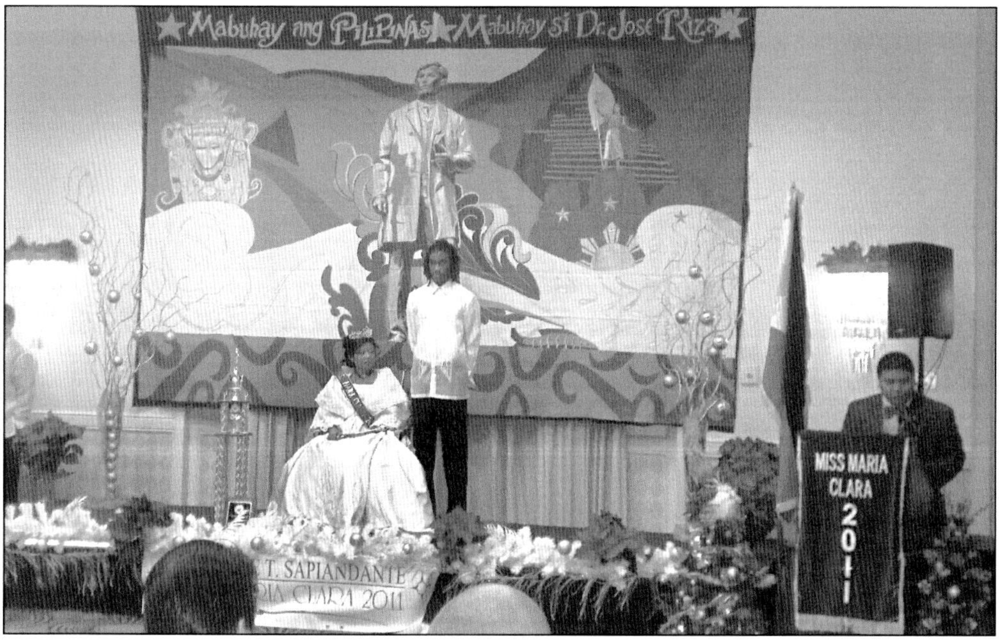

Miss Maria Clara 2011 is Madeline Sapiandante. Emceeing is Stephen Spadaro, FAAPI vice president. Madeline is studying to earn a bachelor of arts degree in communication at William Paterson University, New Jersey, and hopes to join the entertainment industry in the future. She has a good eye for fashion, winning a modeling contest in 2009, which landed her a billboard ad as the featured model, a Pinay, seen by thousands driving down Interstate 95 North in Philadelphia from 2009 to 2010. (Courtesy of Eliseo Art Silva.)

Seven

Emergent Philly Pinoys

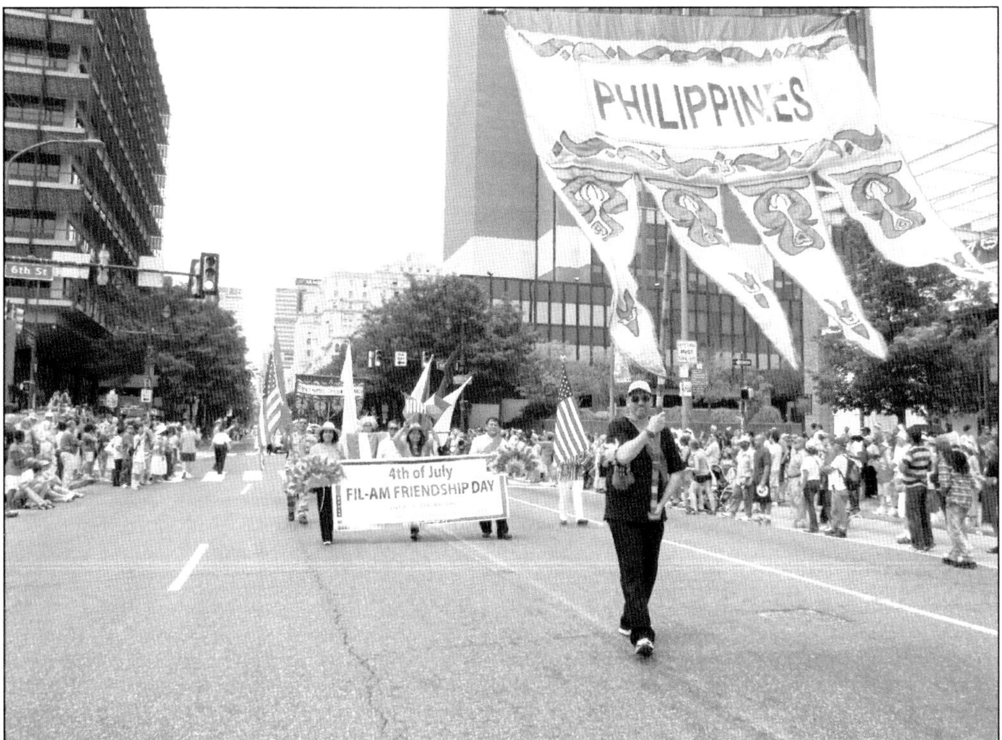

Filipino Philadelphians celebrate the Fourth of July with colorful costumes, flags, cultural dancers, and the current beauty queens. Known also as Filipino American Friendship Day, July 4, 1946, was the day when the United States officially recognized the Republic of the Philippines and reclaimed the legacies of liberty and independence bequeathed by the Philippines' generation of 1898. It also celebrated the liberation of the country by joint Filipino and American forces from Japan. (Courtesy of Philip Reyes.)

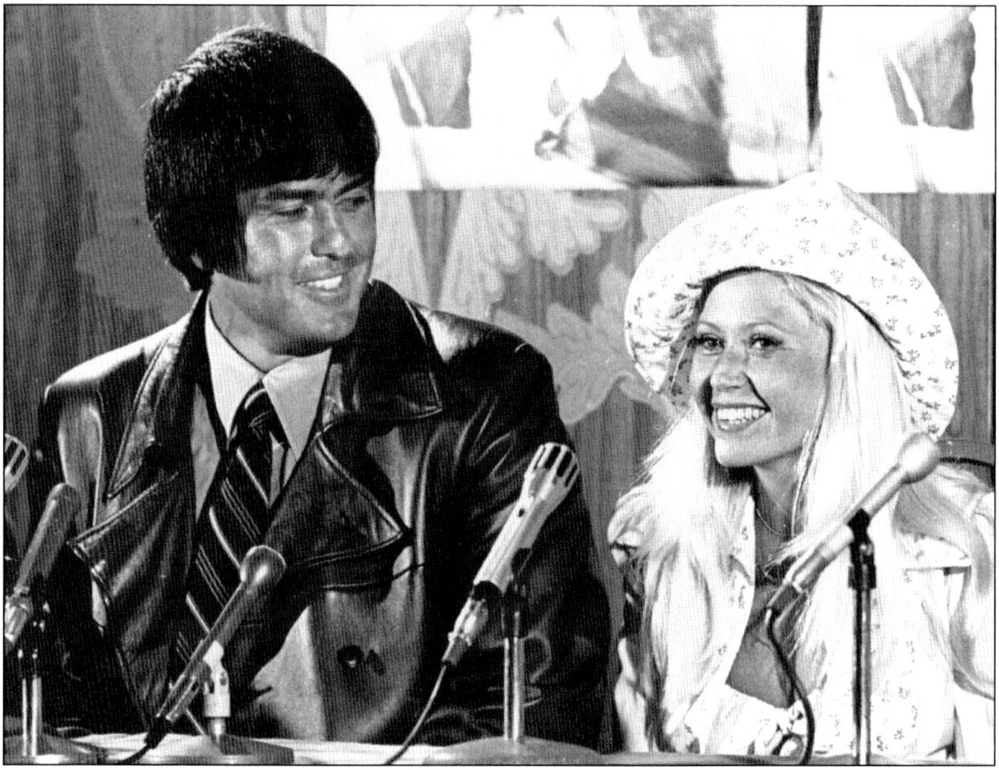

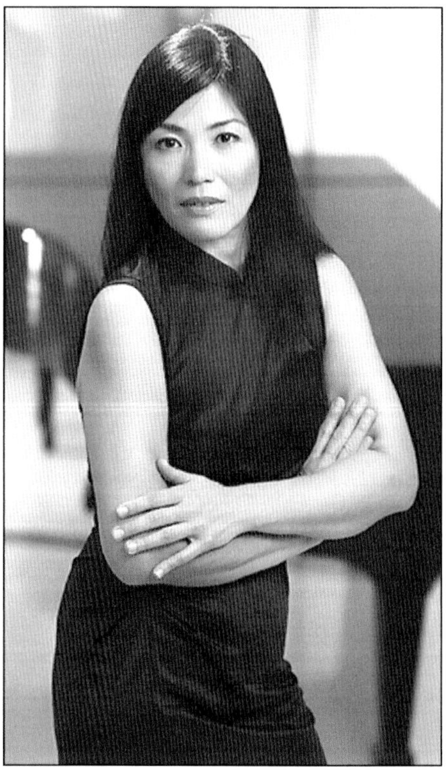

Roman Gabriel Jr. is seen with his wife, Tedra, in Philadelphia in 1978. Roman was called the "world's biggest Filipino," at six feet, four inches and 234 pounds. He was the first big quarterback of the modern era. He was born in 1940 to a Filipino father, Roman Ildonzo Gabriel Sr., who worked as a laborer in Alaska and California before settling down in North Carolina. Roman said, "My dad is my number one hero." He became the Philadelphia Eagles all-time leading passer. (Courtesy of Temple University Libraries, Urban Archives.)

A child prodigy, Philadelphian Cecile Licad moved to the United States at the age of 12 to study piano at Philadelphia's Curtis Institute of Music with three of the greatest performers, Rudolf Serkin, Seymour Lipkin, and Mieczyslaw Horszowski. Hailed by the *New Yorker* as a "pianist's pianist," Licad was one of the youngest musicians to receive the prestigious Leventritt Gold Medal in 1981. (Courtesy of Eliseo Art Silva.)

Rose Tibayan reported for Channel 6 Action News from 1998 to 2002. Her first live shot for Channel 6 was slotted in the rundown of the 11:00 p.m. newscast. Those who watched it saw Philadelphia's first Filipino reporter standing in a park after dark, with microphone in hand, backed by two Philadelphia police officers on horseback. She had been assigned to cover the city's new effort to make public parks safer. Her live shot cue came in the form of a "toss" from veteran anchor Jim Gardner. (Photograph by Akira Suwa, Courtesy of Rose Tibayan.)

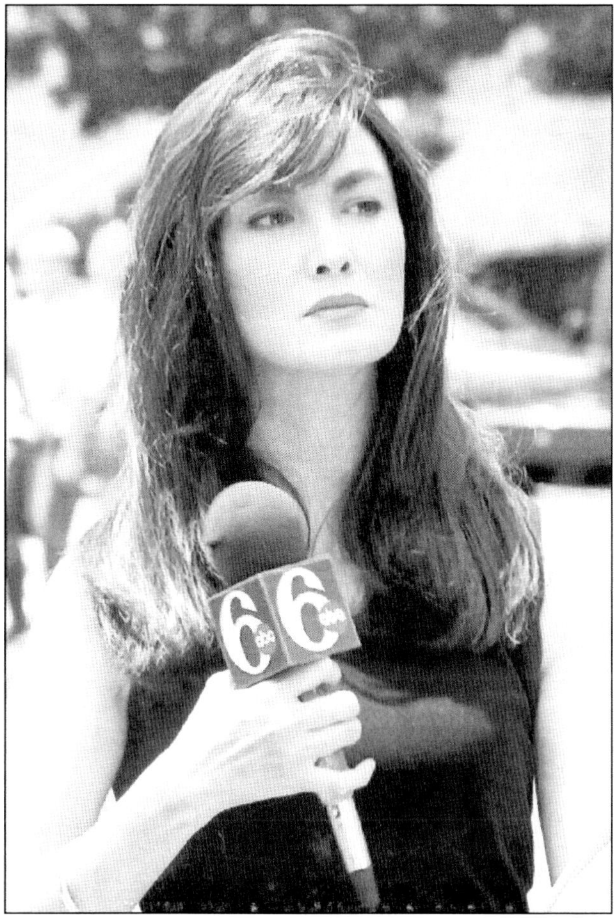

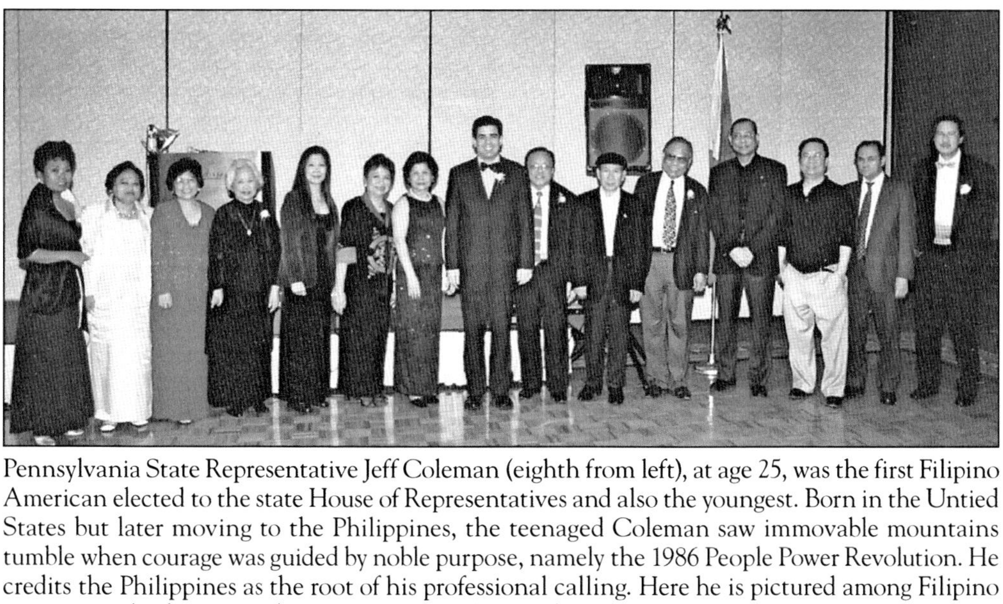

Pennsylvania State Representative Jeff Coleman (eighth from left), at age 25, was the first Filipino American elected to the state House of Representatives and also the youngest. Born in the Untied States but later moving to the Philippines, the teenaged Coleman saw immovable mountains tumble when courage was guided by noble purpose, namely the 1986 People Power Revolution. He credits the Philippines as the root of his professional calling. Here he is pictured among Filipino community leaders in Bucks County, Pennsylvania. (Courtesy of Norma Arevalo Yabut.)

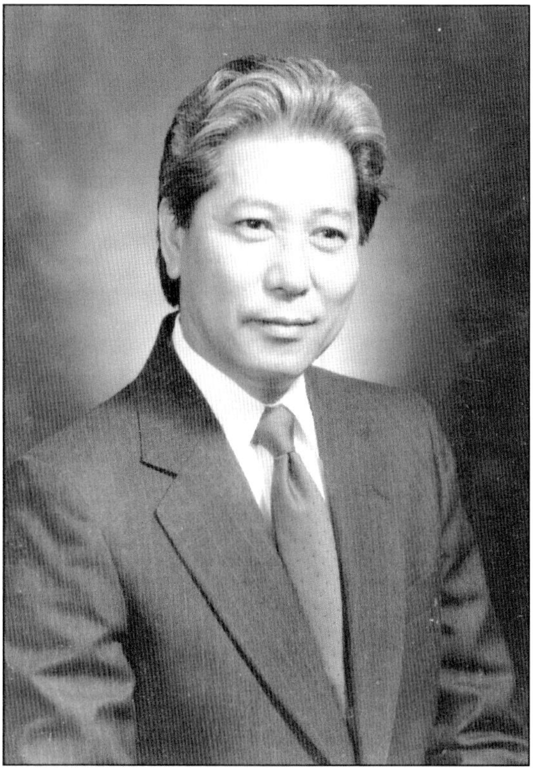

Jose Galura dedicated his life to serving underprivileged neighborhoods. Born in the Philippines, his formative years were shaped during World War II. After the war, Jose cut short his education and took a job without pay for a year in order to pay in advance the medical expenses incurred by his mother, Maria de los Santos. A US immigrant by 1960, Galura worked to pay for his schooling and completed his education at Juniata, George Washington, Temple, and Harvard Universities. (Courtesy of Jose de los Santos Galura.)

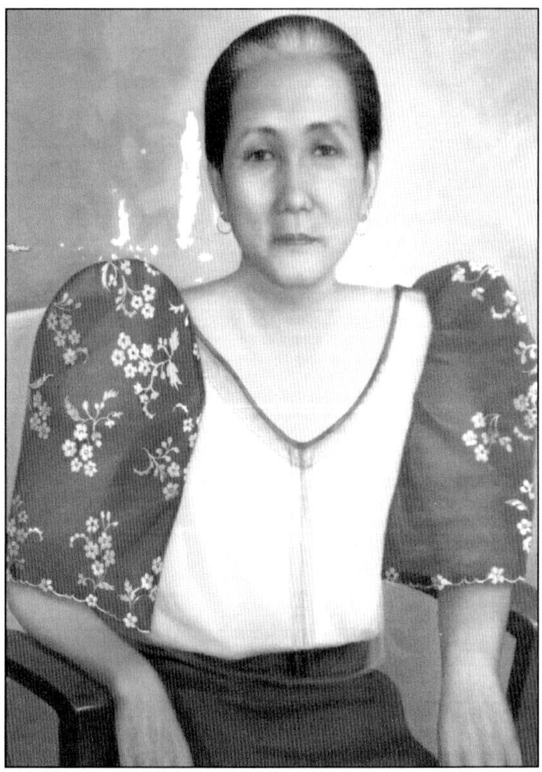

Here is a portrait of Maria de los Santos (September 15, 1894, to April 15, 1971), born in Bacolor, Pampanga, Philippines. She was the mother of 10 children and was well loved by her community. The mission of the Maria de los Santos Health Center is exemplified by an unassuming, devoted, and loving woman who helped so many in her benevolent and caring ways. With deep gratitude, the center was named in her honor. (Courtesy of Jose de los Santos Galura.)

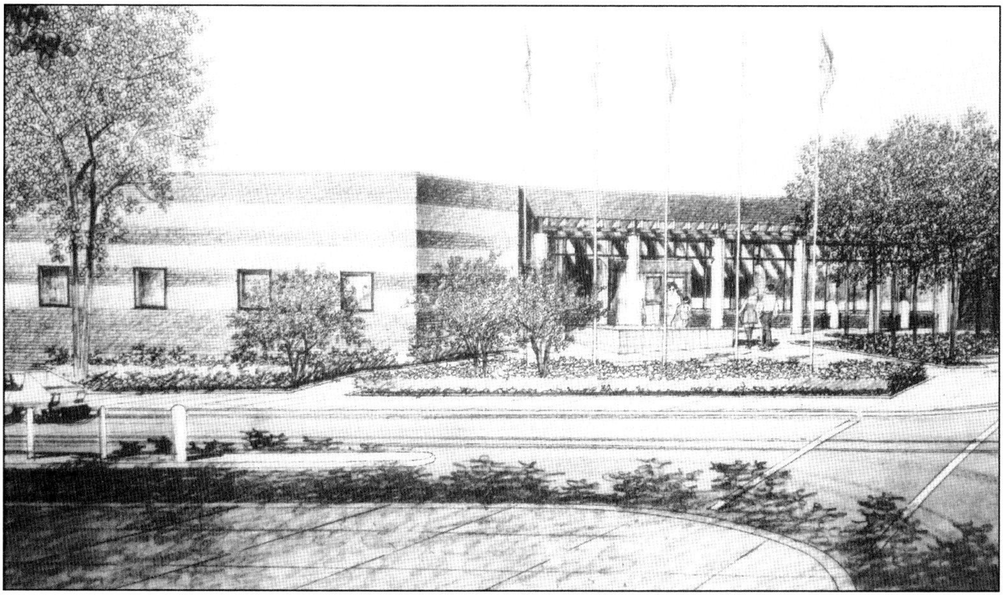

Maria de los Santos Health Center serves as a bilingual and bicultural medical home for generations of Latino residents. While seeking to rehabilitate the facility and set up his own organization, Jose Galura persuaded Hahnemann University Hospital to underwrite the operational costs. He was able to build the new center on Fifth Street and Allegheny Avenue, where most of the Hispanics settled. The new health center became a catalyst for change in the neighborhood. (Courtesy of Jose de los Santos Galura.)

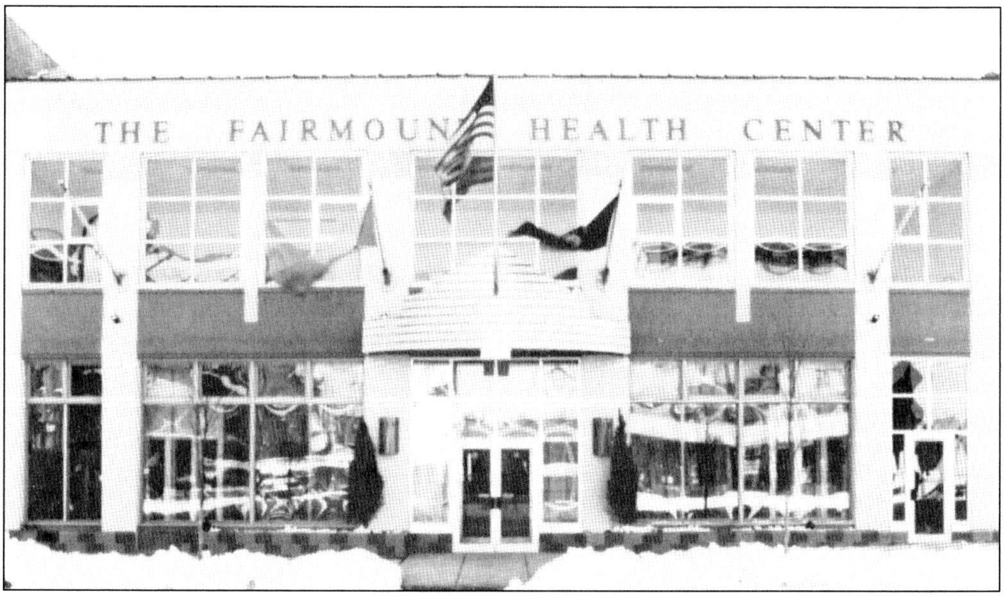

Following the establishment of the Maria de los Santos Center, Jose Galura built the Fairmount Health Center (FHC) on Broad Street and Fairmount Avenue so that the Spring Garden service area would not become abandoned. FHC was converted from an automobile warehouse in a forlorn section and was conceived as an oasis within a decaying cityscape. The center received the Rudy Bruner Foundation Award for causing the greatest impact on the community it served. (Courtesy of Jose de los Santos Galura.)

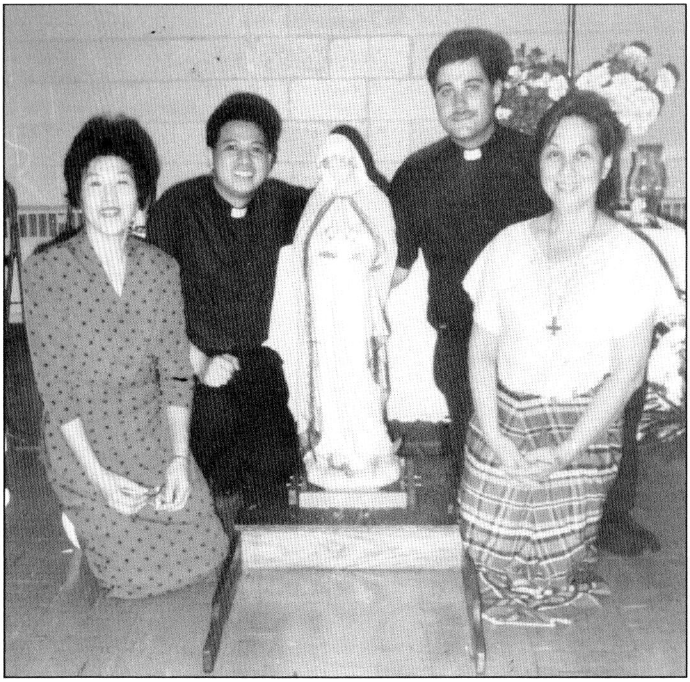

In 1990, Sr. Loretto Mapa arrived in the United States to pursue advanced studies in Cambridge, Massachusetts. After completing her studies, she settled in Pennsylvania to take care of the elderly Assumption Sisters. This photograph is of the Philippine Independence Day celebration at St. Thomas Aquinas Church on June 9, 1991. From left to right are Erlinda Clapano, Bro. Efren Esmilla, Fr. Tom Urian, and Sr. Loretto Mapa. (Courtesy of Filipino Apostolate Philadelphia.)

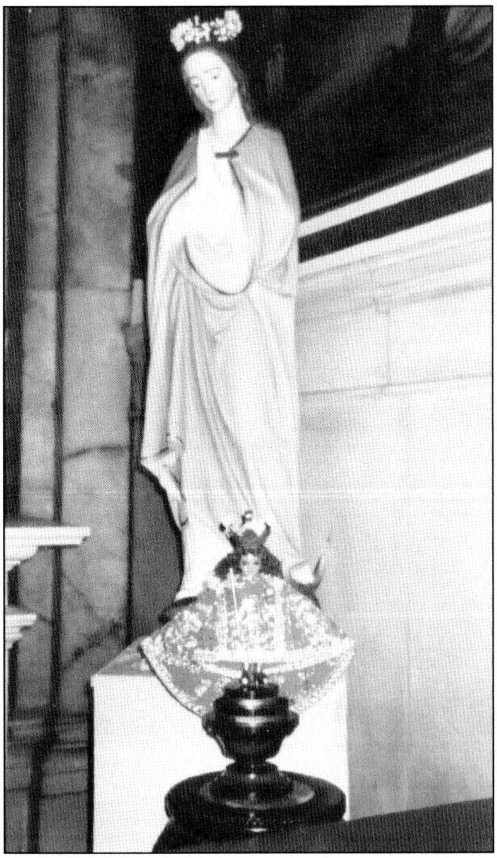

Here is the original Santo Niño de Cebu installed at St. Augustine Church on December 28, 1991. St. Augustine Church, the country's fourth oldest Catholic church, only had nine parishioners attend 1991 Christmas Mass and was scheduled for closure. On January 11, 1992, the Filipino community enshrined the Santo Niño de Cebu and brought the church back to life. St. Augustine's has become a "home church" for Filipino devotees of the Santo Niño. (Courtesy of Dr. Resty Estacio.)

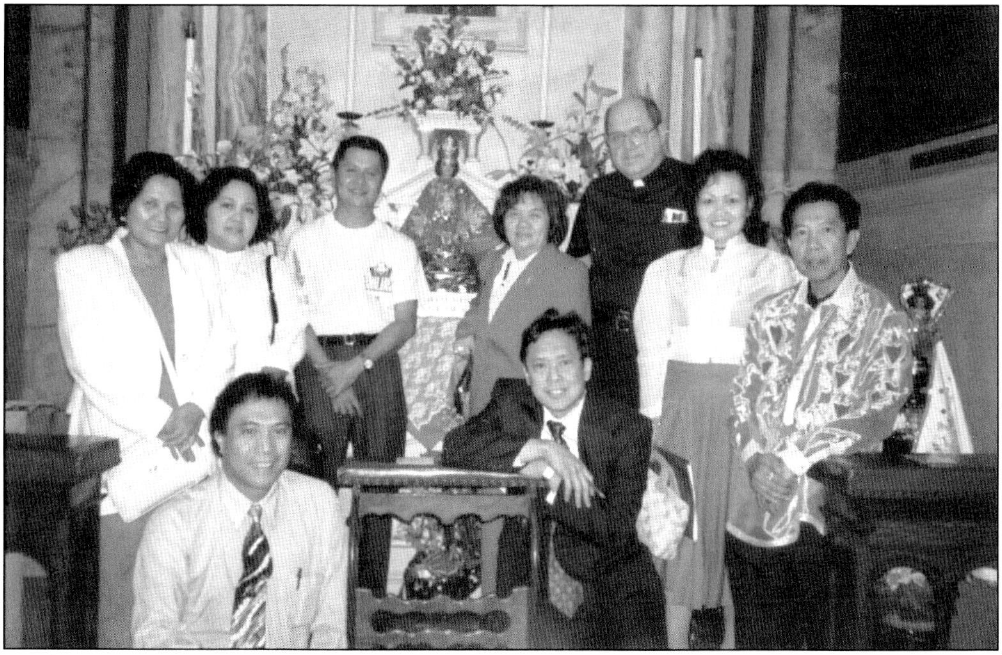

In July 1994, an official replica of the original statue of the Santo Niño de Cebu was commissioned by the Augustinians in the Philippines to be permanently installed at old St. Augustine Church in Philadelphia. Thus, St. Augustine Church, once burned to ashes during anti-immigrant/anti-Catholic riots in 1844, is transformed once again by bringing new life, faith, and culture as a center for Filipino Americans and the national shrine of Santo Niño de Cebu. (Courtesy of Dr. Resty Estacio.)

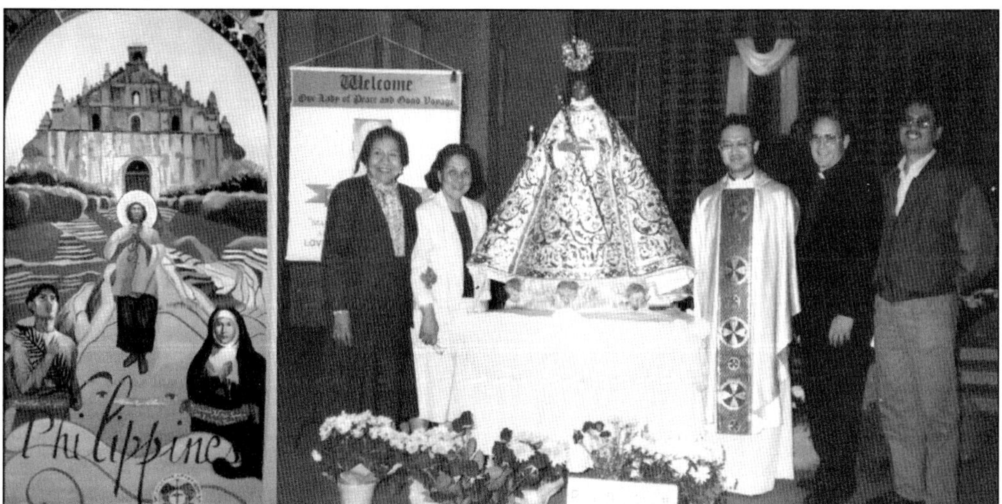

In this photograph, Our Lady of Antipolo, also known as Our Lady of Peace and Good Voyage, visits Philadelphia in May 1995, which is the beginning of the Filipino Apostolate on the Archdiocesan level. Pictured are Victorina N. Peralta and Sr. Lory Mapa. "Mammy" Vicky Peralta, as she is fondly called, served as Philadelphia's director of adult and aging services, where she created the Department of Community Services on Aging in the Archdiocese of Philadelphia. (Courtesy of Filipino Apostolate Philadelphia.)

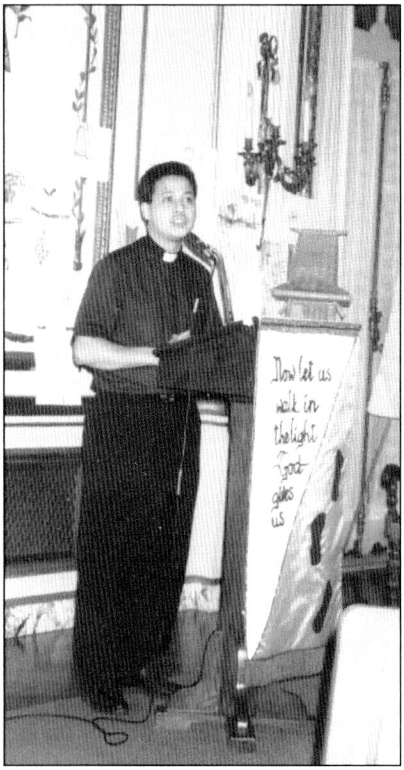

Rev. Efren Esmilla gives an opening talk to FIAT Charismatic Prayer Group, launched in 1993. Ordained as the first Filipino priest in the Archdiocese of Philadelphia in 1993, in 2007, Father Efren was installed as the parish priest of Our Lady of Hope (OLH) making him the first Filipino parish priest in the archdiocese. The Filipino Apostolate also moved its offices from St. Thomas Aquinas to OLH. (Courtesy of Filipino Apostolate Philadelphia.)

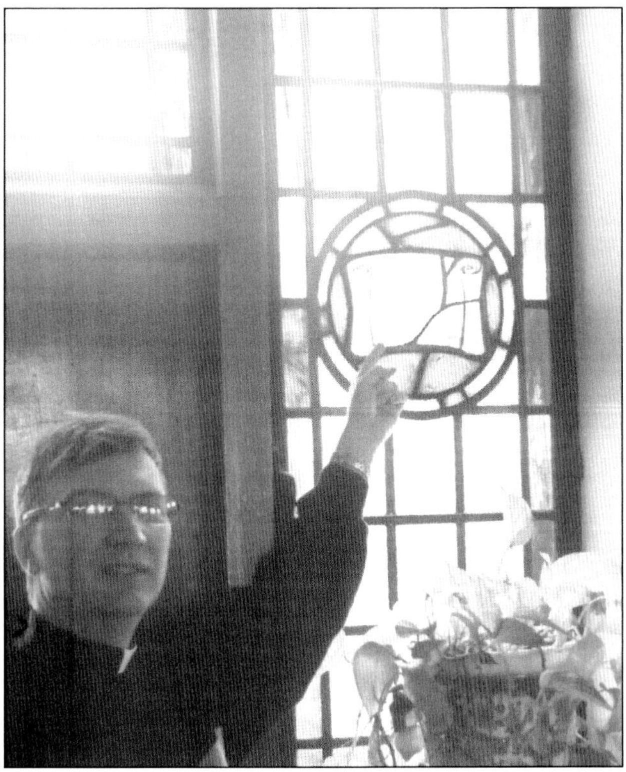

Fr. Tom Betz points to a stained-glass window with a map of the Philippines, located inside the Chinatown Holy Redeemer Church. Its creation in 1941 was due to Cardinal Denis Dougherty, who established the Assumption Sisters in the United States in 1919 through his former parish in Iloilo, Philippines. Father Betz was named director of pastoral care for migrants and refugees and was vital in the flourishing of the Filipino Apostolate. (Courtesy of Eliseo Art Silva.)

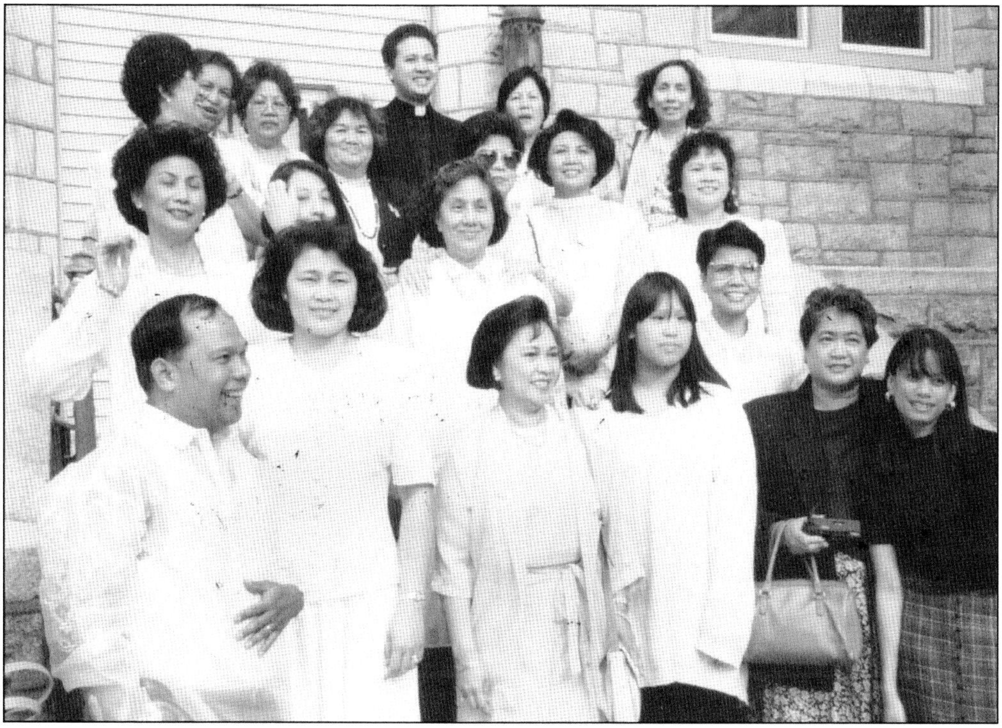

Here are members of FIAT Filipino Charismatic Choir with Fr. Efren Esmilla at a Sunday Mass at Incarnation Church in 1996. The FIAT Charismatic Prayer Group held its first national convention in 1995 in Philadelphia with resounding success. This group forms the core of the Filipino Apostolate community in the Archdiocese of Philadelphia. (Courtesy of Filipino Apostolate Philadelphia.)

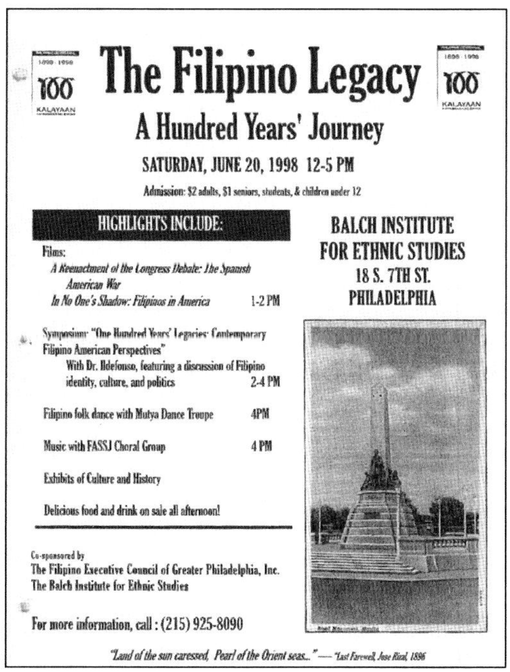

The 1998 Philippine Centennial was celebrated globally. Balch Institute for Ethnic Studics hcld a 3ympo3ium of Philippine exhibits and cultural performances. A centennial ball was held, attended by Philadelphia mayor Edward "Ed" Rendell. FECGP president Dr. Murillo Mangubat said, "We should carry and pass on to our youth the virtues, values, principles and ideals of our forebears. We owe to ourselves to remain faithful to Filipino aspirations demonstrated by our illustrious Filipino heroes." (Courtesy of Emma De Jesus.)

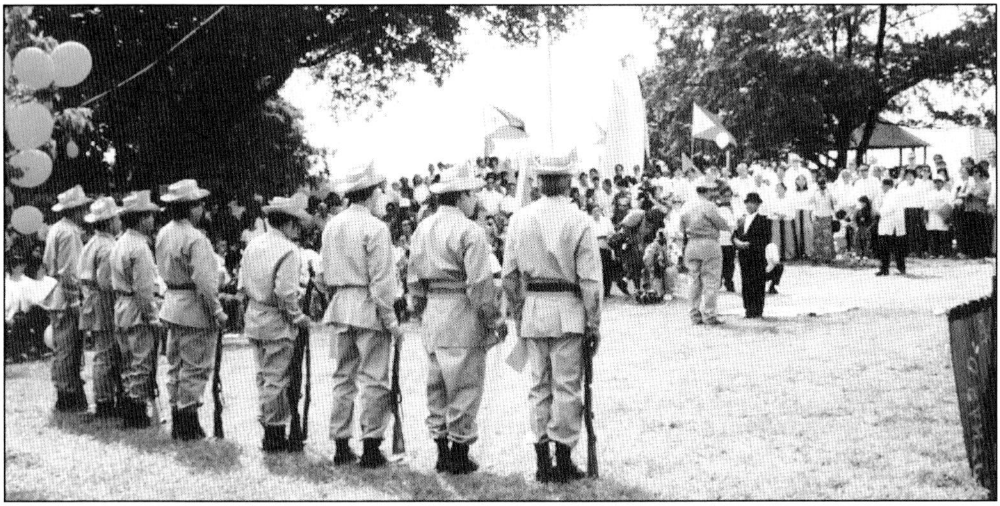

On August 15, 1998, the Filipino American Society of South Jersey, Inc., (FASSJ) contributed a poignant tableau commemorating Rizal's martyrdom at the Dr. Jose Rizal Monument, which celebrated the centennial of the Philippines. Architect Raymundo Benitez wrote the award-winning script. Dr. Alejandro Almario played Rizal, and Raymundo Benitez portrayed the Spanish officer. The 2.2 ton statue was sculpted by Lito Mondejar. (Courtesy of Raymundo Benitez.)

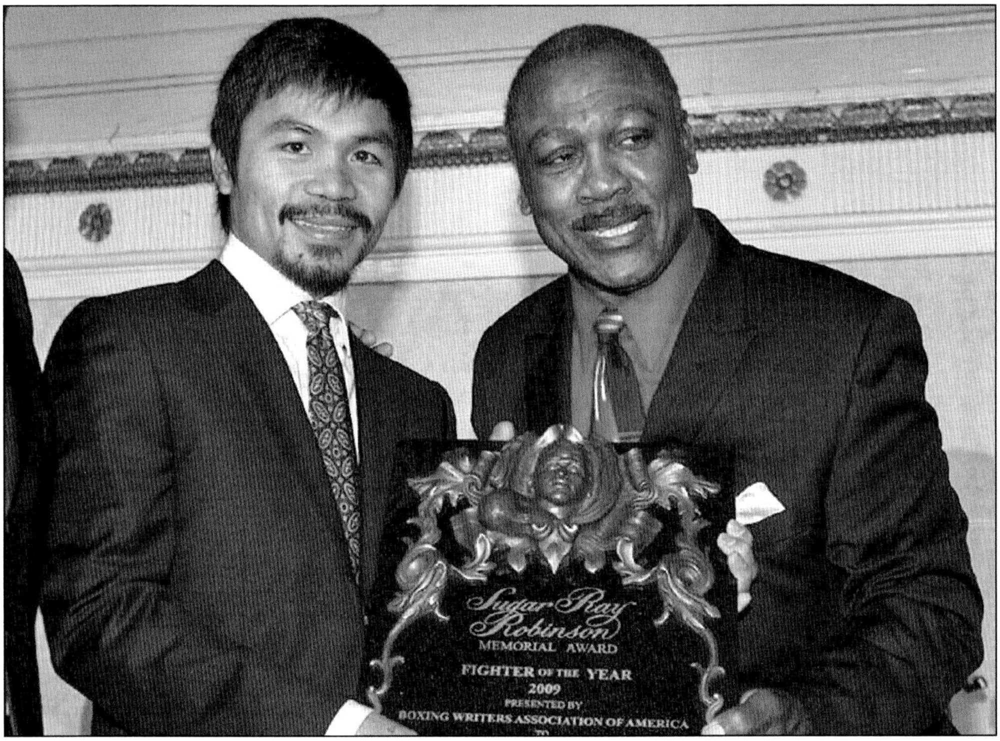

Philadelphia's boxing icon "Smokin' Joe" Frazier (right) gives the 2009 Fighter of the Year award to Filipino icon and eight-division world champion Manny "Pac-Man" Pacquiao. Pacquiao is also known as the Bruce Lee of his generation. Frazier lost the "Thrilla in Manila" in the Philippines to Muhammad Ali on October 1, 1975, after 14 grueling rounds. Ali later said that the fight in Manila was the closest he ever felt to death. (Courtesy of Top Rank Boxing.)

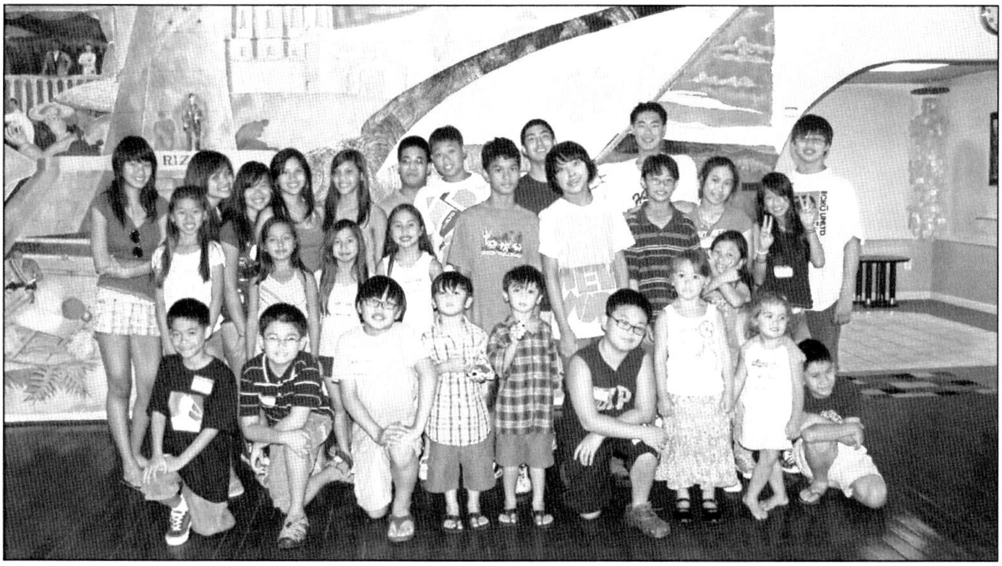

Filipina American youth stand proudly in front of a mural inside the Philippine Community Center of the Philippine Community of Southern New Jersey (PCSNJ) after completing a Filipino heritage workshop conducted by the center. The national anthem of the Philippines and the Philippine flag were both influenced by the United States. Since Aguinaldo was uncertain of American support, he designed the flag so it could be flipped to signal war; the words of the anthem were penned in August 1899 only after the Philippine congress declared war against America on June 12, 1899. (Courtesy of PCSNJ.)

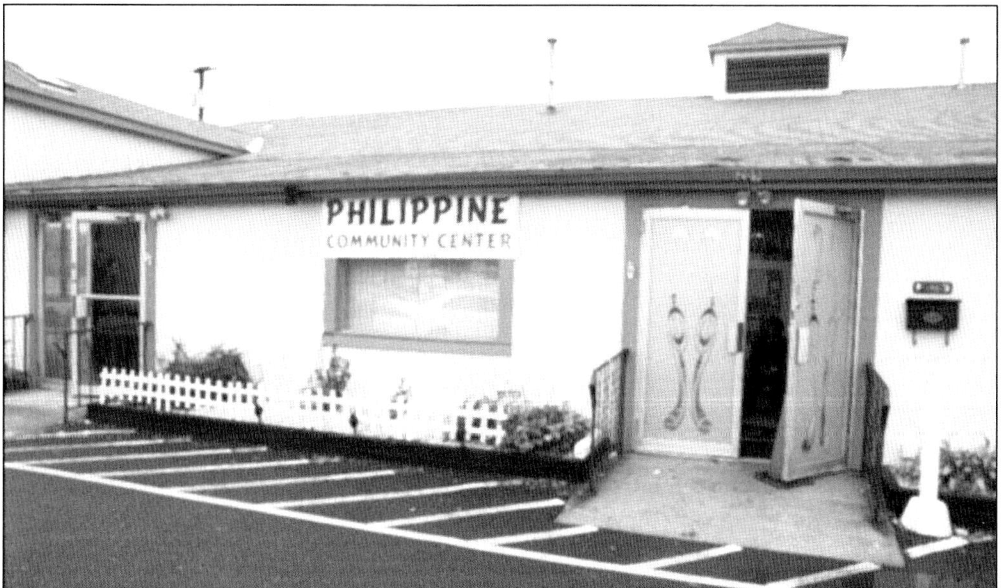

The Philippine Community Center, owned and operated by PCSNJ, develops and offers educational programs to promote cultural awareness, as well as other programs that are beneficial to the members of the community. The center also houses the Filipiniana Library, which was initiated in 1990 by Emma De Jesus and includes over 500 titles, the only one of its kind in the Delaware Valley. (Courtesy of PCSNJ.)

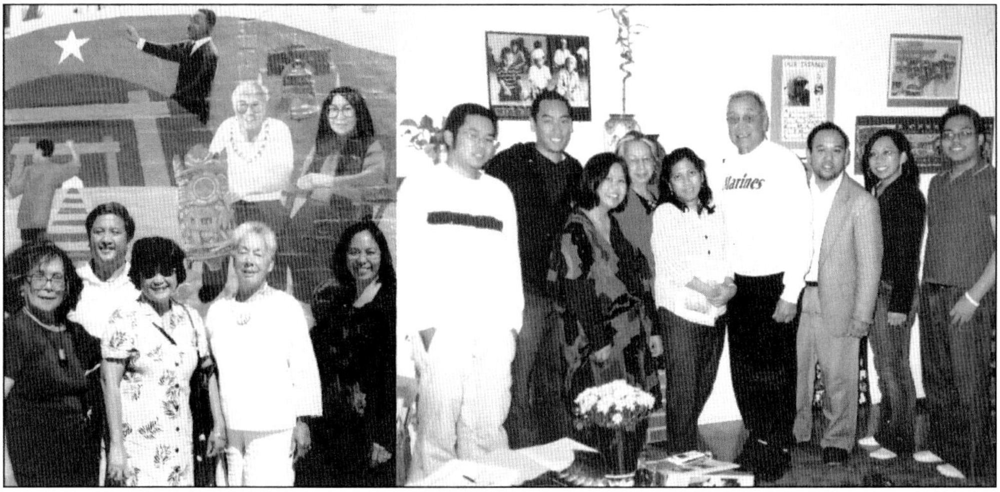

Philadelphia chapter founders of FANHS at right are Jody Aramburo, Brian Redondo, Joan May Cordova, Mary Faustino, Marife Domingo, Skip Voluntad, Brad Baldia, Sheila Cervantes, and Dale Tan. Initiated on July 11, 2005, the local chapter became the 24th FANHS chapter on December 30, 2005. Eliseo Silva served as founding president from 2005 to 2008. According to FANHS executive director Dorothy Cordova (far left), "this founding date is significant in that Pennsylvania being the keystone as the site of the Declaration of American Independence, December 30 (Rizal's martyrdom) also marked the date for initiating Philippine Independence." (Courtesy of Eliseo Art Silva.)

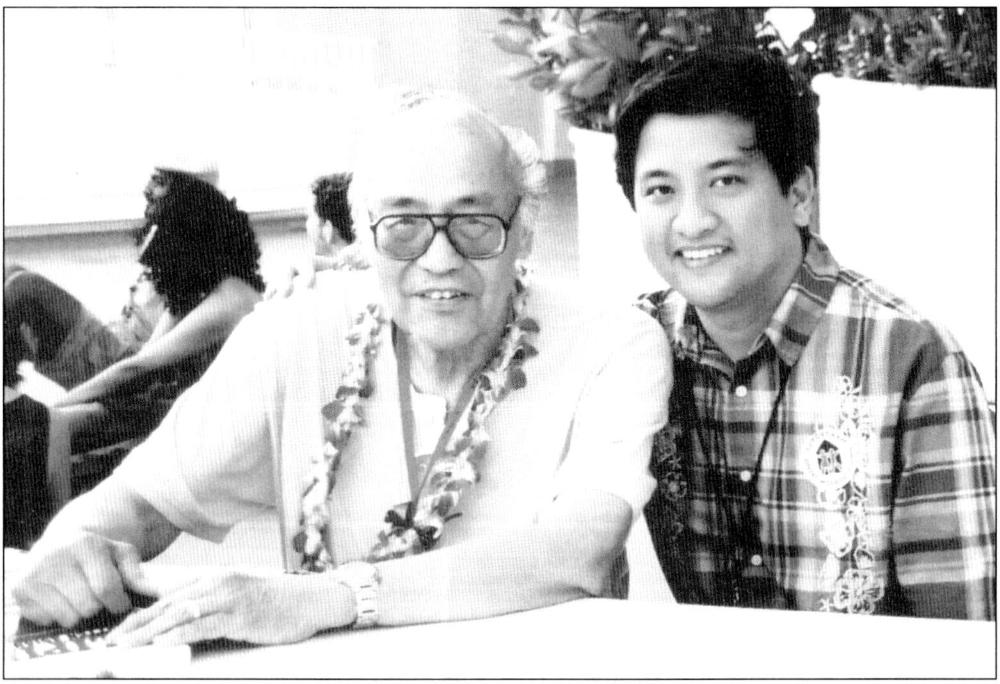

Fred Cordova (left), FANHS founding president emeritus, and Eliseo Art Sliva are at the 11th FANHS Conference in Honolulu, Hawaii. The history of Filipinos of Philadelphia was presented in the conference. (Courtesy of Eliseo Art Silva.)

Deacon Fred Cordova (left) meets Skip Voluntad after delivering his homily highlighting Filipino freedom through unity under the grace of God and "Filipino American solidarity through the Catholic Liturgy and Sacraments." Voluntad said, "I was impressed by Fred Cordova's homily. Fred is a very wise man through the grace of God. We are thankful." It was Voluntad along with eight other Philadelphians who initiated a similar organization on June 1, 2002, called the Greater Philadelphia Filipino Historical Assembly. (Courtesy of Eliseo Art Silva.)

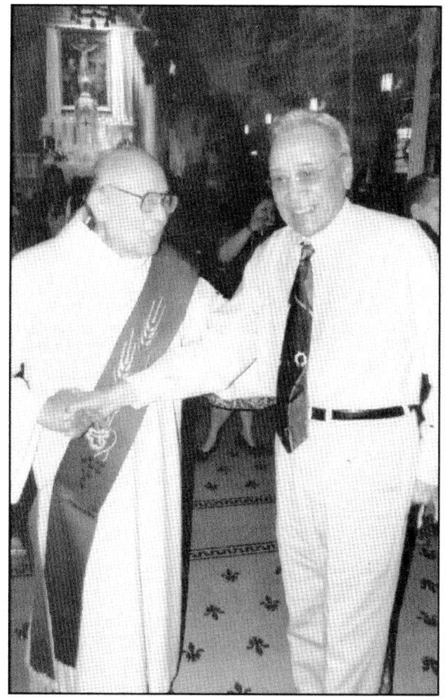

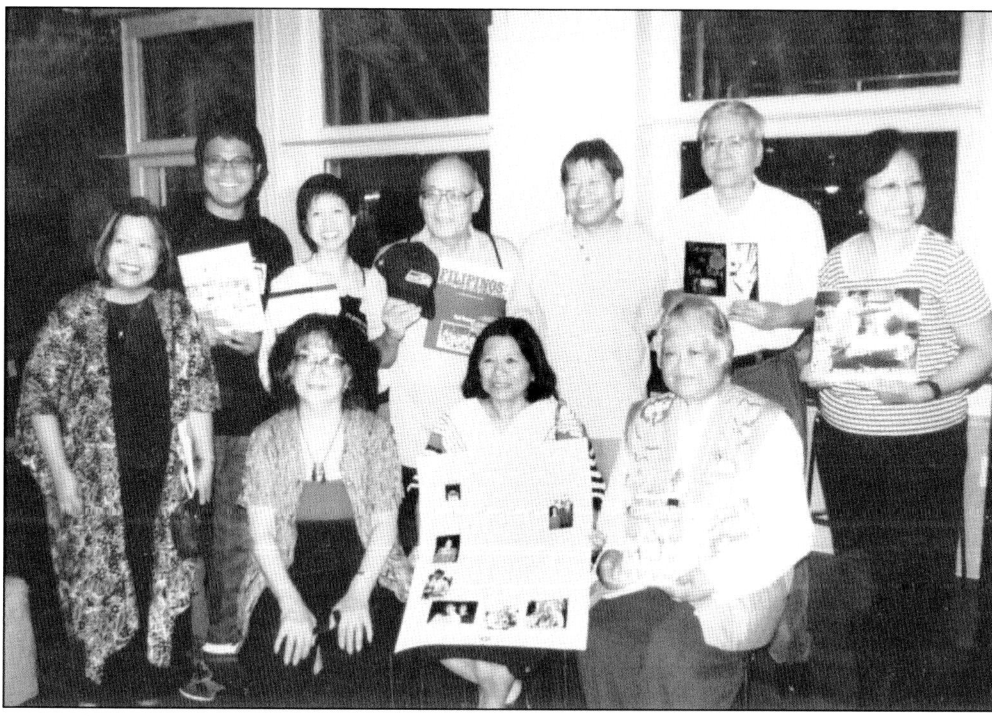

Pictured at an Evening with Filipino American Writers, sponsored by the FANHS Trustees Meeting (June 18–July 1, 2007), are, from left to right, (first row) Dorothy Cordova, Thelma Bucholdt, and Evangeline Buell; (second row) Joan Cordova, Ray Obisbo, Emily Lawsin, Fred Cordova, Romy Dorotan, Oscar Penaranda, and Amy Besa. Amy and Romy lived in Philadelphia in the 1970s and were KDP (Union of Democratic Filipinos) members. Romy developed his passion as a chef in Philadelphia, opening Cendrillion and, later, Purple Yam in Brooklyn, New York, with his wife, Amy. (Courtesy of Eliseo Art Silva.)

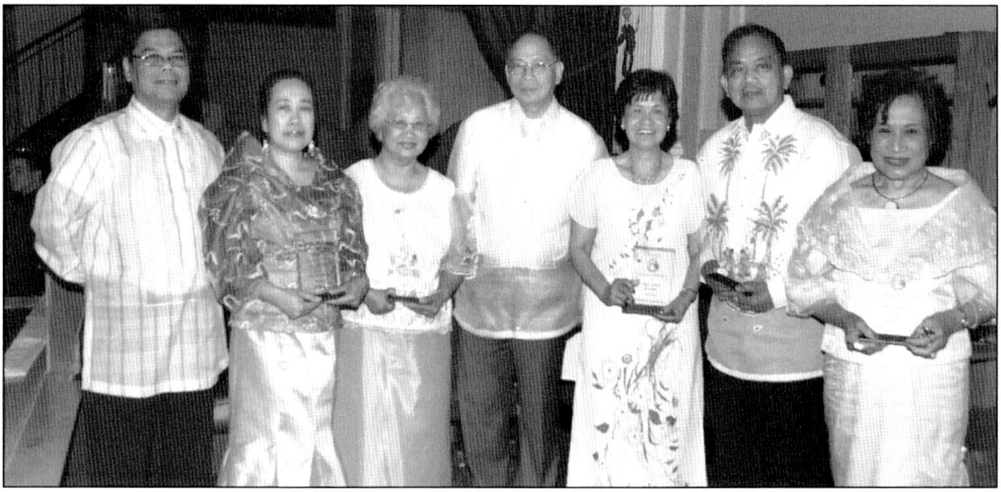

Pictured at the Asian American Heritage Awards "honoring Filipino Americans in the Delaware Valley" at Cebu Restaurant in Philadelphia on May 30, 2007, are 6ABC Community Advisory Board members, sponsors of the awards. From left to right are Dr. Rommel Rivera, president of FECGP and FAAPI; Dr. Aida Rivera, award recipient for arts and culture; Purita Acosta, accepting special recognition on behalf of FAAPI; Philippine ambassador to the United States Willy Gaa, keynote speaker; Erlinda Juliano, award recipient for education; Elias Dungca, award recipient for community service; and Virgie Luz, award recipient for arts and culture. (Courtesy of Dr. Rommel Rivera.)

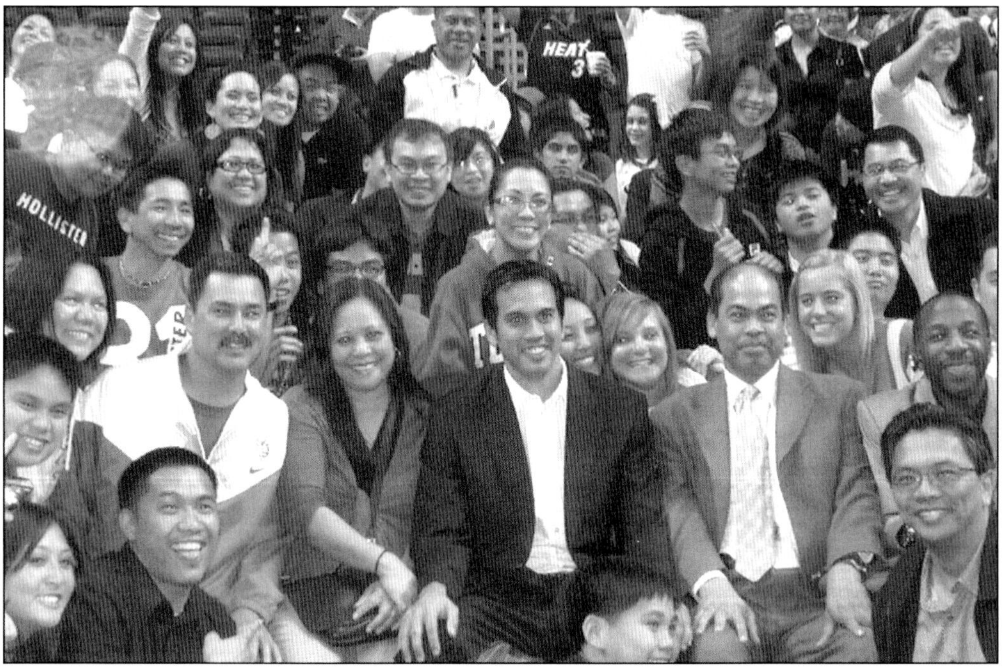

Filipino Night with the Phillies is an annual event organized by the Filipino American Community Athletic Association (FACAA). This particular Filipino event was made even more special when the opposing team featured the Miami Heat with its Filipino American coach Eric Spoelstra, who brought his team to victory in the NBA finals in 2012. Founded in 1995, FACAA has succeeded in uniting Filipino youth in the Greater Philadelphia region through sports such as golf, softball, bowling, tennis, and the popular basketball league. (Courtesy of Noel Abejo.)

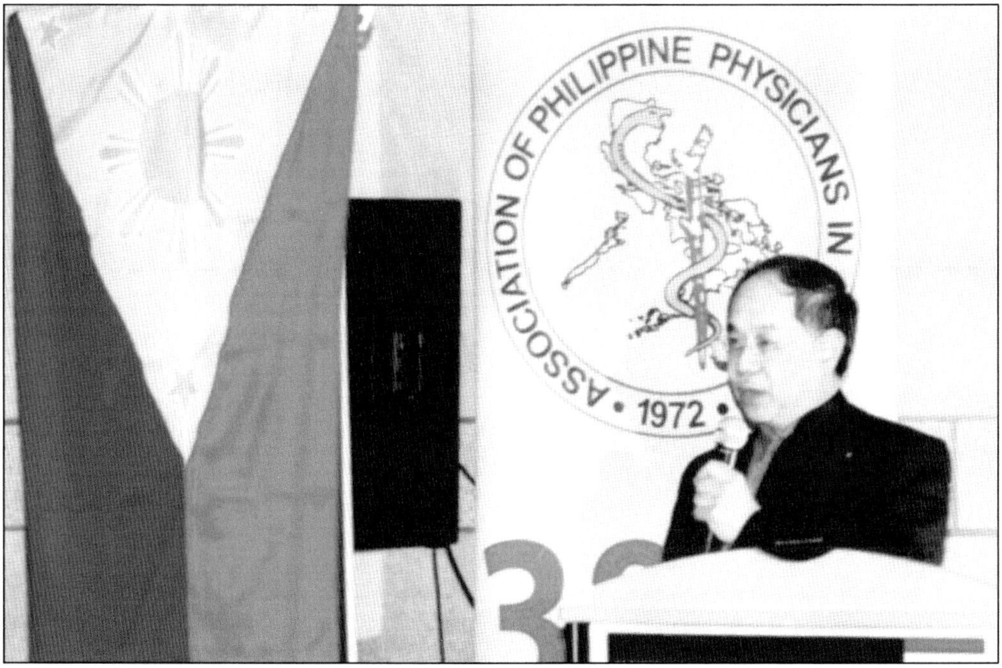

Dr. Francis Talangbayan welcomes delegates attending the Association of Philippine Physicians in America (APPA) 38th annual convention on July 4, 2009, at the National Constitution Center in Philadelphia. More than 300 doctors attended. In 1972, APPA worked to dispel discriminatory practices directed against foreign medical graduates, mainly from the Philippines and India. (Courtesy of April Talangbayan.)

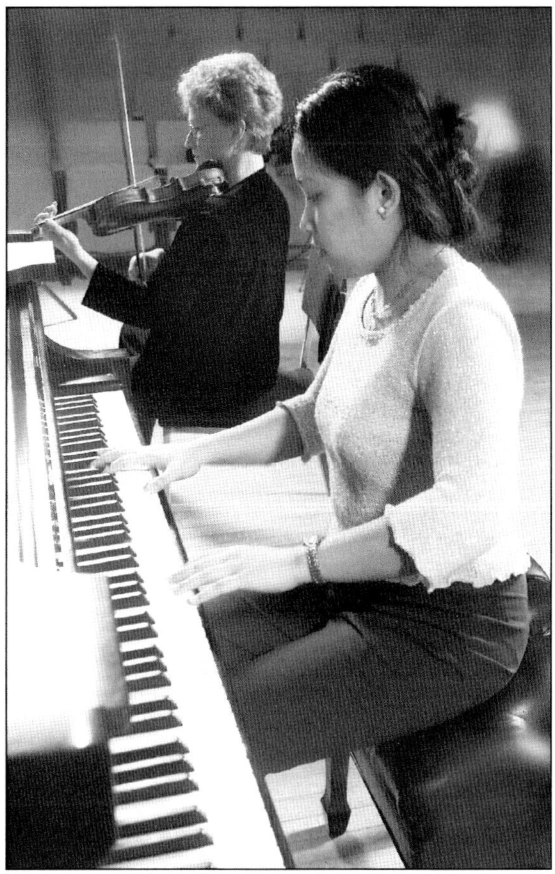

Charisse Baldoria is seen during rehearsal at Moravian College, Bethlehem, Pennsylvania. Charisse graduated as valedictorian at the University of the Philippines and earned her doctorate and master's from the University of Michigan, studying with Logan Skelton under Fulbright and Barbour scholarships. She currently teaches music at Kutztown University. She won first prize at the Society for Musical Arts Competition, was a two-time winner of the University of Michigan concerto competition, and finished among the top 12 at the Sydney International Piano competition. (Courtesy of Charisse Baldoria.)

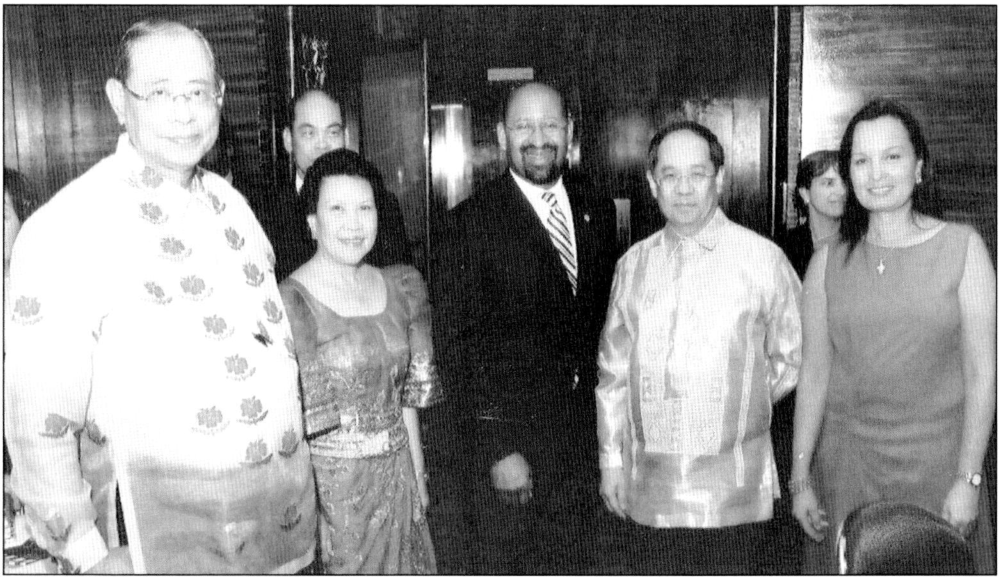

Philadelphia mayor Michael Nutter (center) is pictured with, from left to right, Dr. Alex Cueto, Philippine Consul General Cecille Rebong, Dr. Francis Talangbayan, and 1973 Miss Universe Margie Moran during the 2009 APPA convention. APPA's major victory came in 1982, when the ECFMG succeeded in dispelling racial discrimination directed at Filipino doctors when the American Medical Association finally granted them membership, and doctors who graduated from foreign schools were finally given the same licensing tests as their US-educated counterparts. (Courtesy of April Talangbayan.)

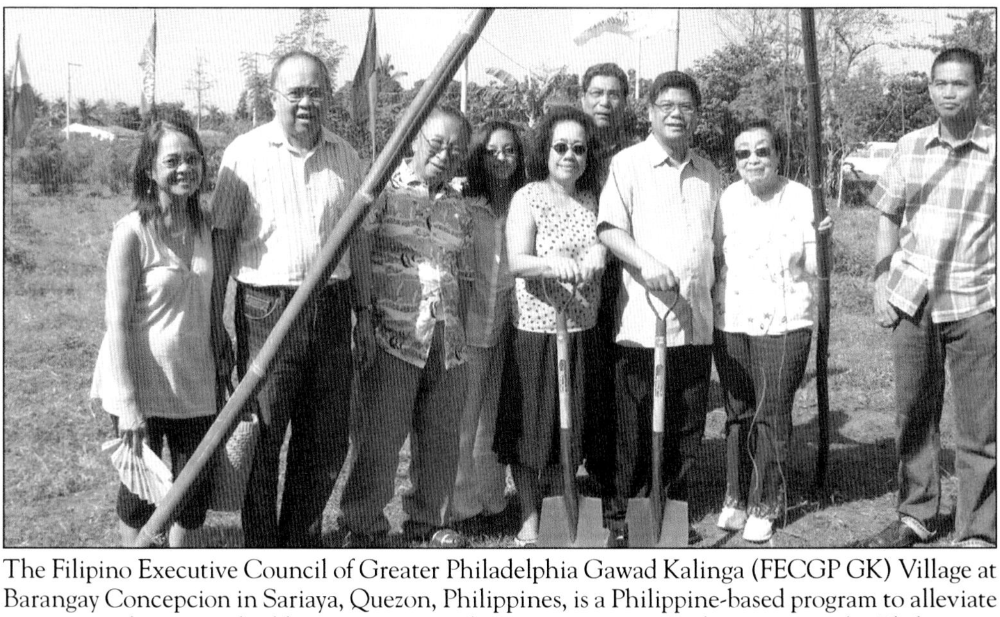

The Filipino Executive Council of Greater Philadelphia Gawad Kalinga (FECGP GK) Village at Barangay Concepcion in Sariaya, Quezon, Philippines, is a Philippine-based program to alleviate poverty, and a nation-building movement whose mission is to end poverty in the Philippines for five million families by 2024. The FECGP GK Village, a project of the administration of Dr. Rommel Rivera, will include a community center and chapel for residents occupying 30 homes. The local GK Pennsylvania coordinator is Roy Calleja, while Eliseo Art Silva was the GK events coordinator from 2004 to 2009. (Courtesy of Dr. Rommel Rivera.)

Philadelphians support Gawad Kalinga (GK) by participating in the Philadelphia Marathon. In the picture are twin sisters Rina Ponce and Rhea Ponce-Borja, joining more than 50 others in a program called the GK Run on November 19, 2006. More than five GK Villages have been produced by Philadelphians in the region, creating homes for more than 300 families in the Philippines. (Courtesy of Eliseo Art Silva.)

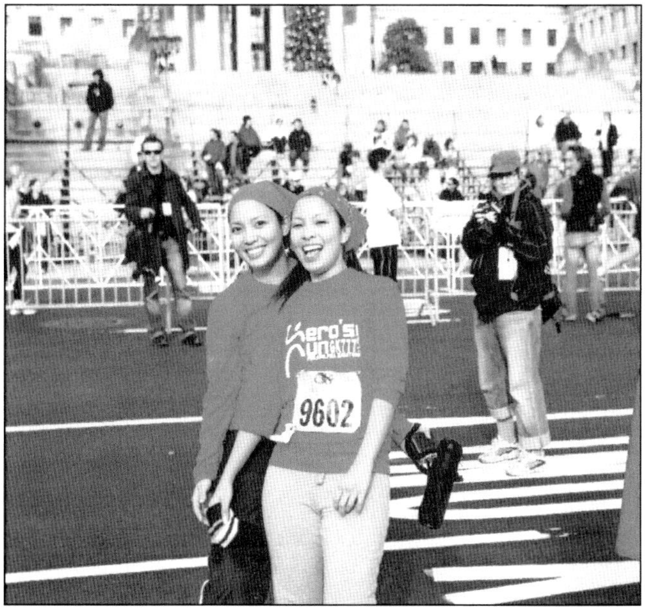

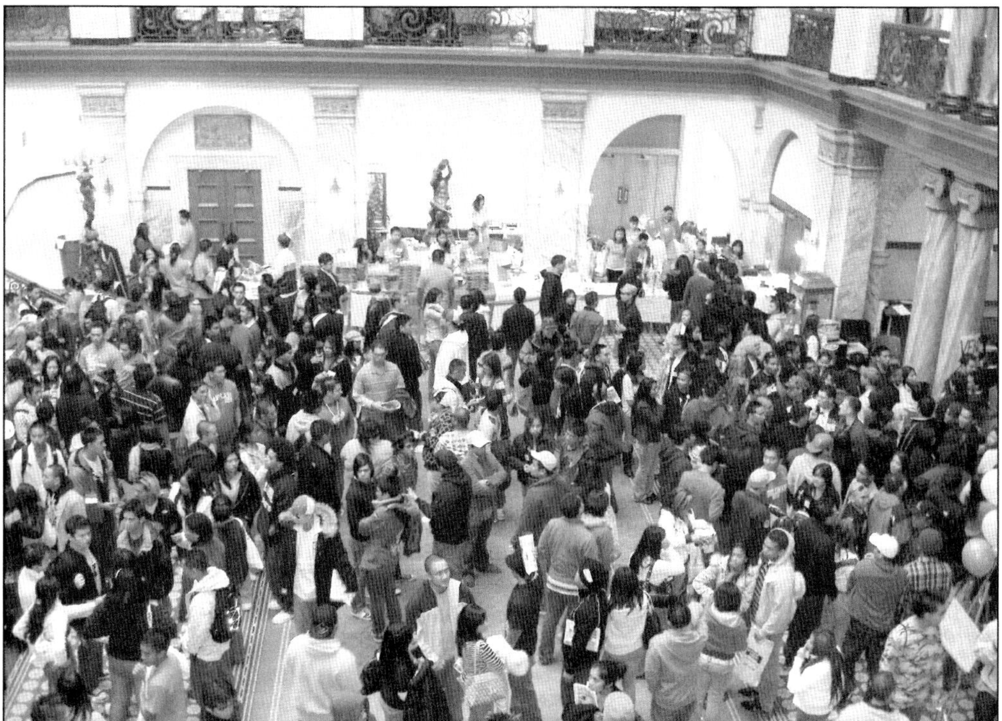

Here is the Filipino Intercollegiate Networking Dialogue, Inc., (FIND) Conference at Drexel University. Every spring, hundreds of students from all over the east coast gather for two days to empower, network, and learn about their roots as Filipino Americans. Founded in April 1991 at Yale University, FIND held its first conference at Harvard University on April 11, 1992. FIND's goals are to offer a channel for dialogue and action and to act as a catalyst for various Filipino organizations. (Courtesy of Noel Abejo.)

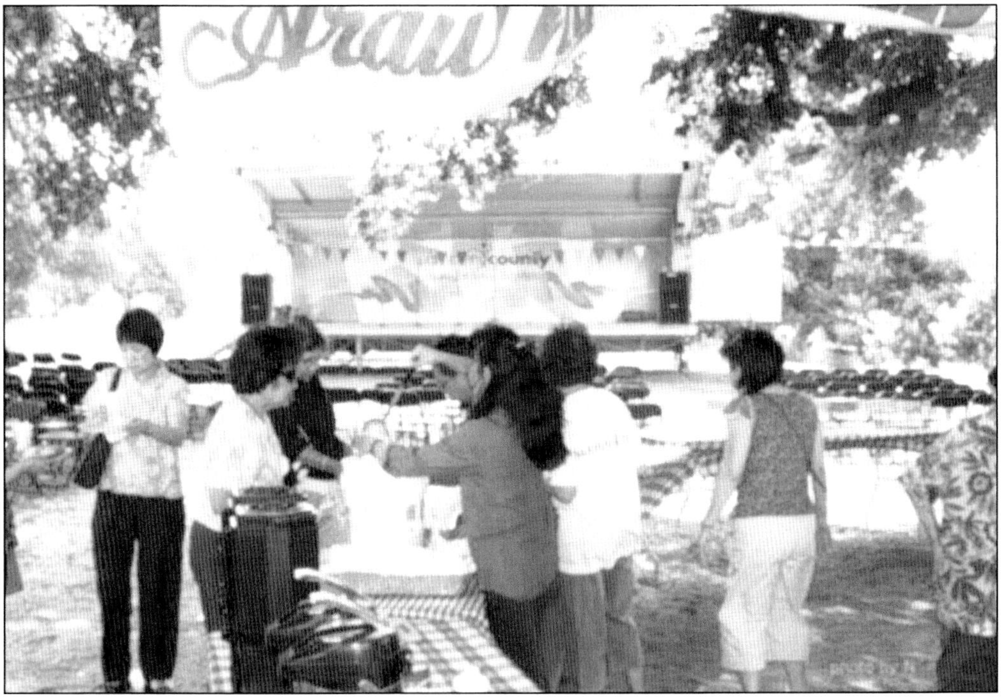

Here is a Philippine Independence Day community picnic at Cooper River Park, Camden, New Jersey. Organized by the Filipino Executive Council of Greater Philadelphia, Inc., (FECGP) as part of Philippine Week, more than 20 member organizations and other groups contribute food, performances, activities, and services to celebrate the Filipino community's national day. All the food, entertainment, and activities are free of charge; it is the largest fiesta organized by the Filipinos of Greater Philadelphia. (Courtesy of Noel Abejo.)

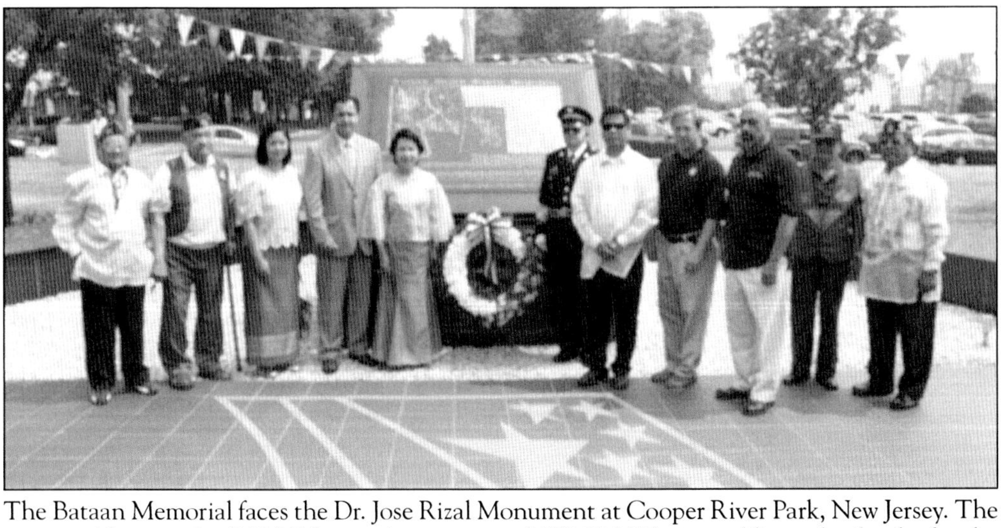

The Bataan Memorial faces the Dr. Jose Rizal Monument at Cooper River Park, New Jersey. The memorial honors the 7,000 Filipino American and 250,000 Filipino soldiers who fought for the United States during World War II. The design incorporates the year Gen. Douglas MacArthur landed in Leyte, fulfilling his promise of returning to the Philippines. The diameter of the granite circle is 44 feet, in reference to October 1944, which was when the final push toward freedom was set in motion. (Courtesy of Philip Reyes.)

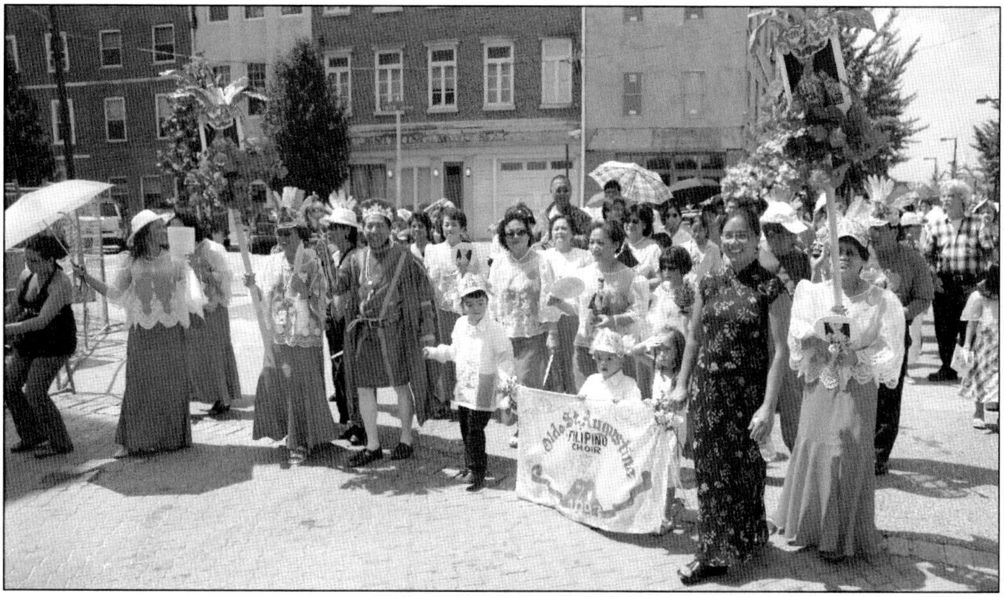

Young and old alike join for the annual summer Sinulog Festival, which is held on the last Sunday of August and attracts busloads of devotees from as far away as Canada and Florida. Because the actual date of the Feast of the Santo Niño de Cebu falls during the third Sunday of January, an indoor winter Sinulog honoring the Christ Child is also held inside the church coinciding with the festivities in the Philippines. (Courtesy of Philip Reyes.)

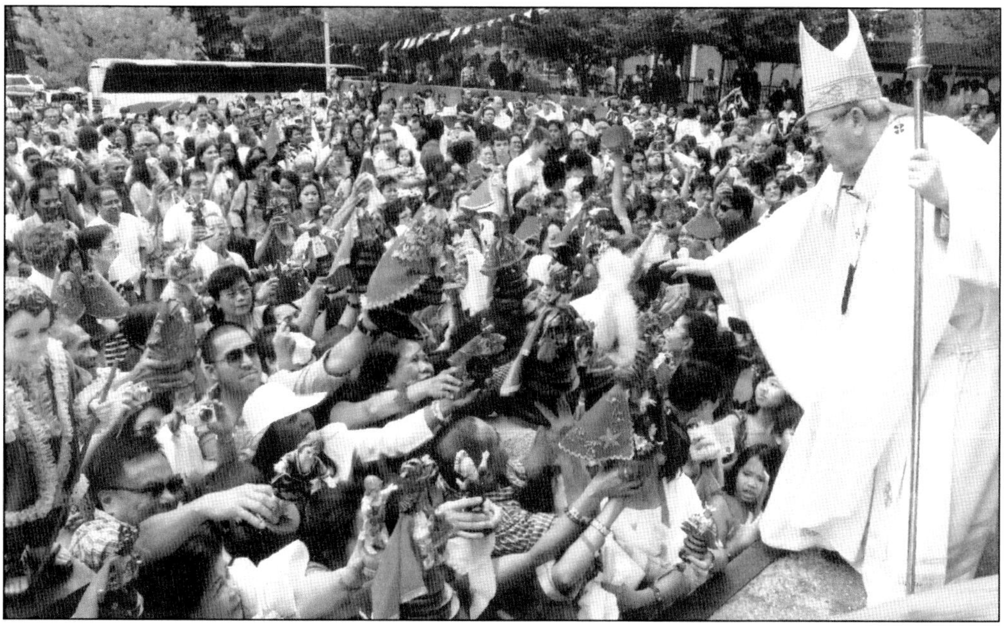

Cardinal Justin Rigali, archbishop of Philadelphia, blesses devotees after the procession. Sinulog comes from the word *sulog*, or river current, describing the ancient dance steps of the parade participants, which were two steps backward and one step forward. Sinulog existed long before Magellan landed in Cebu, Philippines, a veneration of a miraculous "child king" validated by Cebu's Queen Hara Amihan, who initiated the devotion of the child Jesus a century before Prague, Czech Republic. (Courtesy of Dr. Lita Mangubat.)

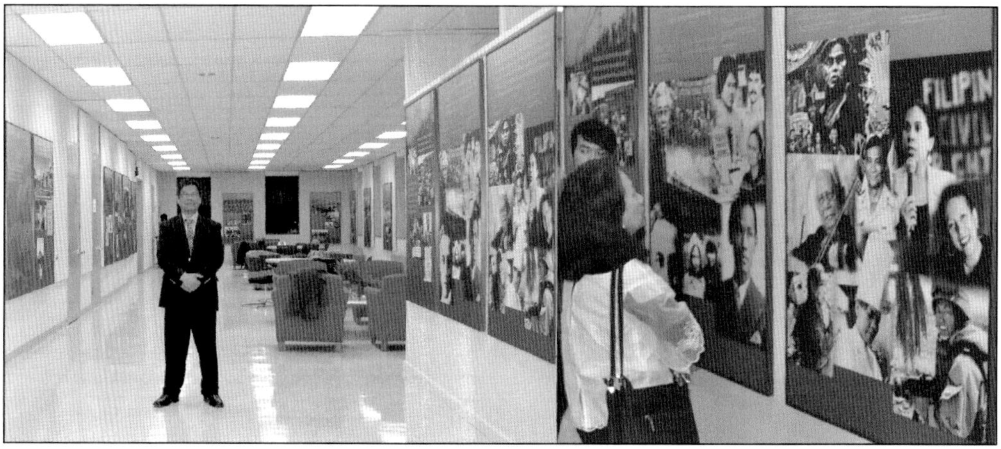

Cecilia Borres views the final panel of the exhibition where Eliseo Art Silva is included among eight Filipino American honorees. "Singgalot: From Colonial Subjects to Citizens," a Smithsonian exhibition celebrating the centennial of Filipino migration to the United States, was brought to Philadelphia from November 19, 2010, through January 14, 2011, by the Singgalot Committee headed by Dr. Rommel Rivera, the Asian American Women's Coalition, the Filipino Intercultural Society of Drexel University, and Drexel University. It was the inaugural exhibit of the new Intercultural Center of Drexel University. (Courtesy of Philip Reyes and Dr. Rommel Rivera.)

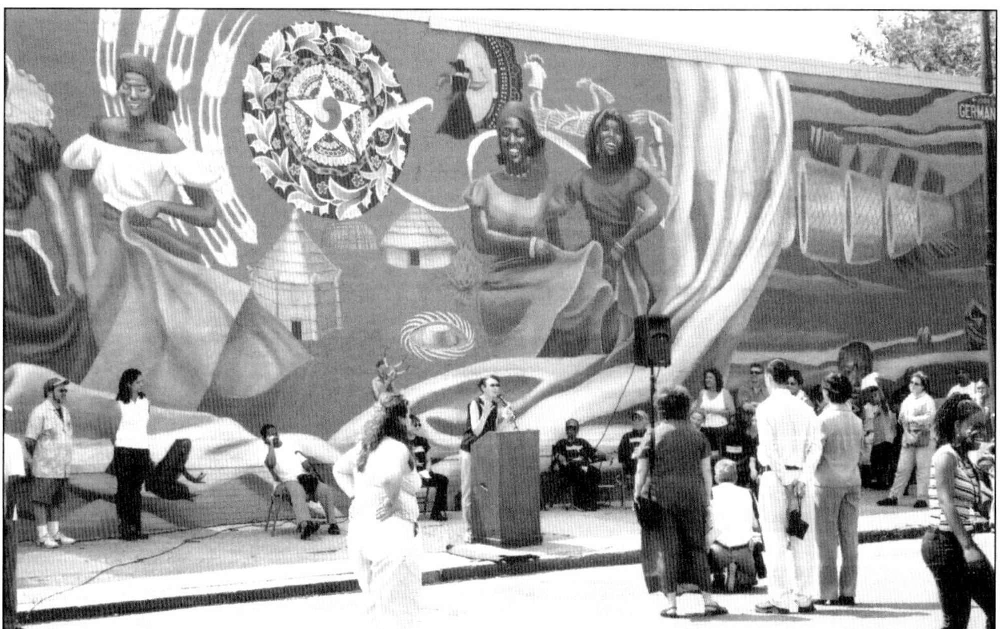

Jane Golden, founder of the Philadelphia Mural Arts Program, unveils *Guardian of An Eden Regained*, a 120-foot mural by Eliseo Art Silva. This is one of the artist's 25 murals in the "Mural Capital of the World" and includes Filipino elements such as Hawaii's *sakadas* and the *ligligan parul*. Silva has completed over 100 murals. (Courtesy of Eliseo Art Silva.)

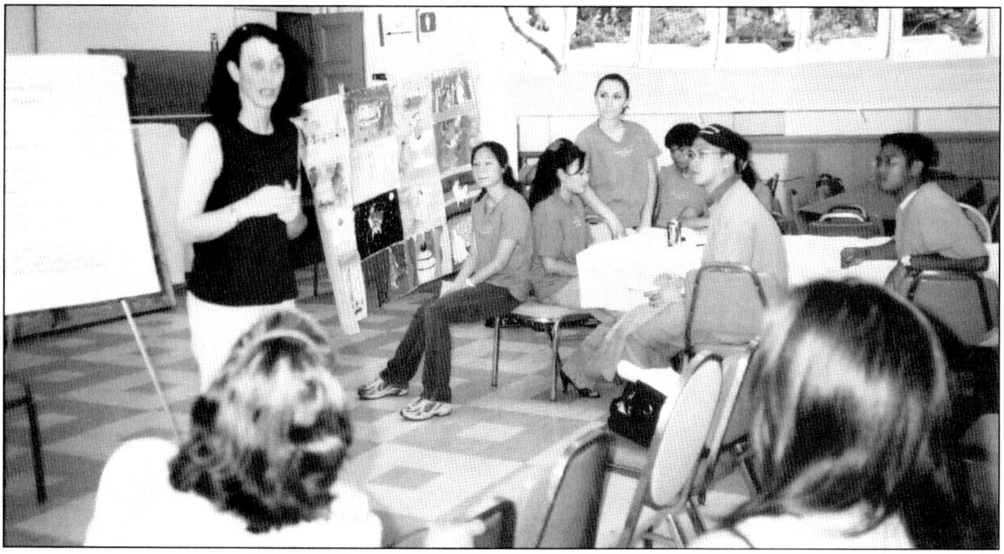

Jane Golden speaks to participants of the Filipino mural workshops, held at the St. Augustine's social hall. Each of the 30 attendees received a *Philly-Pinoy Teach* book, funded by the Association for the Promotion of Philippine Arts and Culture. During the 2007 official visit of Prince Charles to Philadelphia, Eliseo Art Silva was one of only four artists selected by Golden to do a mural demonstration for the royal visitors, held at Heavenly Hall Full Gospel Church. (Courtesy of Eliseo Art Silva.)

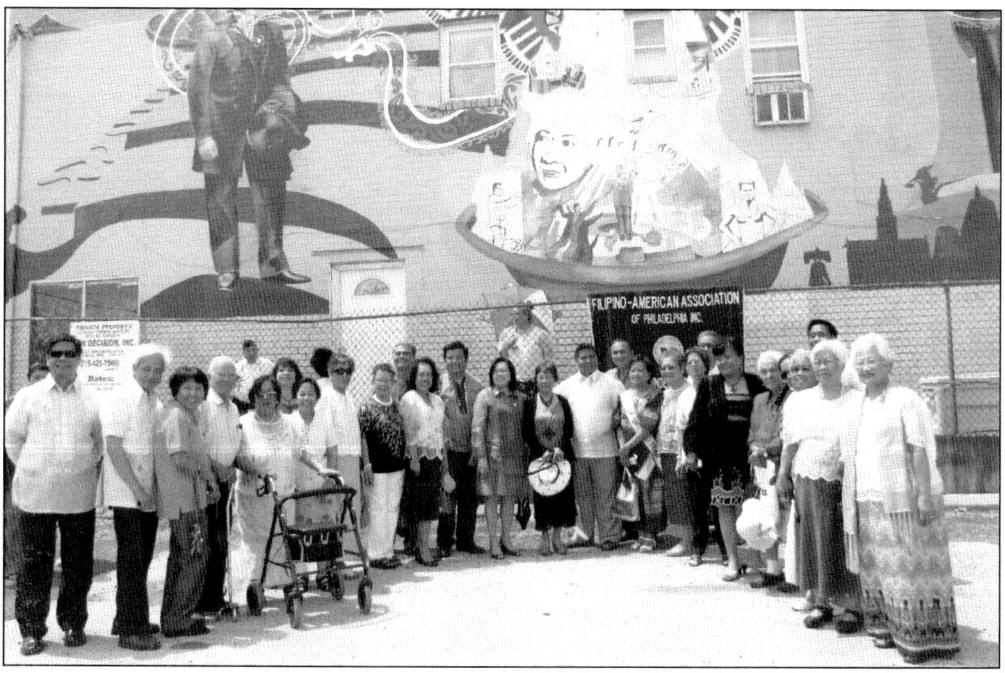

On June 19, 2011, FAAPI unveiled the first phase of the 65-by-22-foot mural honoring the 150th anniversary of Dr. Jose Rizal's birth. The deputy Philippine consul general from New York was the keynote speaker, and Philadelphia mayor Michael Nutter presented a certificate recognizing the mural as the first Filipino mural on the east coast. The mural is 22 feet tall, which corresponds to the number of languages Rizal mastered in his 35 years of life. (Courtesy of Eliseo Art Silva.)

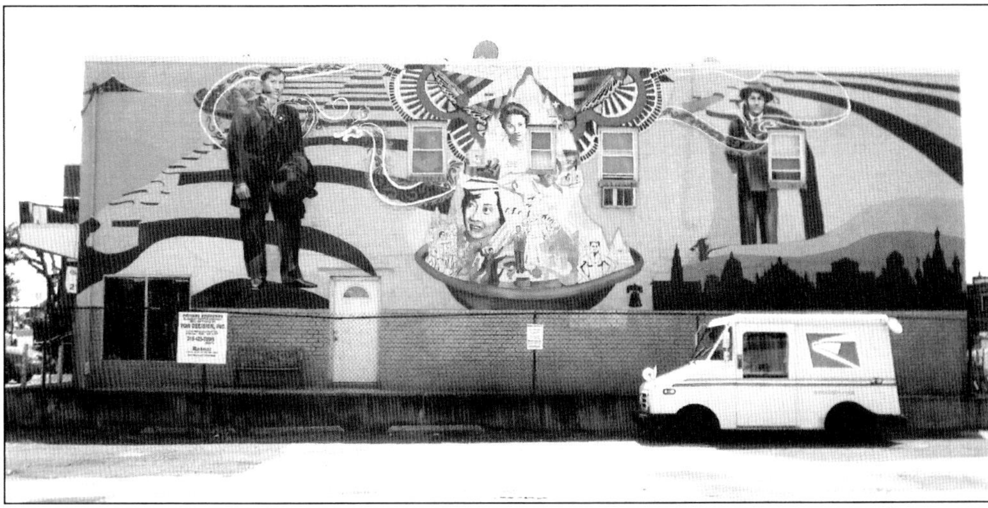

"Alab ng Puso: My Heart's Sole Burning Fire" (pictured 10 percent completed) encapsulates 5,000 years of Filipino and 400 years of Filipino American history, highlighting the history of Filipino Philadelphians. The central image is an eternal flame made up of portraits of "mothers of history," reflecting the Filipino belief that the mother is the light of the home. The two dominating figures function as pillars of the entire mural, referencing the Filipino belief that fathers are pillars of the home. (Courtesy of Eliseo Art Silva.)

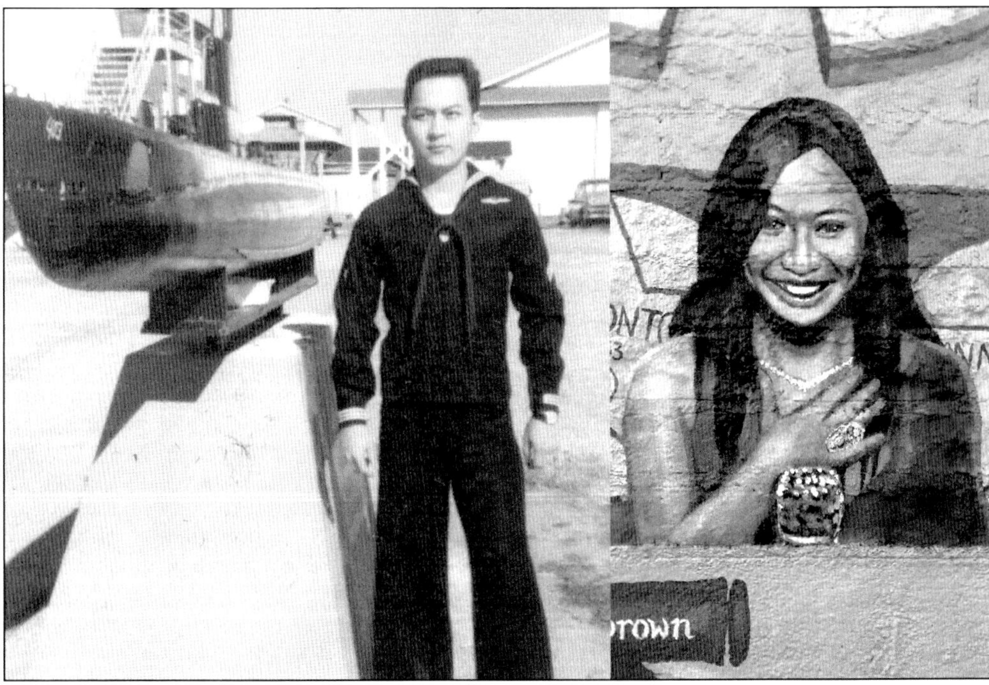

Nestor Palugod Enriquez joined the US Navy and served as a submarine petty officer. He was among many Filipino sailors who trekked to Philadelphia during their liberty weekends. Presently, his groundbreaking research on Filipino American history has enhanced his reputation as a historian and founding president of FANHS New Jersey. American Idol Jessica Sanchez is a hometown girl with Filipino roots and a Navy connection. Her grandfather is Eddie Bugay, a US Navy retiree from Bataan, Philippines. (Courtesy of Ray L. Burdeos.)

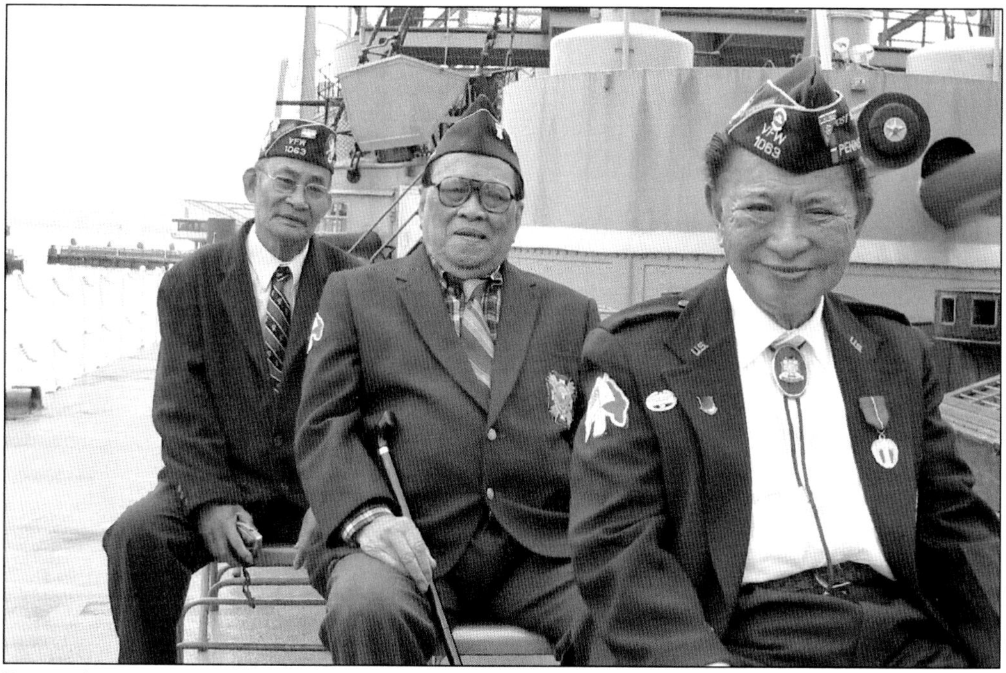

Pictured are veterans on Dewey's fabled flagship. From left to right are Francisco Reyta, Aguinaldo Fontanilla, and Dr. Nacianceno Largoza. Reyta is a Philadelphian member of Pvt. Tomas Claudio Post 1063, Fontanilla was mayor of Quezon Province, Philippines, and Dr. "Nen" Largoza's childhood home in Tiaong, Quezon, Philippines, was burned by the Japanese. Winston Churchill proclaimed "The Filipino soldier is the bravest in the world, second to none." (Courtesy of Sennen Fontanilla.)

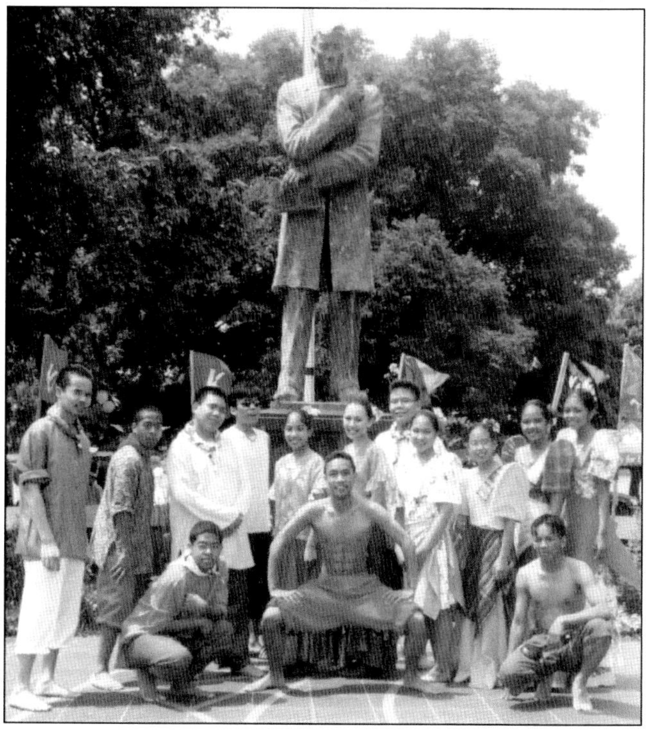

Mutya Philippine Dance Troupe's dancers embody the ideals of nationalism and cultural representation that emboldened the Filipino hero Jose Rizal to attain greatness and proclaim: "the youth is the hope of thy motherland." The dancers are proudly posing in front of the monument honoring Rizal, a beacon to Filipinos wherever they may be. As long as Rizal is unknown to the rest of mankind, so will Filipinos continue to be misunderstood and invisible in the eyes of world. (Courtesy of Virginia Luz.)

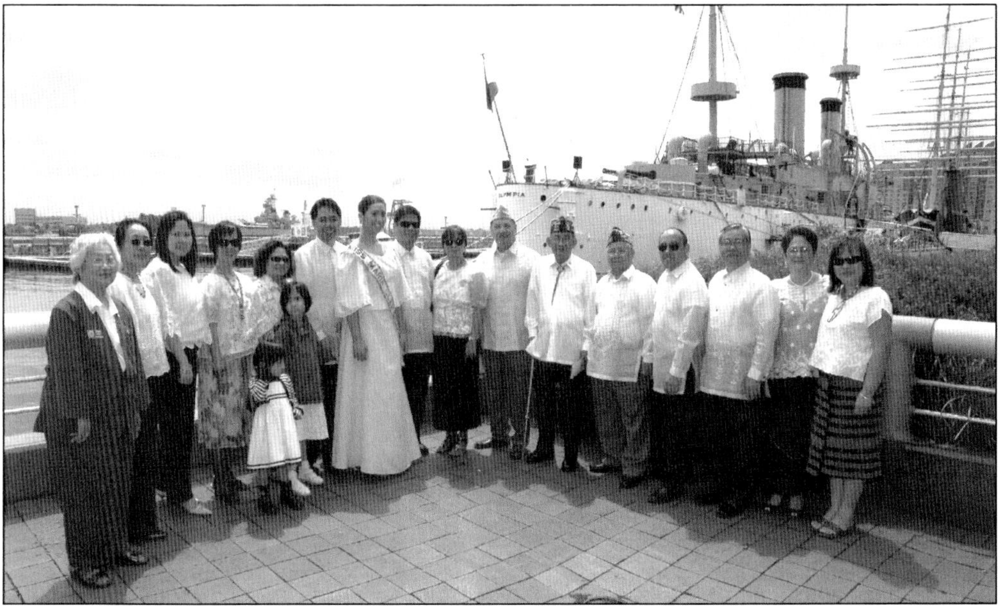

The Philippine flag waves proudly at Admiral Dewey's flagship, the USS *Olympia*, docked at Penn's Landing in Philadelphia's historic Navy yard, the gateway of countless Filipino Philadelphians. The raising of the Philippines "three stars and a sun" at the *Olympia* is the symbolic act of patriotism repeated annually every first Saturday of June by the Filipino community to celebrate Philippine Independence Week, a tradition initiated by FAAPI during the landmark 1976 US Bicentennial celebrations. (Courtesy of Philip Reyes.)

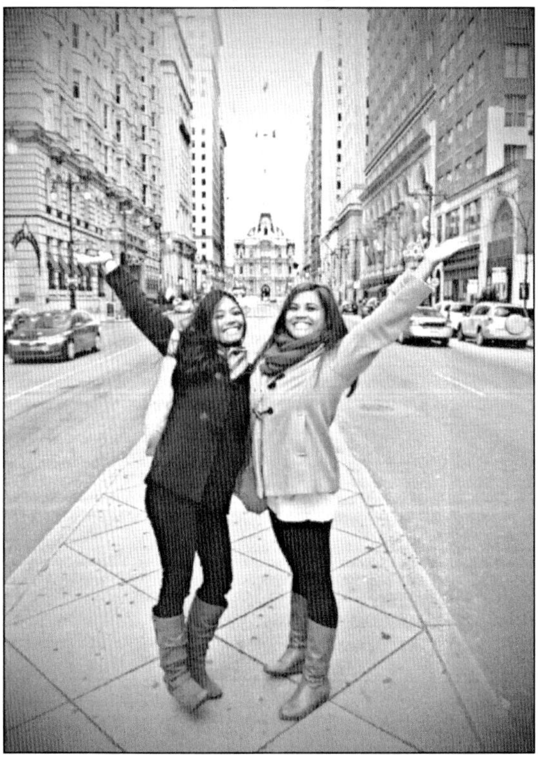

Dana and Lauren Abejo, La Salle University students, are third-generation Filipina Americans. Taken a day before her birthday, Dana chose an iconic landmark, Philadelphia City Hall, the tallest masonry building in the United States, with a 37-foot bronze statue of William Penn overlooking the city. On the 100th anniversary of Filipinos in Philadelphia, Filipino Philadelphians can now stand upon the shoulders of pioneers who were giants, with a clearer view of the future that awaits them. (Courtesy of Noel Abejo.)

ABOUT FAAPI

The Filipino American Association of Philadelphia, Inc. (FAAPI) is currently in the midst of celebrating 100 years in Greater Philadelphia. At the forefront of historic milestones in the city's rich history, FAAPI was designated to represent the Republic of the Philippines during the July 4, 1946, Philippine Independence Day celebration. FAAPI was the lead organizer of the Filipino community during the 1976 Bicentennial celebration of US independence. It has supported many causes including the rightful recognition of Filipino veterans who fought side-by-side with US soldiers in World War II, encouraging our community to register and vote in elections, and advocating for Filipinos and Filipino-Americans in our communities. It started the ever-popular dinner-dances among Filipinos and Filipino-Americans. It has an active senior citizens program, and its youth dance troupe paved the way for the formation of other dance troupes in the area.

First organized in 1912, FAAPI commemorates its centennial in 2012 through a year-long series of events bringing new awareness of Filipino legacies and contributions to Philadelphia. At the kickoff event, the Philippine Folk Arts Society, Inc. (PFASI) sponsored a Multicultural Show on March 17, 2012, that drew representatives from Filipino, Asian, and other communities. A special Centennial Mother of the Year event was held on May 20, 2012, to celebrate the virtues of motherhood as well as leadership. A FAAPI Centennial Scholarship was included in the Asian American Women's Coalition (AAWC) 2012 scholarship program and awarded on June 15, 2012. A Centennial Gala honoring pioneering Filipino-Americans in the region and the launch of this book are scheduled for September 15, 2012. The Rizal Ball, commemorating the Martyrdom of the Philippine national hero, Dr. Jose Rizal, which started in the early 1920s, will be held in December 2012 and will feature the coronation of the Centennial Miss Maria Clara.

As an older organization, FAAPI is constantly looking for self-motivated Filipino youth, not only to maintain its rich history as a civic organization, but also to provide them with opportunities to give back to their community and to understand the value of sacrifice. Collaborative partnerships with local student groups and youth organizations will be strengthened.

The long awaited, first-ever outdoor Filipino mural on the east coast will be unveiled to the public in 2012. FAAPI, the sponsoring organization, thanks the Philadelphia Mural Arts Program and muralist Eliseo Art Silva, as well as selfless civic leaders such as wall owners Van and Ven Kalugdan.

FAAPI continues to develop close partnerships with other nonprofit organizations such as the AARP and the Philadelphia Corporation for the Aging, to provide informational sessions on topics relevant to Filipino seniors.

Finally, FAAPI, the nation's oldest continuously active Filipino organization, has as its long-term objective to reclaim, build, and purchase a new "Philippine Center of Philadelphia," which will provide services to all, especially to Filipino Philadelphian youth and senior citizens.

—Christopher M. Rivera, 1st Vice President
Filipino-American Association of Philadelphia, Inc.